The Christian
Fright Peddlers

THE CHRISTIAN
FRIGHT PEDDLERS

Brooks R. Walker

DOUBLEDAY & COMPANY, INC.

GARDEN CITY, NEW YORK

1964

Excerpt from THE NEW AMERICAN RIGHT, edited
by Daniel Bell, (New York: 1955), copyright 1955
by Criterion Books, Inc. Reprinted by permission of
the publisher.

To KATE R. WALKER (1889–1963),
my aunt, who knew the meaning
of true patriotism, and to
KATE R. WALKER (1963–   ),
my daughter. May she and our two sons
grow up to know the fullness of
liberty in this, the land of concern
for the place of man.

Preface

THE DAY AFTER Adlai Stevenson was struck on the head by a placard-wielding United Nations critic in Dallas I had the opportunity to ask the Ambassador his opinion of right-wing extremism and its effect on the United Nations.

"It has obscured the true face of America," he said. "Extremism, in any form, not only contradicts our policy of peace, but creates an ugly impression of America and Americans abroad."

Mr. Stevenson stated the extremist threat well. His words apply as readily to American institutions of a nonofficial character as to the United Nations. Extremism, in any form, clouds the face of America. It hides from the world the democratic convictions and the commitment to freedom shared by the great majority of Americans.

Extremism also has a way of obscuring our true objectives from ourselves. We become involved with the fears and phobias of the extremist and forget about the objectives we have set for ourselves.

"Human beings," said Ernest Hemingway, "often undergo much needless fear because they are afraid to search out all the facts." This book is about fear and its consequences in the form of right-wing extremism in the Protestant churches, in the private and public lives of Americans. I have attempted to present the facts with as much feeling for the core realities of life and liberty as objectivity would permit. But I have eschewed that pseudo-objectivity which substitutes "available evidence tends to indicate" for "I think," or presents personal experiences as though they were general conclusions. I have attempted to strike a balance between recounting personal experiences with broader implications, and generalizations that may be made from others' experiences and an accumulation of data.

My intent has been to write nonfiction, though there will doubtless be those who disagree and call this work a fabrication. To them I can only say, in words attributed to Lincoln, "A fact deserves respect; it deserves to be truly stated." Go to the facts, separate them from the fables, and form your own judgment. Respect the sacredness of a fact and the integrity of those who must interpret it from their individual viewpoints. Together, then, we may enter into the sort of dialogue that is the foundation for true democracy.

BROOKS R. WALKER

Canoga Park, California

Acknowledgments

MOST OF THE facts in this book have come from the well-springs of right-wing extremism itself: from books, pamphlets, tracts, newsletters, tape recordings, radio and television broadcasts, and the like—all originating with the far right. Some of the data has come from personal interviews with individuals directly involved with the movements discussed; and some, of course, has come from secondary sources such as magazine articles, newspaper accounts and the few books that have been published on the topic. The western edition of the *New York Times*, in particular, has been helpful in its up-to-the-minute reporting of ultrarightist activities throughout the nation.

In those instances in which I have personally attended right-wing events, I have confirmed my quotations, whenever possible, by newspaper accounts or press releases distributed by the group itself. Such, for example, is the case in the chapter on "Armageddon," which includes an account of Project Alert in Los Angeles. In that instance coverage provided by the *Los Angeles Times* and the project's own press kit were indispensable.

In addition, a number of persons have been helpful in putting me in touch with source materials. I would like particularly to thank the following: Steve Allen, the Rev. Dr. Berkeley Blake, the Rev. Dr. John Burt, Ronald Caruso, Fletcher Coates, Congressman James Corman, the Rev. John Crane, the Rev. Robert Haney, Mike Hodel, Carl Keightley, the Rev. Dean Kelley, Dr. Robert Kimball, Haskell Lazere, Robert Little, Gary Marx, Ethel Narvid, Dr. Äke Sandler, Dr.

Fred Schwarz, the Rev. John Simmons, David Vienna, James Wilcox, and Ronald Wyllys, who translated portions of a Spanish-language text quoted in Chapter III. My thanks as well to my wife, who bore with me throughout the project, and to Martha Barcus, who typed and assisted in the preparation of the manuscript.

Finally, I want to thank the Rev. Leon Fay and the Department of the Ministry of the Unitarian Universalist Association, who offered their full support following the bombing of my home in 1962 and the bombing of the San Fernando Valley offices of the American Association for the United Nations in 1963. And above all, I want to acknowledge the warm support which the members and board of the Emerson Unitarian Church have offered following my public encounters with extremism on the right.

B.R.W.

Contents

Barbarous acts are rarely committed out of the blue. . . .
Step by step, a society becomes accustomed to accept,
with less and less moral outrage and with greater and
greater indifference to legitimacy, the successive blows.
What is uniquely disturbing about the emergence of the
radical right of the 1960s is the support it has been able
to find among traditional community leaders who have
themselves become conditioned, through an indiscriminate
anti-Communism that equates any form of liberalism with
Communism, to judge as respectable a movement which, if
successful, can only end the liberties they profess to
cherish.

— Daniel Bell

The Christian
Fright Peddlers

1 Extremism on the Right: Cause Without a Purpose

"BROOKS, THEY FINALLY got to you," said Carolyn Sawyer from the other end of the telephone line.

"What do you mean?" I asked.

"Your house. Someone bombed it."

The fraction of a second that followed my next question seemed longer than any hour I'd ever spent. "How is Sandy—and the boys?"

"Everyone is all right," said Carolyn. "They're here at our house. You'd better come on over. I'd plan to spend the night, if I were you."

My end of that conversation took place at about 10:00 P.M. on Thursday, February 1, 1962, at Temple Sinai in Beverly Hills, California. I had just addressed a public forum, sponsored by the American Jewish Congress, on the topic "The Extreme Right—Threat to Democracy?"

Two other speakers had appeared on the platform that evening—the Reverend John Simmons, a Lutheran minister; and the well-known actress Marsha Hunt. Pastor Simmons had begun the evening with a discussion of some of the personalities involved in the growth of right-wing extremism in America. I had followed with a discussion of the methods employed by the extreme right, together with some suggestions for effective countermeasures. Miss Hunt had concluded the presentation by summarizing the problems faced by public institutions as a result of right-wing activities, and offering a plea for support of the United Nations as a world forum for free discussion. We had just begun a question and answer session when I was called to the telephone.

After the telephone conversation I returned to the auditorium long enough to take my leave of the audience. I doubt if I will ever make a shorter speech than that one—or one listened to with greater attention. I told the audience that I had received word that my suburban home in the San Fernando Valley had been bombed. "My wife and children are all right," I think I said. "I'm sorry, but I must leave you now."

Pastor Simmons muttered, "My God, I'd better call home," in a tone that could only have been called prayerful. And the audience sat—stunned for a moment—then moved with a great wave of shock and concern. "It was almost as though they thought at first that they were watching a television drama," Marsha Hunt told me later. "And then they knew that they were part of the drama. It was life. Real life."

Ed Powell, a friend and parishioner, drove me back to the San Fernando Valley to the home of Paul and Carolyn Sawyer —good friends, the two of them, Paul a fellow Unitarian-Universalist minister. I talked with my wife, Sandy, for a few minutes. She was shaken, but calm. Robert, age five months, was asleep. John, age four, was doing his best to figure the world out through sleep-laden eyes. (He learned of the bombing only the following day, when he saw a reconstruction of the event on a neighbor's television set. How he managed to sleep through the noise of the explosion is still a mystery to us.)

Reporters from the *Los Angeles Times* were waiting, and we saw them. Then we began to speculate. The first question: Was our home the only one bombed? I called John Simmons and learned that a bomb had been planted under the front window of his North Hollywood residence. He reported extensive damage and mentioned that a piece of shrapnel from the homemade bomb had narrowly missed Mrs. Simmons, who was in the kitchen at the time of the bombing.

We talked with the Sawyers for some time that evening. About questions mostly. Who had planted the bombs? What were their motives? Had the bombs been planted merely to intimidate, or to kill as well? Why had the bomber picked this particular evening—and these particular persons?

The link between Pastor Simmons and myself was too clear to be ignored. We were introduced to each other for the first time that evening—five minutes before the beginning of the panel's discussion at Temple Sinai. Our only relationship, to date, was a common speaking engagement which had grown out of a common concern over the excesses of right-wing extremism in America. And then the bombings: the first at my home; the next, about half an hour later, at the Simmons'. "At least," I told Paul Sawyer, "the bomber was ecumenically minded. He picked out a Unitarian and a Lutheran minister, and managed to bomb both of their homes while they spoke at a synagogue."

About 2:00 A.M., Sandy, the boys, and I drove home, but we stopped at the West San Fernando Valley Police Station on the way. "Could police protection be provided," I inquired, "for the one night, at least?"

"Not possible," said the officer at the desk, "but we will have a squad car drive by the house occasionally for a few nights." (The following day the Los Angeles Police Department decided to put the homes of all three panel participants under a twenty-four-hour-a-day guard for an indefinite period.)

Once home, we surveyed the damage and reconstructed the event. At that hour most of Canoga Park was asleep, including our neighbors. The house was empty of police and reporters. A faint, acrid smell hung around the garage. The damage, though real, was not extensive, consisting mainly of a moderately large hole in the outside wall of the garage and several small holes between the end of the garage and the house.

One piece of shrapnel had sliced through the garage wall and the outside wall of the house into Robert's room, its target the baby's crib. Fortunately for Robert, he was in the kitchen at that moment, in his mother's arms, for an unusually late feeding.

Sandy thought at first that the water heater had burst. Uncertain what it was, she called the police and reported an explosion; she was shaken enough to stay in the house until she heard the voices of neighbors outside. Once she was certain of the nature of the explosion, she called the police again, and within minutes two squad cars pulled up. The reporters soon followed.

After talking awhile, we went to bed with a feeling close to philosophical resignation about the whole thing—that, and a firm determination to shut the garage door in the future. Whoever had exploded the bomb, we reasoned, had done so as an impotent gesture of protest. He had felt compelled to answer words not with arguments and debate, but with an attempt at intimidation. We told each other that night that such an attempt would remain just that—an *attempt*, for life could not mean a great deal were we to give up the freedom that was under attack: the freedom to think and to speak without fear of restraint, save for that inner restraint which one hopes will bring with it good judgment and sound thought.

The next morning the really big explosion went off. A small army of reporters, television cameramen, and photographers hit our house with the kind of force it takes to make headlines from one coast to the other and to get full coverage on the major radio and television networks. The morning edition of the *Los Angeles Times* carried this two-inch headline: "TERROR BOMBS Two Ministers' Homes Blasted, Families Safe." Inside, there was a photograph of a leaflet that had been distributed outside Temple Sinai while we spoke —a leaflet that bore the inscription, "Know Your Enemy!"

To the right of the inscription were the United Nations wreath, a Star of David, and a hammer and sickle.

Radio, television, and newspaper interviews continued through the day and into the next. At the time, the attention of the news media seemed out of keeping with the seriousness of the bombings. There is something weirdly disproportionate here, I remember thinking. Two ministers speak out on the extreme right in American politics and religion, and they get their homes bombed by unknown persons. No lives are lost and the damage to property is relatively slight. At worst, two families are badly shaken for awhile. But the mass media go a trifle insane over the fact. There's something strangely disproportionate about it all.

That was the direction of my thoughts the day after the bombings, at least. Looking back now, the disproportion fades —not because there was any more damage than there appeared to be at first, but because it is now possible to see more clearly what was at stake. A constitutional tradition was in question. The right of persons to speak out on issues of controversy had been challenged with the crudest of all possible weapons—physical violence directed against the wives and children of those doing the speaking.

The news media and the American public were outraged. Never mind who set the bombs. They had been exploded. Free speech had been tampered with. The right to criticize was in jeopardy!

Short of some new discovery by the Los Angeles Police Department, it will remain impossible to know who was responsible for the bombings. Many an overly eager commentator has attempted to establish the guilt of the right wing, and not a few persons have suggested that the Communist Party was responsible. Certainly, Carolyn Sawyer's first reaction was that of most people. The right wing was under criticism by both Pastor Simmons and myself at the time of the bombings. Therefore, much of the popular reasoning went toward the assumption that those of the extreme right mentality were responsible.

On the other hand, Edgar Hiestand, one of two acknowledged members of the John Birch Society in the United States Congress, wrote me a personal letter suggesting there was a strong possibility that the bombings were merely "plants" to cast discredit on the right, and pointing out that such maneuvers were a common Communist trick. (Perhaps more significant than the congressman's remark was the fact that I received his letter to me the day after I read about it in a Los Angeles newspaper.) The other U.S. congressman of Birch Society persuasion, Representative John Rousselot, was less concerned with Communist tricks, but assured me in a letter that he would be as militant as my closest friends in urging that full justice be done as soon as the authorities could determine who was responsible for the bombings.

Also without pointing the finger of accusation, Republican Senator Thomas Kuchel, speaking from the floor of the U. S. Senate, deplored the bombings and declared, "The radical right in this country is as grave a danger to the security of our country and the faith of our people in the constitutional system of government as is the radical Communist left." In so speaking, I believe that Senator Kuchel got close to the major truth of the bombings: that although they could in no way be linked with any group, either right or left on the political spectrum, they were nonetheless an integral part of the public hysteria created by the extreme right. At the very least, the radical right served as a powerful stimulus for the bomber or bombers. Hence the national furor. Hence comments on the floors of the Senate and of the House, from Attorney General Kennedy and California's Governor Brown. Hence the concern of Americans of varying political and religious persuasions. The extreme right, religious and political, was recognized as a threat to the American way. The bombing of two ministers' homes in the San Fernando Valley of Southern California proved to be a crucial event in the thinking of many a person already uneasy with the notions proclaimed by the extreme right, but not yet convinced that it represented any threat to organized religion or to the nation.

The important question raised by the bombings was not who was responsible for them, but what kind of thinking made them possible. The bombings were merely one of the most dramatic instances in a whole complex of ideas, men, movements, and events that constitute religiopolitical extremism. The climate of opinion that produced movements capable of giving impetus to such behavior deserves our closest attention.

THE HURLING OF CHARGES

It is almost as though the nation has developed a fever in recent years. Religious and political groups of extreme right-wing persuasion have appeared on the American scene in bewildering numbers. Not that right-wing thought or activity is new to America. It is not. It has been around, in one form or another, for a good many years. But a new expression of ultraconservative sentiment has found its way into the cultural, religious, and political life of the nation. Politicians with such divergent views as Dwight D. Eisenhower and James Roosevelt find themselves sharing the common charge of "conspiracy." Clergymen with such widely differing views as George Buttrick and John Haynes Holmes discover that they have been labeled pro-Communist in their thinking.

Scarcely a segment of American life has not been touched by the resurgence of the radical right. The churches, mental-health movements, the military, the United Nations, humanitarian organizations by the score, and even the Supreme Court are attacked variously as "pro-Communist," "unwitting helpers of the Kremlin," and "treasonous." At no time in recent years have the institutions of our nation been so widely suspect by so many; nor have the loyalty, the integrity, and the motives of so many persons in positions of leadership been questioned with such insistence.

Not the least of the institutions under attack is the Protestant Church. Charges against individual churches and churchmen, together with charges against the National Council of Churches, the major voice of Protestant denominations in America, vary widely, according to who is making them and why. But the charges generally boil down to one critical point: *the person or the institution under attack is accused of aiding Communism.* A militant anti-Communism is the mainspring driving groups and persons on the ultra-right.

In some instances the charge of "Communist" is hurled openly. More often, it is alleged that an individual or an organization is "pro-Communist," or simply "aiding Communism, wittingly or unwittingly."

One widely distributed pamphlet accuses a prominent Methodist bishop of being a "prophet of Marx." Another implies that approximately twelve percent of the clergy in America are in sympathy with Communism. Still another leaflet charges that the National Council of Churches "preaches and advocates Socialism, and is completely opposed to the American (and Christian) system of Individual Freedom." The last charge is followed by yet another, printed (literally) in red ink; still speaking, presumably, of the National Council, the leaflet proclaims: "MANY OF ITS PREACHERS ARE COMMUNISTS."

One single-sheet flyer is a résumé of the activities of Eugene Carson Blake, chief executive officer of the United Presbyterian Church in the U.S.A. Although the facts it reports are, in the main, accurate, the document seeks to put Dr. Blake into the Communist camp by carefully slanting the material it reports.

Charges made verbally are generally more specific than those made in print, but whatever the form, the charges are made. The church is under attack.

But let me offer a more detailed example. On Sunday, December 17, 1961, the Reverend Charles R. Ehrhardt, pastor of the First Presbyterian Church of Phoenix, delivered an unusual sermon. Entitled "Alternative to Flailing and Futility," it was a forceful review of events in his own church—charges that had been made, including whispered innuendos, telephone calls, mailings to the church membership, direct contacts with church members, and so on. "I suppose," said Dr. Ehrhardt, "that most shocking to me was that . . . one of our church members said in all seriousness: 'Did you know that Dr. Ehrhardt was the Number One Communist in the East?'"

A mimeographed sheet mailed to members of First Church was less specific, but fully as unsettling to any minister with a sense of professional responsibility. "We find arrayed against us, or indifferent to our distress and sorrow," it said, "those whom we have always consulted in times of distress, namely our ministers. They tell us we must close our eyes to danger, we must not disturb the peace and tranquillity of those who slumber in peaceful ignorance." Speaking of the mimeographed sheet, Dr. Ehrhardt asked rhetorically, "Can you imagine the distress of your ministers when they are charged with being indifferent to the distress and sorrow of their parishioners? Can you imagine the reaction of your ministers when it is falsely and viciously charged that they have advocated the closing of eyes to danger? Any danger?"

Dr. Ehrhardt, his detractors had claimed, was "sent" to the First Presbyterian Church of Phoenix by the National Council of Churches; and the National Council of Churches, they maintained, was a willing handmaiden of the Soviet Union. It seemed that the chief concern of those launching the attack was to purge the church of all "leftist tendencies," including affiliation with the NCC (a difficult matter, since no individual church can belong, membership being a commitment of the denomination, rather than the local church). Meetings had been called by the "Defenders of the Faith," as the group called itself, in order to consider "church problems" —this, without the pastor's knowledge or the authorization of the Session. With a view to forming a rival congregation in Phoenix, some members had even contacted denominational officials of the Bible Presbyterian Church, an organization founded by the Reverend Carl McIntire of Collingswood, N.J. Other dissenting members of First Church were apparently less interested in founding a rival group, Bible Presbyterian or otherwise. They simply resigned, or canceled their pledges—or both.

The cause of anti-Communism was taking its toll. "Anti-Communism has become a god in the lives of those who do not have the true God as their Lord," Dr. Ehrhardt declared. He concluded his sermon that December seventeenth with a vigorous plea for unity: "Let us not hurl bricks at one another, let us use them to build; let us not fight one another, let us fight in the ranks of Christ our Lord; let us not be fooled by professional detractors of our Lord and of His Church. . . . Let us not join the disciples of dissension, the apostles of discord, the purveyors of hate—let us join hands with Christ our elder brother and in His name work and pray that His will may be done on earth as in heaven. . . ."

So much for the events at the First Presbyterian Church. Now, what truth, if any, was there in the allegations?

Let us begin with the charge that Dr. Ehrhardt went to Phoenix at the behest of the National Council of Churches. The facts here are easy to come by, and the mere charge would be hilariously funny, were it not for the ignorance it reveals. The National Council, an organization whose membership consists of denominations with a common faith in Jesus Christ as Lord and Savior, has no power whatever over the choice of *any* minister serving *any* congregation in *any* denomination. The way in which a minister is chosen is a matter of denominational policy and varies widely according to the denomination in question, but in no instance is the NCC involved. No denomination, no church, no minister would be willing to entrust such a sensitive task to an interdenominational organization, even if that organization wanted the job. The notion that the NCC places ministers is, to state it simply, absurd. As Dr. Ehrhardt gently remarked, "It came as a surprise to the members of our church's Pastoral Nominating Committee when I told them about it."

Now, *was* Dr. Ehrhardt a Communist? On at least one occasion Dr. Ehrhardt is reported to have told his congregation that although he was pained to find it necessary to say so, he could assure them he was *not* a Communist, and that he opposed all that Communism stands for. He went on to say that he was also against "murder, adultery, and theft," but that he did not feel it necessary to announce the fact every Sunday. A self-effacing, weekly repudiation of charges was not Dr. Ehrhardt's way. Like many a veteran of World War II (he served as an officer in the U. S. Navy), he felt that he had demonstrated his loyalty to his country. And like many a clergyman, he believed that an undue attention to the forces of dissent could only mean neglect of the central purposes of the church and its ministry.

The Session of First Church made its position clear in a statement read to the congregation during the service preceding Dr. Ehrhardt's dramatic sermon on December seventeenth. "The Session," said the statement, "has concluded that the allegations . . . are essentially false and misleading and could divide our congregation."

In terms of Dr. Ehrhardt's own statements, then, and in the opinion of the Session of the church he served, the facts are clear. Dr. Ehrhardt's loyalty is firmly established.

Even in making that simple statement I feel dreadfully

uneasy, however. Not because I think that there is any chance
that Dr. Ehrhardt was, or is, a Communist, but because it
seems very wrong to me for any man to have to defend himself against such charges. This is the United States. We have
an old tradition in this country, a constitutional tradition that
says quite plainly that a man is considered innocent until he
is proved guilty. That tradition applies first to our courts.
Should our public life exact any less of us? I think not.

The tragedy of situations such as the one that developed in
Phoenix is that men are said to be guilty before they have
been given a hearing; they are attacked with the flimsiest of
evidence, without so much as a chance to clear themselves.
Grotesque fictions are peddled as facts. And when that happens, something occurs deep down inside of all of us. A bit
of us dies, because a small piece of the American heritage is
forgotten. The heritage I mean is all that is involved in the
simple words "the presumption of innocence."

I wish I could say that the situation in Phoenix was the
product of crackpot patriotism, or something like that. I wish
I could dismiss it with a clever phrase or two. Unfortunately,
I cannot. The trouble in Phoenix is too nearly representative
of the trouble in many another American city. Sometimes the
trouble is less severe; sometimes it is more. The pattern varies.
But the trouble at First Church in Phoenix epitomizes the
sort of concerns, the kind of fears, the variety of images that
move men to strike out against the church and its representatives in the name of patriotism.

FOUNDATION FOR A CAUSE

Behind the trouble in Phoenix lies a deep and festering
problem. Communism, as a rival philosophy of life and as a
competitive system of government, is an established fact. The

Soviet Union is a military threat to the United States and to the western alliance. There can be no doubt of that. There is also little question that the Soviet Union represents a threat to the internal security of the United States. Espionage and sabotage are no idle concerns of U.S. law-enforcement officials. Further, the Communist movement in the United States has long envisioned a day when the U.S. would join the U.S.S.R. in proclaiming an end of "the old bourgeois society." Americans in general have not taken lightly the declaration of the *Communist Manifesto* that ". . . Communists . . . declare that their ends can be attained only by the forcible overthrow of all existing social conditions."

This is not to say that most Americans are unalterably opposed to revolution. On the contrary. It is only that Americans are committed to quite another revolutionary tradition —one which began in 1776, and whose ends are, as yet, unfinished. The revolution of 1776 set in motion enough to occupy this nation for centuries to come. Little wonder that Americans are concerned about the destructive potential of a revolution exported by the descendents of Marx and Engels. All this the American ultraconservative understands. But he takes his understanding one step further. He looks at Soviet military power and reads into it an intent to attack at the first propitious moment. He sees the threat to U.S. internal security and concludes that it is a widespread cancer with little to check its growth. He extrapolates the formulations from the *Communist Manifesto* of 1848 into the year 1965—or '70, or '75—and sees a Marxist revolution in the making. Sedition, he knows, is often a subtle matter, and he is eager to ferret it out, no matter what the cost.

The American ultraconservative is a man who builds his images on real fact, but confuses possibility with certainty. It *is* possible that the Soviet Union is planning to attack the United States at the first opportunity. The question is, is it certain? It *is* possible that espionage agents fill many an industrial job and governmental post. The next question is, is it established fact? It *is* remotely possible that a well-defined revolutionary movement in America is close to overthrowing the government. The crucial question is, is this established fact? What most men regard as possible the ultraconservative sees as probable or certain. On this foundation he builds his cause.

THE RIGHT-WING EXTREMIST

The words *right-wing extremist,* when applied to the religiopolitical conservative, are more than an epithet. They denote a specific syndrome of beliefs—a pattern of convictions which may have variations, but which serves always to describe the man who finds himself defending, in one form or another, some combination of the following propositions:

1) *that Communism is totally evil:* There is no possibility for goodness in a Communist society; all Communists are, by their very nature, irrevocably committed to a course of evil.

2) *that the freedom of the "free world" is a heritage which must be defended AT ANY COST:* It is a question of freedom or slavery. Coexistence is impossible, despite the military strength of the west, because of the nature of Communism. Even if it means entering into full-scale nuclear war, the U.S. must hold its ground. It would be better to sacrifice not only ourselves, but the rest of humanity as well, than to coexist with Communism. Pre-emptive or even preventive warfare *may* represent a valid U.S. approach to the cold war.[1]

3) *that Communism is an acute internal threat to the*

---

[1] Right-wing opinion is divided on the question of preemptive and/or preventive war. Some argue vigorously for such an approach, while others advocate a withdrawal from the arms race by drastically cutting U.S. military expenditures.

United States: It controls, or comes close to controlling the government of the United States and most American institutions, ranging from colleges and universities to civic and religious organizations. Whatever threat Communism poses externally, and the estimates vary, the external threat is plainly secondary.

4) *that all tendencies toward government regulation are "collectivist" and are, as such, evil:* It would be better if the world were governed only in terms of trifles. Free enterprise, above all, must be left alone. A regulated economy is to be eschewed at all costs.

5) *that the Soviet Union is bent on "world domination," and will stop at nothing to achieve its ends:* Modern Communists follow the teachings of Marx, Engles, Lenin, and Stalin without significant deviation, and nothing—including global holocaust—will deter the Communists from marching toward their goal of physically occupying the U.S.A. and enslaving its population.

6) *that the Judeo-Christian heritage, a "Christian-style civilization," or simply Christianity, is the only final answer to Communism:* All other religions, moralities, or philosophies are intrinsically unsatisfactory, heretical, blasphemous, or downright evil.[2]

Less general propositions held in common by most of those on the extreme right include opposition to the United Nations, the U. S. Supreme Court, and the U. S. State Department, all of which are seen as following, in some measure, Communist or pro-Communist policies. Also generally opposed are continued diplomatic relations with the U.S.S.R.,

[2] Often, a narrowly defined Christian sectarianism is cited as the *only* alternative to Communism, and the one means for achieving victory against the "Communist foe." Billy James Hargis and Fred Schwarz typify this approach. On the other hand, some, like Robert Welch, maintain that all religions and moral philosophies may be integrated into a Christian-style civilization based on the moral precepts of all great religions. The wholly nonreligious cannot, of course, be integrated.

U.S. foreign aid, and the possible admission of Communist China to the United Nations. On the domestic scene, right-wing condemnation descends heavily on most civil rights and social legislation, and on almost any attempt to increase federal expenditures for health, education, or welfare. Finally, the wrath of the extreme right wing finds full expression in attacks on the income tax, public schools, fluoridation of public water supplies, and the National Council of Churches.

The positive objectives of the right wing are more difficult to discover, although Robert Welch, the founder of the John Birch Society, probably summed them up as well as anyone in his statement of the purpose of that organization: "to promote less government, more responsibility and a better world." The only difficulty with such a summary is that it not only includes all those on the extreme right, but encompasses everyone else as well, including the Communists. Even the Marxist has his eye fixed on the day when the machinery of the state will no longer be needed and men may become more responsible, thus bringing about a better world. Such a belief is basic to his philosophical system.

It *is* true that most persons on the far right vigorously support the concept of free enterprise, heartily endorse domestic patriotism, and firmly believe in God. But these positive items of belief are still not enough to sustain a definition. Those of moderate or liberal persuasion may be equally convinced of the values to be found in free enterprise, patriotism, and belief in God.

It would appear, then, that we must do without a summary of the positive objectives of the extreme right wing. Perhaps one exists somewhere. If so, I have not seen it.

The religious beliefs of persons on the extreme right vary widely. No major religious group in America has avoided completely the effects of right-wing extremism. There are right-wing Jews and right-wing Roman Catholics. The greatest diversity by far, however, is to be found within the limits of

Protestantism. Here, the spectrum of belief ranges from a warmed-over nineteenth-century liberalism to a militant twentieth-century fundamentalism, from passionately defended variations on Episcopalianism to new versions of Presbyterianism and Methodism. But whatever the denominational affiliation of the right-wing extremist, he is convinced that the church is the victim of conspiracy. It has fallen into Communist hands.

The typical right-wing extremist has a host of documentary evidence buttressing his contentions. One right-wing group, concerned with ferreting out evil in the form of Communists and Communist sympathizers in the churches, proclaims that, as of 1955, no less than 1411—20.5%—of the Protestant Episcopal rectors in this country had in some way identified themselves with the program of world Communism. In another "compilation of public records," it is claimed that 42% of all Unitarian ministers, and no fewer than 450 rabbis are in league with Communist causes in one way or another.

The best that may be said for such claims is that the public records on which they depend are apparently extensive. They are so extensive, in fact, that they often list persons dead or out of the ministry; and they commonly include organizations never heard of by those individuals who are alleged to have belonged to them. Thus, the right-wing organization responsible for the compilations mentioned above—Circuit Riders, Inc.—has alleged that Dr. Luther Weigle, chairman of the committee concerned with translating the Revised Standard Version of the Bible, belonged to a total of six subversive organizations. Dr. Weigle's sinister associations were as follows: He had never heard of two of the six organizations before he read of his alleged membership in them. He had never attended any meetings held by the other four organizations, had never contributed to their work, and had never given permission for his name to be used by them. Yet, according to the Circuit Riders, Inc., Dr. Weigle's affiliations were established "fact."

Did the Circuit Riders claim that Dr. Weigle was a Communist? No. Nothing so direct may be found in the organization's lists. They are "compilations of public records." They are listings of "facts," which the reader is left to interpret for himself. That these facts may be irrelevant to the person's life does not matter. They are there for all to read.

Circuit Riders, Inc. is headed by Myers Lowman, a Methodist layman, whose first objective in founding the organization in 1951 was "to oppose Socialism and Communism in our [Methodist] church." He has long since taken on all of Christendom. That he has not endeared himself to his fellow Methodists is indicated by the following quotation from a report adopted on May 6, 1960, by the General Conference of the Methodist Church: "We regret that any Methodist contributes either money or leadership to such organizations as Circuit Riders, Inc., which utilize the 'guilt by association' and 'fellow traveler' approaches as they stir up unjustified suspicion and develop unfounded fears. We direct attention to our general rule concerning 'uncharitable or unprofitable conversation, particularly speaking evil of magistrates and ministers.'"

The right-wing extremist may turn to the Circuit Riders, Inc., or to any one of several similar organizations, for confirmation of his views on the condition of American Protestantism. Or he may simply pick up a pamphlet such as one printed by *The Independent American*, a paper published in New Orleans. One of the paper's tracts, labeled "Communist Infiltration in Religion," begins with this startling headline (printed in red): ATHEISTIC COMMUNISM IS SUBVERTING THE CHURCHES. Under the subheading "How Many Red Sympathizers in the Churches?" the tract cites J. B. Matthews as an established authority. According to the unnamed author(s) of the publication, Matthews has observed that a Gallup poll discovered that "88% of the clergy [in America] expressed the view that 'it is impossible to be a good Christian and a member of the Communist Party.'" Mr. Matthews, in the light of the poll, is said to have raised the question, "What about the 12%, or 30,000, of the Protestant clergy who were either unable, or refused to affirm the complete irreconcilability of Christianity on the one hand and the Communist conspiracy on the other. . . ."

What about it? The tract quotes Mr. Matthews. "I confess," says Matthews, "that I find something alarming in the situation that finds 30,000 confused Protestant clergymen ministering to the minds and morals of the more than six and a half million members of their congregations."

Does Matthews think that there are Communists among the clergy? The tract is careful not to say. But "30,000 confused Protestant clergymen," the reader must surely know, are not confused with a dull fog of ignorance and uncertainty.

Abruptly, the tract then leaves the observations of J. B. Matthews and goes on to quote the testimony of Manning Johnson before the House Committee on Un-American Activities:

> It is an axiom in Communist organization strategy that if an infiltrated body has 1% Communist Party members and 9% Communist Party sympathizers, with well-rehearsed plans of action, they can effectively control the remaining 90% who act and think on an individual basis. In the large sections of the religious field, due to the ideological poison which has been filtered in by Communists and pro-Communists through seminaries, the backlog of sympathizers and mental prisoners of socialistic ideology is greater than the 10 percent necessary for effective control.

Is the tract saying that the Communist Party controls the churches with a small group of members in key positions and a modest number of sympathizers in the rank-and-file membership? It does not make its position plain, but the inferences seem clear enough. The churches, the pamphlet seems to be saying, have been infiltrated by Communists and their fellow travelers.

The next subheading reads "Communist Clergymen," and deals with testimony, before the House Committee on Un-American Activities, during which it was estimated that "there are up to 600 members of the Communist Party among the clergy in America."

A colorful quotation from the well-known anti-Communist, Matt Cvetic, follows, on the "infiltration" of the churches "planned by a secret group of high-level Red agents, labeled the 'Clergical Commission of the Communist Party' . . . composed of Soviet Agents and American Reds, posing as ministers, preachers and priests. . . ."

The rest of the tract is concerned with Communist motivation for infiltrating individual congregations and the National Council of Churches.

Two things seem to me to be especially significant about the tract. First, like the Circuit Riders' publications, it avoids libel by never saying that anyone actually is a Communist. Second, the tract doesn't even spell out what it *does* say. Not in a straightforward manner, anyway. Having given the reader a hearty shove in the right direction, the author(s) leaves him to develop his own conclusions by inference. No one with an I.Q. over 75 could fail to draw the conclusions that the author(s) has in mind. But libel has been avoided. Nothing —absolutely nothing—has been said directly.

I could continue to quote pamphlets and books of the sort published by the Circuit Riders and *The Independent American*. Such literature seems to appear in an endless stream, and the buyers continue to thirst for more of it. But another question presents itself: What truth, if any, is contained in the heady charges delivered by the extreme right wing? Just how many Communist clergymen *are* there in the United States?

"It may be stated factually and without equivocation," says William C. Sullivan, Assistant Director of the Federal Bureau of Investigation, "that any allegation is false which holds that there has been and is, on a national scale, an extensive or substantial communist infiltration of the American clergy. . . ."[3]

Mr. Sullivan, please note, does not shilly-shally. He speaks in plain language. Unless one is willing to argue that the F.B.I. has been infiltrated by Communists, or by their fellows, and that Mr. Sullivan is in the F.B.I. as an agent for the Communist Party, we must take his statement at face value. But let me quote him at greater length:

> According to estimates, there are 300,000 ordained clergymen in the United States, the great majority of whom are Protestant. When this large figure is compared with the total number of clergymen who have had communist affiliations, joined communist fronts, engaged in communist activities, supported communist causes, signed communist documents, or otherwise—unwittingly or wittingly—aided and abetted the communist movement during the past four decades, the proportion is actually exceedingly small. Moreover, many of the most active, most vocal, and most publicized of these clergymen who have worked so diligently on behalf of communism do not have or never have had their own churches or congregations. Of those who did have, many were removed when their procommunist backgrounds and connections became known.[4]

Several years ago the Fund for the Republic commissioned Ralph Lord Roy to conduct a research project and write a book on Communism and the churches. Roy, a Methodist minister with a capacity for careful research and

[3] William C. Sullivan, in a lecture entitled "Communism and Religion in the United States," delivered October 19, 1961, at the Highland Park Methodist Church, Dallas, Texas.
[4] *Ibid.*

evaluation, arrived at conclusions not unlike those reached by F.B.I. Assistant Director Sullivan. In *Communism and the Churches* Roy cites names, dates, and places, examines evidence with the care of a seasoned scholar, and delivers to the reader what the *Christian Century* (December 7, 1960) has termed "a discriminating and objective account by a competent educator and historian." His conclusion is succinct: "The notion that America's churches and religious leaders are significantly influenced by Communists or Communist sympathizers is absurd."[5]

Behind that terse conclusion stands the statistical summary which Roy includes in the Introduction to *Communism and the Churches*:

> Since 1930, there has been an estimated total of well over 500,000 ordained clergymen in the United States. Of these, approximately 85 per cent have been Protestants. The proportion who have been "affiliated" with Communist efforts in any way whatever has been exceedingly small— perhaps slightly over 1 per cent. Conversely, almost 99 per cent have had no such "affiliation." The number who have been Communists, or persistent—and identifiable—fellow travelers, has been minute, in spite of continual efforts to involve clergymen in the Communist apparatus. Today, perhaps twenty-five of this number remain—or approximately seven one-thousandths of 1 per cent of American ministers, and most of these are not serving pulpits.[6]

A possible seven one-thousandths of one percent of the ministers in America is not an alarming number. It is, in fact, just large enough for the fantasy builders on the far right to take hold of. There is enough reality in such a minuscule figure to provide the right-wing extremist with a small anchor

[5] Ralph Lord Roy, *Communism and the Churches* (New York: Harcourt, Brace and Company, 1960), p. 421.
[6] *Ibid.*, pp. 9–10.

in reality as he begins to spin his web of fabrication. Not that this touch of reality is necessary for him! It isn't. But it helps. It helps him convince himself that he is on the side of truth and righteousness when he attacks one, or ten, or twenty percent of the clergy in America, labeling them as Communists, pro-Communists, or fellow travelers. It helps him to believe that he is promoting the cause of religion and helping to defeat the world Communist movement whenever he takes on the local ministers' association, or exposes the National Council of Churches as "Communist dominated."

The germ of reality behind the extremist's charges is reassuring to him, and by clinging to it as though it were the whole of reality, he is never forced to ask first questions: How do I know? What is the evidence—the real evidence, based on careful, intelligent research and analysis? Such questions are of little importance. His mind is made up.

IN THE NAME OF ANTI-COMMUNISM

I began this study of right-wing extremism on the American religiopolitical scene with a short excursion into solid, though somewhat personal, fact. Outcroppings of hatred, direct or indirect, may be violent, but in their very violence, deceptive. Violence tends to obscure the more subtle damage done to men and social institutions whenever charges are made without substantive foundation. Ministers and churches may well find that they have been undermined by the phantasms of the imagination that take their toll among large numbers of persons and organizations under attack by the ultra-right. No segment of American life has been exempt from the hysteria of the extremists on the right. The difficulties experienced by the First Presbyterian Church of Phoenix are illustrative.

There are reasons, of course, for the extremist's overpowering anxiety. There are reasons for the feelings that give rise to his unrealistic behavior and to his still less realistic viewpoints, many of them valid reasons. But even valid reasons, pushed far enough, become inane, frantic cries of desperation. When a person takes things that are barely possible, and accepts them as established fact, we have the man with a cause, the "true believer," for whom the true facts become irrelevant.

It is impossible to say precisely what constitutes the positive platform of the right-wing extremist. This may be because he has none. And it may also be because his negative program is so extensive. In any case, the right-wing extremist finds himself opposing nearly everything that stands for social progress—or indeed, characterizes the twentieth-century world as a very different place than the nineteenth-century world. The list of things which the right-wing extremist is against is tediously long, and ranges from the income tax to a large segment of the Protestant clergy and the National Council of Churches.

Extensive compilations of "facts" are a favorite weapon of the right-wing ultra, but the "facts" are generally rather fragile and subject to disintegration under scrutiny. At any rate, they seldom hold up under impartial examination.

The chief charge leveled against the churches by the extremist on the right is this: The churches are dominated by Communists and/or Communist sympathizers. A substantial number of persons are collaborating with Satan—i.e., Soviet Communism. Some significant persons disagree, among them William C. Sullivan, Assistant Director of the F.B.I., and Ralph Lord Roy, author of *Communism and the Churches*.

Judging by the evidence, then, the Communists have made no discernible impact whatever on the over-all life of American Protestantism. Not so, however, with the anti-Communist extremists. Their impact, while not remarkable in scope or depth, has been distressingly real.

In the name of anti-Communism, discrimination has been condoned and sometimes praised, programs calling for social justice have been muted, and truth has been forced to take cover. In the name of a singularly pervasive, self-righteous anti-Communism, constitutional principles and ethical maxims have given way to a multifaceted attack. We turn now to the methods used for that attack.

2   The Attack on Practically Everyone

"I'VE LONG GOTTEN used to being called a Communist, and I'm aware of the various subtle forms of intimidation that can be used," wrote a friend of mine early in 1962. Although he was a respected Unitarian minister in a venerable New England church, organized long before the American Revolution, he had made an uncomfortable discovery about himself, the members of his church, and the community he lived in. He had discovered that beneath the placid façade of New England respectability, there was a malignant suspicion of anyone who dared to suggest reform of the status quo. A dark distrust of motives haunted persons who might normally have been expected to offer their full support in efforts to achieve social justice. Their numbers were not great, nor was their voice particularly effective. All the same, they were there, convinced that anyone whose ideas were innovative, or whose proposals for reform were creative, must necessarily be a member of an alien conspiracy. The status quo must prevail.

This state of mind is not peculiar to New England. Distrust of the new, the original, or the unfamiliar is part of the human condition and is likely to turn up anywhere. The congealing of distrust into a militant anti-Communism, which finds its targets everywhere, may be unique to the present epoch, but it knows no geographical boundaries within these fifty states. There are points of concentration to be sure, but the attack of the ultra-right is a national dilemma.

It may be found in a respectable midwest suburb, where a program chairman for the P.T.A. feels compelled to declare in the course of his defense of the film "Operation Abolition" that ". . . everybody knows that the National Council of Churches is a leftist body." It may turn up in tempestuous Orange County, California, where a public meeting, held at a Methodist church and sponsored by the American Association for the United Nations, is disrupted by two superpatriots who are put out of the meeting for refusing to conduct themselves in an orderly fashion, only to return waving an American flag. The impact of the attack may be felt in small, unpretentious towns like Norborne, Missouri, where Robert Bolivar DePugh lives with his wife and five children, and ponders stratagems for the organization he founded, the Minutemen.

Wherever the impact of the ultra-right is felt, the tools and methods of attack are similar. Many are legitimate facets of our free heritage and as such constitute an important part of the democratic dialogue. Others are unworthy of persons who presume to call themselves free.

The verbal assault is certainly the most common and, generally speaking, the most legitimate weapon in the arsenal of the ultraconservatives. Often, however, the verbal attack is more effective in provoking community acrimony than in convincing the unconvinced, or changing the minds of the opposition.

Representative of many a similar meeting in other American communities was a May 1961 gathering called by the Council of Churches in Pasadena, California. The subject was "Communism and the Churches." In what were reported to be excellent and brief speeches, a local minister, the Executive Secretary of the Pasadena Council of Churches, and a well-known layman presented the facts as they saw them, drawing as they did so largely on Ralph Lord Roy's book *Communism and the Churches* and J. Edgar Hoover's *Masters of Deceit*. The churches in America, they pointed out, are a "major bulwark against Communism," rather than its victim. They concluded by emphasizing the churches' role in clarifying social issues and their responsibility in working for reform.

Dr. Harmon Gehr, one of the ministers present at the meeting, later described what followed the presentation: "Then the house fell in. What happened was shocking. At least a dozen persons, each of whom identified himself as a church member, attacked the speakers and the National Council of Churches as enemies of the nation and humanity in general, because they are for disarmament, international aid, integration, the United Nations, etc. . . . One speaker . . . actually said, 'Let people stick in the mire! It does not matter that they are enslaved! Our only work is to save their souls through the blood of Jesus!'"

Dr. Gehr's indignation bordered on prophetic wrath. "It seems to me," he said, "[that] this issue is clear-cut—between cowardice and courage, between retreat and advance. If the religion of the prophets and Jesus is only a . . . mechanism for saving souls, I want none of it. . . . To me, this is not religion, but a serious spiritual disease."

The point may be made that the clergy in Pasadena's Council of Churches gave the opposition little, if any, place on the program, and that they presumed too much in answering charges before they had been voiced at the meeting. They saw their role in terms of preparing a defense for the churches and providing a rationale for the place of religion in public affairs. They knew that the churches were not contaminated by Communism or Communists. But they had not reckoned with their opposition.

A barrage of charges, wholly unsupported for the most part, followed their presentation. Then came an emotionally driven counterrationale for noninvolvement in public life on the part of the churches. If integration and aid to the hungry are the objectives of the "genteel establishment" of conventional Protestant Christianity, reasoned those on the far right, the way is plain: We must return to the pure religion of saving souls "through the blood of Jesus," without regard for the material estate of man.

Despite such an unreflective willingness to turn the world over to the forces of evil while saving the souls of men, the position maintained by the opposition group may not have been without theological integrity. Yet if theological integrity, or ethical concern, were present, they never had a chance to emerge. The concentration on the attack was too consuming. The hated "liberals" had to be put down.

Unfortunately, the putting down of the so-called liberals involved a heated, verbal assault on the integrity of the churches and churchmen in the mainstream of Protestantism. Evidence to support the assault was not provided. The attackers believed too deeply in the guilt of those attacked to bother with the presentation of objective evidence supporting their contentions. They *assumed* the guilt of those they attacked, and in so doing, violated the American constitutional tradition of the presumption of innocence. With apparent disregard for the Biblical admonition, "Thou shalt not bear false witness against thy neighbor," the Christian ultra-rightists hurled their epithets.

But what if, by some chance, those on the far right in Pasadena had bothered to look for evidence to buttress their allegations? Where would they have turned? That is precisely the predicament of any extremist on the religious right. As we have seen, he has no facts at his disposal—none that may be examined dispassionately and added up to his unshakeable conclusions, at any rate. He must make his point, and his point is almost wholly a child of emotion. The method of attack follows from the measure of his passion.

Attacks from the ultra-right range from slanderous or libelous denunciations of persons in public life to paramilitary activities ostensibly designed to protect American institutions. They range from well-planned heckling campaigns at public meetings to the use of scripture itself as a weapon for the

Cause. What follows is something of a systematic review of the stratagems employed by the ultra-rightists in their campaign to protect America from a variety of "enemies."

THE VERBAL ASSAULT AND ATTACK BY LETTER

When attacks-in-general, of the sort that took place in Pasadena, spill over into attacks-in-particular, they may prove to be slanderous in content.

Almost a year before I met the Rev. John Simmons at Temple Sinai in Beverly Hills (on the night our two homes were bombed), he discovered what it meant to be on the receiving end of a sharply worded verbal attack. Pastor Simmons was, at that time, minister of St. Matthew's Lutheran Church in North Hollywood, and active in a number of community organizations of a more or less controversial character in Southern California, such as the American Civil Liberties Union and the American Association for the United Nations.

At a meeting in early 1961, a speaker introducing the film "Operation Abolition" described the "Communist situation" in the San Fernando Valley. He charged that there were Methodist, Presbyterian and Lutheran churches sympathetic to Communist goals and specifically singled out Simmons as one clergyman who "followed the Communist line" and "spread the Communist philosophy."

Less than three weeks later this speaker retracted his statements in the presence of witnesses, acknowledged that his allegations concerning the churches were unfounded, and admitted that he had had no information indicating that Pastor Simmons was not a completely loyal and patriotic American. Simmons, he acknowledged, had never followed the Communist line, nor had he spread the Communist philosophy.

Regret was expressed in this statement for any damage that might have been done to the churches or to Pastor Simmons' family and friends by the previous remarks, which were described as "hasty and unfounded."

Such a signed retraction is rare, although the sort of charges which made it necessary, unfortunately, are not. Generally speaking, they go unchecked and unrefuted, doing whatever damage the occasion may provide for. It is seldom that an indiscriminating critic of the churches or the clergy is forced to prove his statements or retract them, to admit that he has "no information" on the topic at hand. Normally the damage is done and beyond recall. The verbal assault is often difficult to verify, tedious to track down, and expensive to refute if legal services are involved, and they often are. For this reason alone a verbal assault that borders on the slanderous, or is, in fact, slanderous, remains one of the most effective methods of attack employed by the right-wing extremist.

Closely related to the verbal assault is the attack by letter. Periodically swamped by right-wing letter campaigns of a hysterical sort, Senate minority whip Thomas Kuchel observed in a 1963 speech on the Senate floor that ". . . in every day's deluge of mail at my office, which sometimes means as many as 5000 letters, telegrams, and postcards— there are generally a hundred and even two hundred letters which I describe simply as 'fright mail.'" His colleagues, the Senator added, refer to such mail "in much stronger terms."

Most of the letter writers insinuate that Kuchel or his Senate colleagues are joining in one plot or another to subvert the government of the United States. Some openly charge treason. "I still cannot believe my eyes," says Kuchel, "when I stare at the ugliest word in the American lexicon tossed about in a letter as casually as the 'Dear Senator' salutation which opens it." The conspiracies imagined and detailed by the radically right letter writers are as various as the human imagination can make them, but they all add up to one con-

clusion in Kuchel's judgment: the letter writers have been
swindled by the "fright peddlers," the right-wing purveyors
of hysterical, uncritical anti-Communism. They have been
diverted from the nation's most crucial problems—foreign and
domestic—by "manufactured hobgoblins." The result is confusion, dissension and a tragic loss of responsible leadership
in shaping the American dream into reality.

Anyone who is involved in any way with public issues today
must inevitably receive his share of fright mail. In my own
experience, and in the experience of most of my colleagues,
it accounts for only a small part of the total volume, but it is
nonetheless significant. Each public appearance, in person or
on radio or television, each published article will bring a
response, part of which will certainly be the work of the fright
peddlers.

Following the bombing of our homes in February 1962,
both Pastor Simmons and I received a small flurry of postcards and letters with fright messages ranging from a cryptic
scrawl declaring, "The American Nazi Party is watching you,"
to a carefully typed letter which stated with finality that "a
government of usurped powers has been set over us. The
enemy—the leftist-oriented intellectuals who are driving to
submerge us into one-world socialism through destruction of
the American Republic and its Constitution, which by now
has been critically wounded. . . . Once this central fact is
understood," said my correspondent, "everything else falls
into place. . . . From all indications, the President [Ken-
nedy] and his Harvard crew are at least Fabian Socialists."
The letter concluded with the ejaculation, "Let the Eagle
scream."

One note writer was concerned about the state of my
soul and convinced of the truth of the extreme right-wing
cause. "If you repent, O.K.," the writer said, and then observed that "Unitarianism is the devil's religion . . . comes
from the very pit of hell and I really feel sorry for you. The

extreme right is going to always be O.K. Our worry is [the] extreme left and people like you." The note was signed, "Disgusted."

Another letter, copies of which went both to Pastor Simmons and myself, began with the familiar John Birch Society refrain, "Let me get you straightened out on a point. The United States of America is *not* a democracy, it is a *REPUBLIC*." The writer went on to raise this question: "What really are you driving at or for? Could it be possible . . . that you are part of or being used as a D-U-P-E of the Godless schemers of Communism and the so-called 'Zionist' Jew 'One-World' Conspiracy?"

Such letters comprised no more than perhaps five to ten percent of the total mail we received. The fright extended only to the fright peddlers themselves, since such letters are singularly ineffective as a method of harassment. No man need ever read a letter he doesn't want to read, nor need he change his opinion beyond the point that good judgment indicates. Most of the fright mail, which tends to be tediously long-winded and poorly written, is not worth reading through, much less worth serious consideration. It is, I suppose, more a key to a state of mind than anything else.

THE PRINTED ATTACK

Far more effective than the letter of attack is the printed attack. As with the verbal assault, a printed attack may or may not transgress legal limits. Libel tends to be somewhat less common than slander, if only because the evidence is more tangible.

Religious and political groups with a message have sought to make their viewpoints known in print since shortly after Gutenberg devised moveable type. I find myself seriously wondering, though, if any movement, religious or political, has ever exceeded the printed output of America's religiopolitical right wing. The volume, in terms of sheer tonnage alone, is incredible. It ranges from badly composed and crudely reproduced mimeographed smear sheets to well-illustrated, typographically sophisticated volumes of several hundred pages. Each group seems to have its newsletter and its supply of pamphlets.

"Conservative" bookshops, operated by enterprising right-wing enthusiasts, may be found dispensing literature across the country, although most of them apparently are clustered in the Southwest. One may purchase a newly printed edition of McGuffey's *Reader*, a pamphlet telling the "truth" about fluoridation (a Communist plot), an exposé of the Protestant clergy, or a copy of the latest edition of the Washington newsletter *Human Events*.

Over-the-counter sales account for only a small part of the flow of right-wing literature, however. The bulk of it is delivered by the United States Post Office and distributed in the neighborhood, passed out at meetings, or remailed on an individual piece basis.

Christian ultra-rightists intent on informing an apathetic citizenry about Communism in the churches are urged at every turn to increase their consumption of rightist publications. As Billy James Hargis, crusading right-wing evangelist from Tulsa, Oklahoma, put it in his February 1963 newsletter, "Counterattack with literature. Read recommended literature, buy vast quantities of it, and distribute it far and wide. . . . Distribute anti-communist 'propaganda,' and lose no opportunity to speak out against communism."

Hargis' use of the word "propaganda," even as cushioned by his quotation marks, is revealing. He has named the literature that he and his fellow far rightists distribute for what it is.

Typical of local church groups with a right-wing propaganda mission are chapters of the Committee of Christian Laymen, an organization with national headquarters in Phoenix, Arizona. I first became conscious of the local chapter of the Committee when I read a long letter by its secretary, Mrs. Arveta Bosnian, in a local newspaper. Mrs. Bosnian had some searching questions about the National Council of Churches and about the Protestant clergy. Her letter seemed to invite an inquiry.

Since I was in the midst of preparing a radio commentary on the topic, I telephoned Mrs. Bosnian and obtained a fairly full report on the activities of the local group. She offered to supply me with some of the committee's literature, and brought it by that evening.

One pamphlet, written by a retired Presbyterian minister, the Rev. Charles S. Poling, and published by the Committee at its Arizona headquarters, charged that "the National Council of Churches is leading us down the road to Socialism and that she, unless halted by the Christian laymen, will destroy our churches. . . . That destruction," said Mr. Poling, "will mean the destruction of America as the last citadel of freedom."

Another pamphlet, printed by the Sword of the Lord Foundation in Wheaton, Illinois, but bearing the imprint of the local Committee, spoke of the General Assembly of the National Council of Churches held in San Francisco in 1960 as the "largest collection of heretics, modernists, pinks, scoffers, higher critics, false prophets, and religious subversives in the triennium. . . ."

Local advertisements run by the Committee are less severe in their judgment, although they tend to be more guarded in their statements. Let me offer an example: An advertisement published in a local newspaper seeks to prove that the National Council of Churches is influenced by Communists and that many nationally prominent clergymen are at least pro-Communist in their outlook. The clergymen under attack are put in what is made to appear to be a questionable situation. Then it is noted that they are connected not only with what has been made to appear to be a dubious cause, but that they are also active in the National Council of Churches.

The cause in question is a petition, presented to Attorney General Kennedy on November 8, 1961, by a delegation headed by Clarence Picket of the American Friends Service Committee, which argued, in essence, for the right of persons to refuse to testify, on First Amendment grounds, before Congressional committees in instances which involved their freedom of belief, speech, or association. Behind the petition is a philosophy of constitutional government, perhaps most clearly articulated by Alexander Meiklejohn, one of the foremost constitutional authorities of the present century and a recipient of the Presidential Medal of Freedom:

> The First Amendment seems to me to be a very uncompromising statement: it admits of no exceptions. It tells us that the Congress, and by implication, all other agencies of the government, are denied any authority whatever to limit the political freedom of the citizens of this nation. It declares that with respect to political belief, political discussion, political advocacy, political planning, our citizens are a sovereign and the Congress is their subordinate agent.

Those who composed the newspaper advertisement ignored the niceties of such constitutional theory. They concentrated simply on the personalities involved, listing the names of petitioners together with the names of those who had been convicted of contempt of Congress for refusing to testify on First Amendment grounds. This question was raised, but never answered directly: "We Ask the National Council of Churches *Why all this Interest on the part of Churchmen?*"

Fortunately, such newspaper advertisements are, in themselves, seldom very effective. Not so, however, with the mass circularization of congregations. The same advertisements, when mailed by a local committee to the membership of a particular church, may do considerable damage. Thus, the local Committee of Christian Laymen reports that following its first mailing to a Presbyterian church in the area, ". . . the Church office was swamped with calls from members. . . . Overtures," says the Committee, were made to get it to "discontinue its mailing of literature," but they were unsuccessful. The Committee continued to inform the church membership of new Communist perils in the churches.

Measured by Committee standards, its mail propaganda campaigns are sometimes extremely successful. "On October 8, 1961," the Committee reported, "the North Hollywood Presbyterian Church split, with some 200 members (conservatives and the principal financial supporters) pulling away to form the Valley Presbyterian Church, which is unaffiliated with the U.P.U.S.A. [United Presbyterian Church in the U.S.A.] or the National Council." Commenting on the background for the split, the Committee observed, "The Liberals in control . . . are promoting a Socialistic economy and a so-called 'Social Gospel.' Theirs is a materialistic, one-world, one-church, planned Church-State relationship. Many church members, at present, are supporting this position not knowing what is involved."

The Committee sees its responsibility in terms of informing the many church members who, unknowingly, are supporting the "liberals," and in so doing, are promoting a "Socialistic-planned economy." The number of persons involved in the schism within the North Hollywood Presbyterian Church may, as denominational officials indicate, be somewhat exaggerated, but there can be no question about it—the local Committee of Christian Laymen and its counterparts in other communities have gotten through.

Periodically, a beleaguered church will invite one of its highest-ranking denominational officers to address himself personally to the causes of dissension within the congregation. Thus, Eugene Carson Blake, Stated Clerk of the United Presbyterian Church in the U.S.A., addressed the Presbyterian

Church in Santa Barbara, California, on March 19, 1961: "I am asked to come and preach to you in Santa Barbara today," said Dr. Blake, "because this congregation is being subjected to a campaign of false witness about the leadership of your Church, both lay and ministerial, and about the leadership of the National Council of Churches. . . ." In the course of his sermon Dr. Blake carefully analyzed and refuted a series of charges that had been made in a circular mailed to members of the congregation. "I challenge this congregation and this Session to wake up to what is happening to you under the guise of anti-Communism," said Dr. Blake, who made it clear that the Ninth Commandment, forbidding the bearing of false witness, had in his judgment been violated by Santa Barbara's Christian ultra-rightists.[1]

Dr. Blake has personally been the object of printed smear campaigns on more than one occasion. One mimeographed sheet, put out by the American Council of Christian Churches, a dissident anti-National Council organization founded by the Rev. Carl McIntire, traces Blake's career from 1951 to 1961. The entry under 1956, which is typical of the sheet, declares, "Dr. Blake, as president of the NCCC, invited a team of eight Iron Curtain church leaders, headed by Metropolitan Nicolai, to visit the U.S. This team did visit the U.S. in June, 1956. Blake saw to it that these Communist agents in religious garb were paraded around our nation and presented to the American people as dedicated servants of Christ from the Communist world."

That apparently was enough to indict the man in the view of persons who hold that there must be no rapprochement between the United States and the Soviet Union, or who maintain that all Russians are inherently evil because they are Russians. The anonymous writer of the sheet holds what would seem to many to be a curious presupposition—that is, that no one, or at least not Eugene Carson Blake, can deal

[1] For an account of other measures taken against right-wing extremists in Santa Barbara see Chapter V.

with persons who *might be* Communists without being taken
in by them.

But let us suppose, just for the moment, that the Russian
churchmen were all Communists—a point by no means
proved—and that their sole intent in visiting the United States
was to do violence to American ideals. What then? Are those
who play host to them promptly going to throw over the
whole of their religious heritage, together with their national
loyalty? I think not, and I am troubled by an assumption that
casts such grave doubt on the substance of American religious
and political convictions. We have, I suggest, nothing whatever to fear in a peaceful encounter with Soviet churchmen,
whatever their politics, provided that we are secure in our own
loyalties and commitments. Given that, it is the Soviets who
should be troubled.

Another publication, also distributed by the American
Council of Christian Churches, is written by McIntire himself and is concerned with the late Methodist Bishop G.
Bromley Oxnam. The title of the twenty-four-page tract is
Bishop Oxnam—Prophet of Marx. The text of the tract claims
that "as perhaps no other man, Oxnam represents the popular,
radical, pro-communistic element in religious circles in America. . . . In the name of Christ, Oxnam has championed the
socialist principles of Karl Marx and become, I believe, the
leading 'religious disciple' of Marx in the free world."

The tract is a hodgepodge of quotations taken out of context, of biographical material used without regard to its proper
sequence in the life of the Bishop, and unsupported claims
about his alleged adherence to the Communist party line.
There is no hint that the House Committee on Un-American
Activities has said—following Bishop Oxnam's voluntary testimony before the committee—that it had ". . . no record of
any Communist Party affiliation or membership by Bishop
Oxnam." There is no suggestion that his leadership in such
organizations as the National Council of American-Soviet
Friendship was confined to a period when the United States

and the Soviet Union were allies and the Council was endorsed by such respected persons as Secretary of State Cordell Hull, Governor Leverett Saltonstall and General Dwight D. Eisenhower. Nor is there any suggestion that in criticizing the House Committee on Un-American Activities, the Bishop declared his opposition to Communism in such unequivocal fashion as the following: "I believe the Communist party is a conspiracy and that conspirators should be discovered, tried, and, if guilty, punished." Granted, Bishop Oxnam had further stated his belief in the ineffectiveness of the committee in dealing with such a conspiracy by observing that ". . . the Federal Bureau of Investigation is far better qualified for that duty than Mr. Velde's committee."[2] But such criticism, together with the other facts of the Bishop's biography, scarcely prove that Oxnam was pro-Communist in his outlook. An outspoken civil libertarian he may have been, but any identification of Bishop Oxnam with Communist purposes requires a calculated stacking of the evidence.

It is difficult to assess the damage done to persons or institutions by such printed attacks. But there can be little doubt that some churches have been split by them, and that many public figures have had their reputations significantly marred. Beyond that, we may only be certain that the printed assault massed by the Christian ultra-rightists has seriously troubled, and so dissipated the energies, of a significant segment of the Protestant community.

PATTERNS OF HARASSMENT

It is altogether natural, I suppose, that the more vitriolic verbal and printed attacks should, on occasion, spill over into more concrete expressions. Speaking specifically of Southern

[2] Quoted in Ralph Lord Roy, *Apostles of Discord* (Boston: Beacon Press, 1953), p. 243.

California ultra-rightists, Bruce Bliven once observed in *The Reporter*, "They are masters of the anonymous telephone call, the threat of economic boycott, the mobilizing of letter-writing squads." And so they are!

I know that I shall never forget a "Faith and Freedom Rally," sponsored by the American Council of Christian Churches, which I attended on June 23, 1961. Midway in the meeting, the Rev. L. W. Linnerson, pastor of a nearby Lutheran church, rose and inquired whether he might ask a question, since he would be unable to stay for the entire rally. The Rev. John Dekker, pastor of the Bible Presbyterian Church in North Hollywood, who was chairing the meeting, indicated that no question period had been scheduled. The audience responded with, "Let him be heard," and Mr. Dekker changed his mind.

Pastor Linnerson's question was this: "Does the ACCC approve of the way in which J. Edgar Hoover is handling the Communists in the United States?"

The ACCC ministers on stage went into a huddle. When they emerged, the answer, to no one's surprise, was affirmative.

Pastor Linnerson then asked if he could read a statement by J. Edgar Hoover, strongly disapproving of "self-styled experts on communism." Someone on stage announced that there was no time for discussion of this sort at the meeting, and Pastor Linnerson made his way out, accompanied by several members of the audience.

Once outside, a group formed around the pastor, who then read the text of Mr. Hoover's statement. Later, Pastor Linnerson reported that at some point during the reading of the statement two men told him to move on, punctuating their directive with the words, "You had better leave if you want to leave in one piece."

Pastor Linnerson made the alleged threat known to the police department, and on Sunday *The Valley News* carried a front-page story that began, "Police will be on standby for

trouble at a Woodland Hills church today, following reports
that a group of hecklers may try to disrupt the worship service
as a 'revenge' move against the minister."

A number of local ministers, including myself, had made
statements to the press deploring the whole incident. The
night the statements were published our telephones began to
ring. My first call came at 2:00 A.M., the next at 2:30 A.M.
The following night there were five calls between 2:00 and
5:00 A.M. And so it went. Each time the caller remained
anonymous, breathing into the telephone and tying up the
line. (At that time telephones on Pacific Telephone and
Telegraph circuits in the west San Fernando Valley remained
connected until the initiator of a call hung up.) When I tried
to get onto the better side of the caller (Who could say what
his problem might be? Dope addiction? Potential suicide?)
all I evoked was a laugh, calculated to sound like the graveyard, I suppose, but conveying more of the ham actor than
anything else. When I attempted a frontal approach and connected a tape recording device to the telephone with a pre-
recorded message for the caller, it so delighted him that he
called back repeatedly.

Pastor Linnerson, whom I telephoned the day after the
calls began, reported a similar pattern of harassment. It continued for both of us until my family and I left for summer
vacation, and it resumed for us, at least, shortly after we returned. Our ultimate solution was to put in an answering
service.

The pattern of harassment was not confined to telephone
calls for Pastor Linnerson. Cars would cruise steadily around
the block late at night, slowing down or stopping in front of
the house, then repeating the circuit. Men would sit in an
automobile parked across the street, staring at the Pastor and
his family, watching and observing by the hour, saying nothing, but being constantly, obviously present—and then, with
no more announcement than when they came, they would

drive off, only to appear again on another day, or another night.

All this in response to an attempt to ask a question at a rally for "Faith and Freedom"? Apparently so. I have no reason to suppose that Pastor Linnerson invented the stories, and he has no reason to suppose that the pattern of harassment was linked to anything other than the "Faith and Freedom Rally."

In all fairness to the clergymen who set up the rally, however, I must confess that the Rev. M. H. Reynolds, the third speaker of the evening, who spoke after Pastor Linnerson's exit, had a point in observing that Rev. Linnerson was "trying to make a sounding board out of the meeting." Reynolds went on to say that "It became obvious that the pastor was out of order," and again, I must agree that there is merit in his contention. Reynolds was no doubt more than a little perplexed when he told the audience that ". . . they would see how he [Linnerson] appreciated someone standing up in his church on Sunday and asking to speak when he was preaching." (It was this remark that caused police to stand by lest hecklers disrupt the services at Linnerson's church.)

In retrospect, the whole affair seems absurdly trivial—certainly not worthy of the deep feelings and sentiments that went into it. It seems especially so when one remembers that the principal actors in the farce called themselves Christians, and were, for the most part, clergymen.

All the same, it seems that an inability to distinguish between the important and the trivial is one of the chief characteristics of a virulent anti-Communism. When a man gets anxious enough, reality becomes misshapen; he loses his perspective; all manner of stratagems seem to be proper means to the end of eradicating evil and exposing duplicity.

I don't think that I shall ever fully understand what causes one human being to harass another—not as part of a systematic campaign, anyway; and I shall continue to be puzzled by what happened during and after the "Faith and Freedom Rally," just as I am puzzled by what happened at another public meeting in California's San Fernando Valley.

It was a P.T.A. president who arose, in this instance, to protest charges that the P.T.A. was promoting Socialistic ends. Some of the persons attending the meeting asked her her name and she gave it to them. Why not?

According to one newspaper account, she received four critical calls the next day, all of them anonymous. The fourth was from a woman trying to sound like a man.

"We've had a chance to check your background," the voice is reported to have said, "and we find you have teen-agers in your family. Aren't you concerned with their safety?"

"What do you mean?" the lady asked.

"You should know," said the voice. The caller hung up.

THE PUBLIC FACE OF HARASSMENT

Patterns of harassment are not confined to the San Fernando Valley in California, of course. One minister in another area—a Methodist—reports that he got up one morning to find a hammer and sickle neatly stenciled on the sidewalk in front of the parsonage. Another minister was called by the police and informed that he had been hanged the night before —in effigy, in front of the church. Still another, in Columbus, Ohio, found that the number of hecklers at public meetings was getting so numerous that special procedures had to be set up to ensure order. In Houston, a prominent church official arrived in town only to be greeted by protest marchers and pickets.

The last word in harassment, however, is the well-engineered, economic boycott, which in the case of a church can mean the difference between a balanced budget with building-loan installments and salaries paid on time, and serious organizational dislocation. When pledge income is cut off suddenly, even the most smoothly administered church program may rapidly fall to pieces. In point of fact, I know of no means for harassment that has been used with greater precision or with greater effectiveness.

In instance after instance, withdrawal of economic support, or threatened withdrawal, has been accompanied by a vigorous insistence that the churches purge themselves of alleged Communist influences. What has amazed many an extremist, however, was the plain fact that the church is not often for sale. Not for any price. A few churches *have* capitulated to economic pressures, of course, and chosen institutional acts of public expiation in preference to the loss of needed income, but they have generally done so with the uneasy knowledge that they were relinquishing their responsibility to be relevant to the world.

A typical approach works something like this: A prominent member of a local church will write to the President of the National Council of Churches, or another high-ranking official, sending carbon copies of his letter to the minister of his church, denominational officials and local officials of the NCC.

The NCC will then be charged with offenses ranging from pro-Communist activities to the promotion of salacious literature. The writer will probably observe that most, if not all, of his friends feel as he does and declare that the NCC should speak neither in the name of its "thirty-eight million members," nor in his.

He will inform the NCC that he is canceling his pledge to his local church so the NCC will have no way of receiving his support. He will reinstate his pledge, he is likely to observe, whenever the NCC comes around to his point of view.

Economic blackmail of this sort is, unfortunately, a good deal more common than one might think. But economic pressure, valuable as it may be in attempts to coerce institutional conformity, is not often possible in relation to individuals. And in any case, other means may be far more practicable in dealing with persons in public life.

Let us examine one method for dealing with a public figure. Suppose for a moment, if you would, that you are a member of a right-wing group, and that members of your group are seriously distressed over the beliefs and activities of a particular public figure. Let us further suppose that members of your organization honestly believe that the man in question is doing a good deal, in the course of his public appearances, to promote Communism—that he may, in truth, be a Communist in disguise. What action will you take?

If you happen to be a member of the John Birch Society and have read the Society's manual carefully, you will probably advise your group to proceed in the following fashion: Two or three persons will be asked to attend one or more of the lectures of the man about whom you are concerned. They will sit apart from one another and give no indication that they are acquainted. Then, during the question-and-answer session, each will begin to ask questions such as the following:

"Mr. Hall. According to this printed record, you once spent several months passing out anti-Semitic literature. Is that true?"

Another member of the trio will then rise. "Mr. Hall. According to this announcement of your speech, obviously based on information you yourself gave the program chairman, you worked for a while for the XYZ Agency. But I have here a published statement I happened to run across, in which Mr. X says that you never worked for the XYZ Agency at all or in any capacity. Is Mr. X mistaken?"

Neither the questions nor the technique are hypothetical. They are straight from the John Birch Society's *Blue Book*, which concludes its description of how to heckle with the observation, "Let the barrage . . . go on for a few nights . . .

[and Mr.] Hall may still be finding some other way to serve Communist purposes, but it will not be as a speaker."[3] Search the *Blue Book* as carefully as you wish and you will find no directive cautioning you to make certain, before you begin your heckling campaign, that your target is, in fact, a Communist. You will find no indication that your questions should be based on solid fact, rather than on conjecture or inventions of "fact." Nor will you find any hint that such a technique might not be in the best American tradition of fair play. It is simply commended to you as a workable technique, as a means for discrediting a speaker, justified by the end of destroying the effectiveness of one more alleged Communist.

It would be impossible to count the number of times the *Blue Book* strategy for heckling, whether practiced by John Birch Society members or by others, has been used at church meetings over the past several years. It would be still more impossible to know how many times such strategy has been augmented by hissing, booing, feet-scraping, paper-rattling antagonists whose sole interest was to see to it that a speaker was silenced. Meetings have occasionally been broken up by such tactics. More often, the antagonists, who are generally in the minority, have been discredited by their own unmannerly behavior.

In talking with persons who acknowledge membership in organizations on the far right one is often assured that neither they nor their friends would engage in tactics of harassment, but in light of the *Blue Book's* explicit "counsel to heckle" one wonders where the line is drawn and by whom. Someone is doing the heckling and a good deal of it is boisterous. That much is certain. If it is not being done by the John Birch Society or its members it is surely being carried out by their fellow ultra-rightists. The presence of the shock troops cannot be denied.

[3] Robert Welch, *The Blue Book* (Belmont, Mass., privately printed, 1961), p. 107.

Let anyone inadvertently omit a patriotic observance, such as the pledge of allegiance at the beginning of a program, and a chorus of protest goes up with the clear implication that subversion is afoot. Let a speaker talk disparagingly about the United States—something the ultra-rightists reserve for themselves—and he may have trouble finishing his remarks. Schedule a speaker who is left-of-center politically, concerned with social reform, or in some way controversial, and the hecklers will appear.

Sometimes the intimidation attempts are subtle and difficult to interpret. A woman may send the speaker a note, if there are written questions, informing him that she is writing to the House Committee on Un-American Activities, informing the Committee of what he has said (her privilege, of course). A group of "strong men" may arrive just after the meeting has begun and plant themselves prominently in the front row, never taking their eyes off the speaker. A crew of evidence collectors may move about during and after the meeting with portable tape recorders and motion-picture cameras, ostentatiously making certain that every remark, every gesture is taken down. All these techniques have been used and are being used by radical right wingers, and none of them are anything that anyone can object to—much. They are the subtle and not-so-subtle tools of harassment, violating no one's civil liberties, but providing a continuing nuisance factor.

After a few experiences with those intent on heckling and harassment, most ministers, and others whose ideas may be anathema to the radical rightists, invent their own techniques for defense. Not long after arriving in Southern California, I learned that when speaking on a topic related to right-wing extremism it was often prudent to devote part of my talk to explaining some of the methods of harassment used by the radical right. This kind of pre-emption had the virtue of serving notice to any ultras in the crowd that good manners were in order, both during the talk and the question-and-answer session, while at the same time providing the audience with information on the operational techniques of those whom Hoover has called "self-styled experts on communism."

Again and again, however, I find that the best defense against public harassment is to assume that the extremists are human beings—which they are—and to speak to them as honestly and as openly as to anyone else in the audience. The extremist often has a legitimate point to make, and to grant him that point, without embracing his whole system of beliefs and convictions, is to grant him a basic right held by any human being—to be considered as a person.

PREPARING FOR THE COMMUNIST TAKE-OVER

Unfortunately, some ultra-rightists seem determined *not* to be treated as human beings. A number of the more hostile sort may be found studying weaponry and engaging in the war games of the Minutemen. Founded by Robert Bolivar DePugh of Norborne, Missouri, following a 1959 duck hunt, the Minutemen is a loose federation of independent guerrilla warfare groups ready to defend the United States against a Communist invader or a Communist *coup d'etat.*

According to *Newsweek,* DePugh is a member of the John Birch Society. His personal convictions are unreservedly ultra-conservative. He is convinced that it is only a question of time until the Communists will move in, and is therefore critical of rightist organizations that talk about anti-Communism, but which have no machinery for direct action.

The November 12, 1961, edition of the *New York Times* quotes DePugh as saying, "We must be willing to continue the fight for liberty even though we no longer have the legal support of established authority . . . [and] prepare ourselves to take any action—no matter how brutal—that may be required to renew the protection of the United States Constitution for future generations."

DePugh has his own notions as to who the enemy may be. "A lot of people in this country are Communists without knowing it themselves," he says. The Minutemen are in a better position to discover who is a Communist without knowing it, DePugh maintains, than the F.B.I. or the C.I.A.—at least on the local level. As a consequence, the Minutemen keep their own files.

In the view of the Minutemen, nearly everyone should be investigated, and DePugh wastes no verbage on the fact. "We must investigate, by means of our own secret memberships," he says, "the possible infiltration of Communist sympathizers into American organizations of government, business, labor, religion or education."

Minutemen pride themselves on their ability to be self-sustaining. They live off the land during their "wilderness" exercises and take extreme care to leave no trace of their maneuvers, even burying used pocket matches. Many of the training exercises are held late at night when detection is least likely, and members are advised to stay on friendly terms with the "native" population. Numerous manuals on guerrilla warfare methods have been prepared and distributed.

DePugh estimates national Minutemen membership at figures as high as 25,000, but concedes that the organization's loosely-knit structure makes an accurate membership count impossible. Membership recruitment, which is carried out largely by means of classified newspaper advertisements, suffered a setback following the widely publicized arrest of two Minutemen leaders in San Diego on a charge of failure to register as sex offenders.

DePugh is careful not to endorse other right-wing groups such as Fred Schwarz's Christian Anti-Communism Crusade. All the same, the *New York Times* indicates that DePugh disseminates the literature of such organizations. Nor is his tacit endorsement of Schwarz the limit of his concern with the Christian ultra-rightists. Donald Janson and Bernard Eismann report in their book *The Far Right* that DePugh attended one of Billy James Hargis' five-day anti-Communist meetings held at the Mayo Hotel in Tulsa. If his presence at the meeting was noticed it was neither heralded nor acknowledged, however.

By no shaping of the evidence may the Minutemen be regarded as a present threat on the American political scene. Its organizational lines are too diffuse for the group to control any measurable portion of public opinion. Its war games, so much like the vacant lot exploits of boys who have taken up soldiering, have become something of a national joke—the "Mi-nute" Men, Pogo calls them. Whether a surge of ultra-rightist sentiment would bring with it a corresponding growth in paramilitary activity of the Minutemen brand is doubtful. All the same, the activities of the organization will bear watching. We must be alert to the possibility that those who assume they know the shape of the political scene better than the experts may also decide that they know how "law and order" may best be assured, and then proceed to establish it.

FROM PRAYER TO SEDITION AND INTRIGUE

We have not yet exhausted the arsenal of the right-wing extremist. So persuaded is he of the justice of his cause that nearly every facet of life, spiritual or secular, is regarded as one more weapon in his fight. The most central elements of personal and public piety are unhesitatingly reshaped into bludgeons for attacking the "enemy." Thus the evangelist Billy James Hargis advises, "Counterattack with prayer," and insists that "The Word of God is one of the weapons most feared by anti-Christ Communism."

Even as one who is somewhat outside the mainstream of Christian life in America, I cannot suppress the observation that the unflinching use of the primal elements of Christianity as mere instruments for achieving given ends demeans the religion. When the Bible is used as a "weapon" and prayer as a means for "counterattack," even the most worthy of purposes becomes as naught. To *use* religion, rather than being shaped by it, to see it as a means to an end, rather than as a way of life and a system of commitments, is to repudiate religion. It is to begin to worship the golden calf anew and to commit the error of Adam, who assumed that man might define for himself the ground of his ultimate commitment and tell ultimate reality how it might best serve his ends.

Hargis is not alone in his attempt to harness the energies of Christianity to the cause of anti-Communism. Fred Schwarz, Executive Director of the Christian Anti-Communism Crusade and author of the book *You Can Trust the Communists —To Do Exactly As They Say*, observes that ". . . the Communists have proved themselves superlative organizers, organizers of Revolution, terror, war, oppression, sedition and intrigue. . . . Similarly," says Schwarz, "the Christian forces opposing Communism must be organized and disciplined."

The question must be raised: are we to expect Schwarz to follow through on his observation that Christians must be similarly organized to Communists, whom he tells us are "superlative organizers . . . of Revolution, terror, war, oppression, sedition and intrigue"? I hope not. I assume not— particularly in the light of Schwarz's further comment that his concern is with "*organization*". This is so that the "gasoline of conviction, consecration and courage may move the mountain of lethargy, self-indulgence and ignorance which provide the inflammable debris through which the Communist fire is consuming the earth." (!) From that hyperbolic statement I take it that Schwarz is talking about the ability of the Communists to get organized, and the necessity for

Christians to find a like *ability* (with the gasoline of conviction). I take it that he would not include his catalogue of Communist turpitude in his own organizational plans.

Whether the Christian ultra-rightists have or have not been responsible for the sort of organized violence which Schwarz attributes to the Communists is an unanswered question. Further, we are not likely to discover whether or not the new American right wing has adopted the techniques ordinarily accepted by Communist insurrectionists—not in the foreseeable future, anyway. Short of some good detective work following an act of violence, and the subsequent judicial processes which are necessary to establish guilt in the American tradition, we must leave unanswered the question of the Christian ultra-rightist's dependence on violence for achieving his ends. Obviously, extremists on the right—Christian or otherwise—are not going to advertise their illegal activities, if such exist. We can only wait to see what happens and in the meantime judge those on the radical right by a principle of justice applicable to all citizens of these United States: We must assume that they are innocent of acts of violence until they are proved guilty.

THE ATTACK SUMMED UP

I seriously doubt whether the Christian fright peddlers have introduced any new principles in the art of controversy, public or private. Their weapons are the classic ones, occasionally updated for an age of technology, but as ethical or unethical as the persons who use them. They range from sometimes slanderous attacks at public meetings to anonymous midnight telephone calls, from printed smear sheets to well-organized campaigns to convince the members of a local congregation that they should repudiate the National Council of Churches or the parent denomination. They include economic levers and public heckling campaigns. Nothing, apparently, is outside the scope of the ultra-rightists' storehouse of weapons, including prayer and the Bible, both of which are commended to the faithful as effective means to their religiopolitical ends.

The weapons of the more unethical among the radically right are not those found among men who simply disagree and in their disagreement propose reform within the disciplines and responsibilities of a free society. The weapons of the Christian fright peddlers far too often are the weapons common to men who prefer innuendo to straightforward presentation, defamation of character to analysis of ideas, unsupported charges to careful examination. They are the weapons of those who are so concerned with making wrongs right (as *they* have defined them) that any method will suffice. They belong to the sort of men whose whole purpose consists of establishing their point, because they assume that any other point is wrong.

The emphasis among some ultraconservatives is on organizational diffusion; and for others, it is on organizational efficiency. But whatever the organizing principle, the attack is primary. The battle must be won.

Whether or not the extreme rightists have resorted or would resort to violence in their war of intrigue is unknown, and for the present we must assume, in keeping with the American tradition of jurisprudence, that even the most extreme among them are innocent of violence unless they are proved guilty.

Of this much, however, we may be certain: The Christian fright peddlers have done untold damage. They have attacked free institutions and free men in an open society without regard for the disciplines of responsibility acknowledged by those who cherish liberty. They have sounded the alarms of distrust with unrelenting insistence, knowing full well that the only environment capable of sustaining freedom is one that begins with a trust in persons and ends with a deep confidence in the democratic process. Their offense, their true offense, is in their tampering with that process, in their attempts to coerce it—in short, in their antidemocratic bias.

Perhaps the following judgment by the Rt. Rev. John P. Craine, Episcopal Bishop of Indianapolis, is too severe, but it is entirely relevant:

> It is interesting to note that the far right has adopted the same tactics as the Communists—the repudiation of democracy, the fundamentalist, dogmatic attitudes, the theories of guilt by association. Any clergymen who has any liberal inclinations, who is concerned about housing or segregation or even supports the National Council of Churches or the United Nations is accused of softness toward communism. I can only say that if I were intent on destroying this great nation, I can think of no better way than to create distrust, hate and fear, as is being done today.

Also speaking of the radical right, New York's Governor Nelson Rockefeller declared on July 14, 1963, "These people have no program for . . . the American people except distrust, disunity and the ultimate destruction of the confidence of the people in themselves. They are the purveyors of hate and distrust in a time when, as never before, the need of the world is for love and understanding."

I believe that Governor Rockefeller is right, and yet I must grant that such is not normally the objective of the right-wing extremist. The creation of distrust, hate and fear is not often, I am sure, the conscious intent of those involved. But it is nonetheless real. That is the tragedy of it.

3 Emergent Fundamentalism

FRED SCHWARZ DOES not like to be identified with the right wing, and strictly speaking, he is correct. He is not a member of the movement in terms of any precise definition of the right-wing syndrome. As an Australian citizen, he comments selectively on U.S. domestic issues, and one can only guess whether he would favor urban renewal or oppose federal aid to education; unlike most ultraconservatives, he sees Communism as an external threat as well as an internal menace; and he is altogether unwilling to compile his private list of American subversives. Schwarz is open in his presentation of evidence and straightforward in his arguments. For all that, he still derives his greatest support from acknowledged members of the right wing and participates enough in the ultraconservative world view to deserve at least honorary membership in the movement.

The main components of Schwarz's Christian Anti-Communism Crusade are a fervent commitment to a very conservative kind of Christianity and an unrelenting dedication to anti-Communism. Judging entirely by his emphasis, the latter is, by far, the more important of the two.

Schwarz is not a man on whom religious labels may easily be pasted. For one thing, it would be difficult to discover his doctrinal stand from reviewing either his lectures or his books. Apart from evoking a kind of faith in evangelical Christianity in general, he says little about the content of Christian belief. Although he accepts the appellation "evangelical Christian," I am not certain that he would care to be called a fundamentalist. His offense, however, would come from the word, not from the movement or its beliefs. He readily assents to all of the following articles of belief, common to both fundamentalist and evangelical Christianity:

I. The Bible is the revealed Word of God, is without error, and must be understood literally.

II. Man is inherently sinful, his sin having been contracted by the disobedience of Adam in the face of God's commandment.

III. Men are either saved or they are not; there can be no ambiguity about the state of salvation.

IV. Men are saved only by faith in the risen Lord, who was crucified and suffered, spilling his blood in order to atone for man's sins.

V. There is a clear line between the evil and the good; hell is the certain punishment of the former, heaven the sure reward of the latter.

VI. Jesus of Nazareth arose bodily from the tomb and ascended bodily into heaven.

VII. Miracles are historical facts, as recounted in the Biblical narratives.

VIII. The virgin birth was a historical occurrence and, as an article of faith, is an altogether essential part of Christian doctrine.[1]

The list is not exhaustive, but it covers the main points of fundamentalist doctrine. Other beliefs tend to be peripheral, such as the common confidence among fundamentalists that the King James Version of the Bible, translated in 1611, is

[1] Schwarz assented to this summary of evangelical, or fundamentalist, beliefs in the course of an interview in North Hollywood, California, on July 18, 1963. One additional article was in the original summary, but has been deleted from this version since Schwarz said that he had never taken a position on the question—*i.e.,* belief in the premillennial return of Christ.

vastly superior to any other, if indeed it is not the only authentic version in existence. The value system of fundamentalism —or more accurately, its catalogue of moralities—stresses the personal virtues: abstention from the use of alcoholic beverages and tobacco, the worthfulness of the simple life, and the impropriety of dancing should it involve anything more than a folksy, community affair. In an earlier day fundamentalism energetically fought the Darwinian heresy, but although it has not conceded defeat, the troops are now largely deployed on other fronts. The movement scorns anything intellectual and is certain that relativism, pragmatism, and empricism are the works of Satan. At root, fundamentalism nurtures a serene confidence that even the most complex aspects of reality may be reduced to simple explanations. Good is good and evil, of course, is evil; although God alone may be able to make final distinctions between the two, the moral Christian can make a reasonably certain judgment as to which is which in any given instance.

This, then, is the religious context from which Schwarz speaks. *Time* magazine quotes him as describing himself (rather ungenerously) as "a narrow-minded, Bible-believing Baptist." Narrow-minded or not, Fred Schwarz is a lay evangelist of unusual talent. He is not the first in the family. His father, a Viennese Jew who was converted to Christianity, was a lay preacher in the Pentecostal tradition.

THE MAN AND THE MOVEMENT

Fred Schwarz was born in Brisbane, Queensland, Australia, on January 15, 1913. He took degrees in both science and in arts at the University of Queensland, and while lecturing at the Queensland Teachers College in mathematics and science, he completed the medical program at the University. He entered medical practice in suburban Sydney and continued there as a psychiatrist and general practitioner until 1953.

He first became seriously interested in anti-Communism while still a student at Queensland, following an unfortunate debating encounter with Max Julias, a prominent Australian Communist. The experience sent him back to the books, this time to study Marx, Engels, Lenin and Stalin. More Australian debates and speeches followed, until 1950, when Schwarz's combination of Christian fundamentalism and anti-Communism brought him in contact with two North Americans, the Rev. Carl McIntire of the American Council of Christian Churches and Dr. T. T. Shields, a Baptist minister from Toronto. At their suggestion he made a U.S. tour that year. He returned to the U.S. in 1953 to join W. E. Pietsch, a Waterloo, Iowa, radio evangelist, in founding the Christian Anti-Communism Crusade.

Why did Schwarz give up a successful medical practice in Australia? His more severe critics call him a "patriot for profit" and point to the large earnings of the Crusade. The *New York Times* reports the Crusade's 1961 gross earnings at $1,250,000, and Schwarz declared on December 12, 1962, that gross earnings for that year would be close to $1,000,000, despite what he termed "virulent, vicious attacks" on the organization.

Midyear in 1963 Schwarz reported that, with the exception of its anti-Communism schools, the Crusade was having its "best year to date," both in terms of attendance at rallies and income.

Schwarz himself contributes generously to the Crusade, turning over all of his royalties and speaking fees (more than $140,000 in one year alone), and is careful to say that his own salary is a meager $5000 per year—plus expenses. "I'm not boasting about this," he says. "I don't consider myself a martyr. I'm enjoying it up to the hilt."

Critics aside, Schwarz offers his own summary of his motivation. First, he has a wife and family of whom he is understandably fond. The Communists, he says, consider them "diseased social animals," and since he believes that Communism will have conquered the world within a generation—unless there is a general awakening to the danger—he is eager to see to it that his family will not be among the first to be liquidated. Second, Schwarz finds that his belief in God and in the redeeming power of faith in Christ impels him to preach the gospel in the face of the enemy of God and Christ —Communism.

THE TRUSTWORTHY COMMUNISTS

Schwarz regards Communists as incredibly intelligent, capable, resourceful and well-organized, and at the same time, as insane. "The achievements of Communism are unprecedented in the annals of human history. The Communists have repeatedly achieved the impossible," he says in *You Can Trust the Communists*. And in testimony before staff members of the House Committee on Un-American Activities, he declares, "They have reached the point of insanity. . . . I believe that paranoia is at the heart of Communism and that their theoretical concepts are far more convincing to them than the evidence of the facts."

Communists, Schwarz believes, behave in accordance with a kind of inexorable, inner logic, according to "laws of their being," which, if understood, make them wholly trustworthy and predictable. He compares that predictability to the law of gravity, and observes that once we understand the nature of Communism, and the techniques it uses, we may even use those same techniques against it. The Communists' primary objective is simply to fulfill their inner destiny—that is, "to create a new world and regenerate mankind." To do so they must, of course, conquer the world, something which Schwarz feels they are doing handily.

The Australian evangelist enjoys tracing the statistical success of Communism, charting its development from 1903 to the present. Schwarz contends that since its inception Communism has grown from a movement consisting only of a leader and seventeen supporters to a world-system dominating more than 900 million people. And nearly two thousand years after the birth of Jesus what do we see? Only one third of the population of the world is even nominally Christian, he reminds us.

So is the world divided; and the Communists are winning the contest. Their success is achieved, says Schwarz, through the application of three "scientific laws."

First, atheism. The Communists, he says, ". . . are proudly, unashamedly atheistic in theory and in practice. When they deny God, they simultaneously deny every virtue and every value that originates with God. They deny moral law. They deny absolute standards of truth and righteousness. An entire civilized code of moral and ethical values is destroyed so that they are free to erect in their place new moral and ethical standards as the occasion demands."

"The second law of Communism," says Schwarz, "is that man is a material machine. He is matter in motion and nothing more. Man is a body, and he is completely describable in terms of the laws of chemistry and physics. Man has no soul, no spirit, no significant individual value, no continuity of life. He is entirely an evolutionary product, the specie Homo sapiens, and subject to modification, adaptation, and transformation by the applied, established laws of animal husbandry."

Schwarz contends that the "third law of Communism is economic determinism," and adds, "It states that the qualities

of human intelligence, personality, emotional and religious
life merely reflect the economic environment. . . . In the
final analysis, man is a determined economic being."

A SIMPLISTIC REDUCTION OF DOGMATICS

While it is plain that Schwarz is rather too generous in
conceding global real estate to the Communists, his greatest
fault is in his facile, simplistic reduction of Communist
dogmatics to a few terse lines. Unfortunately, Communism
is far more formidable as a philosophical system than his
exercise in word magic would have us believe. You do not offer
an effective criticism of a philosophy by summarizing it as
an absurdity.

While atheism is an integral part of Communist philosophy, it is scarcely the touchstone of Communist morality.
While Communists are committed to scientific empiricism,
and some may have committed the reductionist fallacy of
describing man purely in terms of his physiological makeup,
not all Communists are so naïve as to dispose completely of
man's capacity for transcending his physiological being. Finally, economic theory does, without question, occupy a disproportionate place in the Communist view of the world. It
often serves as an uncritical (and mistaken) monocausal explanation of complex historical developments. But it is *not*
the sole explanatory principle used by Communist theorists.
To represent it as such is to slay the paper dragon.

I have still another objection to Schwarz's summary of the
"scientific laws" of Communism. It has to do with atheism.
To suggest, as Schwarz does, that there is an intimate connection between atheism and the repudiation of ethics and
morality is to impugn the good names and ethical standards
of a multitude of persons who are atheists and, at the same

time, ethical and moral. Similarly, to insist that there is a necessary connection between atheism and Communism is as unfair and as illogical as it would be to declare that there is a necessary connection between Christianity and the German Nazi movement, which unabashedly proclaimed "Positive Christianity" as the state religion. Atheism and Communism may coincide with each other. "Positive Christianity" may have been embraced by the Nazi Reich. But a coincidence of belief is not the same as an identity. It does not necessitate a relationship. No more than belief in Christianity implies belief in the Führer principle does atheism imply Communism. That atheism and Communism should be so linked is one of the minor tragedies of our era.

To say, as does Schwarz, "It has always been my endeavor to show . . . gatherings the logical connections between atheism and Communism," and to add without hesitation, "There is also a historical link between liberal theology, Modernism and Communism," is to engage in the kind of assassination of ideas that must inevitably spill over to the character of any who happen to be atheists, or who care to identify themselves as religious liberals.

Schwarz is not so unworldly as to be unaware of the great men who have been both atheists and persons of integrity. It was not, after all, so many years ago that Robert Ingersol, whose moral character was admired by even his most ardent critics, nominated a Democratic candidate for President of the United States. Ingersol was an atheist. Supreme Court Justice Oliver Wendell Holmes remains one of the most admired jurists ever to sit on the bench of the highest court of our nation. He was an atheist.[2] John Adams, Thomas Jefferson and John Quincy Adams were all religious liberals.

[2] Holmes has also been counted as an agnostic. Whatever the label used, Mark DeWolfe Howe, one-time secretary to Holmes, has this to say about the Justice's religious philosophy and its relationship to his character: "[Holmes] could retain belief in morality without belief in God and accept the standards of gentlemanly conduct as self-justifying principles of taste." See Mark DeWolfe Howe, *Justice Oliver Wendell Holmes—The Shaping Years, 1841–1870* (Cambridge: The Belknap Press, 1957).

Is anyone bold enough to suggest—even for a moment—that the thought of Ingersol and Holmes had a "logical connection" with Communism? Is anyone willing to say that three of the first six Presidents of the United States were part of a "historical link" to Communism because they were theological liberals? I doubt it. Not even Fred Schwarz would claim so much.

I will grant that atheism is not a popular belief at the moment and that theological liberalism is not the majority faith. All the same, the right to be an atheist or a theological liberal is guaranteed by the Constitution of the United States, and at least implied by Christian charity.

COMMUNISM AND HUMAN NATURE

If Schwarz misses the mark in his attack on atheism, he is nonetheless discerning when it comes to identifying one of Communism's main appeals: It has a program to change human nature. It proclaims that the old human nature will die with the passing away of bourgeois society. As it dies, new men will emerge. No longer will there be strife and class warfare; no longer will there be any need for legal restraint; men will live together in peace and freedom; an ordered society will develop without compulsion. Abundance, made possible by the sharing of surplus value, will eliminate the greed of the past. Leisure time, made possible by a fully productive economy, will enable men to become the modern Greeks, devoting themselves to a new birth of the arts, a renaissance in human values.

As Schwarz describes it, "There will be no need for a police force; there will be nothing for police to do. There will be no need for an income-tax department because everyone working, according to his natural impulses, gives of his best for the general well-being, and out of the abundance thus created retains only his own personal needs. Farewell anger, lust and greed, envy, malice and strife, pestilence and war; enter golden, companionable, cooperative brotherhood; mankind will live together in the glorious day of communism that has dawned on the earth."

Schwarz's apocalyptic description is not extreme, as anyone will know who has read the Soviet periodicals over the past few years or listened to American Communists who have returned recently from visits to the U.S.S.R. The "fatherland" of Communism, it is said, even now is moving from the phase of socialistic development to pure Communism. The machinery of the state, the encumbrances of industrial management are being eliminated piece by piece.

No matter where I encounter the apocalyptic vision—whether in the writings of Fred Schwarz, in a Communist periodical, or in a speech by an American Communist—I find it frightening and profoundly disturbing. Behind the vision of the world made over, behind the image of all men living together in the fulfillment of the collective, is the certain knowledge that one man must be sacrificed, and he is the most important man of all—the individual. Human nature has been redefined by someone, some group, other than the only person who has a right to say what human nature should be—the individual. The nature of man has been placed in the keeping of an elite, now called the Presidium, which is entrusted with deciding what is best for man. Insofar as that trust is acted upon, man must be remade for good or for ill.

But suppose for a moment that the transformation were for the good; suppose that the means were at hand for making it possible. What then? The offense to humanity is still as great. The anguish is just as deep, because freedom has been vanquished. It is dead.

As Hallock Hoffman, staff member of the Center for the Study of Democratic Institutions, once put it, "If somebody is to decide what kind of man is good, and if that somebody appears to have the power—or even the knowledge—for making men over into his idea of what is good, what has happened to freedom? Are we men, if other men make us what we are? Or are we less than men, objects somehow at the mercy of controls we do not understand, helpless in the grasp of powers beyond our reach?"

The answer is plain. Soviet society, or any other that would act as the creator and custodian of the "true" image of man, must deliver to the world a human who is not a human being, but is simply a frail caricature of a man.

Fred Schwarz sees this and sees it clearly. He perceives the flaw in Soviet utopian idealism because his Christian faith maintains that sinful human nature may be transformed, but only in Christian liberty. "Stand fast," said Paul, ". . . in the liberty wherewith Christ hath made us free, and be not entangled again with the yoke of bondage."

That is the root of Schwarz's conviction. For others of us, who recognize the too frequent reality of human bondage, but not its inevitability, freedom is still the important thing. It is essential to the fulfillment of the human spirit. The man who speaks with the voice of a concerned humanity, whose life relationships and values are more than passing reflections of the condition of the race, the man who has distilled his own deepest identity from out of the joy and pain and anger of life itself is no mere casting from a mold of ideal prefigurement. He is a person who has the courage to meet the questionings of existence with answers that may be found only within the freedom, and therefore the destiny, of his true self.

THE FAILURE TO TAKE COMMUNISM SERIOUSLY

I only wish that Schwarz's understanding of the failure of Communist first assumptions extended to his appraisal of Communism as a movement and its relationship to democratic culture. Unfortunately, the greater part of his writings is given over to the description of one atrocity after another, to repeated analogies between Communism and disease syndromes (usually cancer), and to cries of despair over the alleged success of the Communist conquest of the free world. The total effect is a picture of the world neatly, but falsely, divided into the forces of evil and the forces of good.

Were Communism nothing but a diabolical system of evil, intent upon perpetrating one barbarism after another, successful in the abolition of all moral principles within its boundaries and capable of exercising an uncompromising tyranny over its proponents, it would not be the threat it is today. It is precisely because of its successes in raising standards of living, in furthering scientific and to a lesser extent artistic achievement, that Communism represents an alternative to the world's uncommitted peoples. If the choice were between freedom and barbarism there would be no difficulty in choosing, no matter how carefully the barbarism might be disguised. By failing to give Communism its due Schwarz has committed that error he finds most scandalous—he has underestimated the power of the "dread opponent."

The Crusade's rallies and schools are perhaps the best illustration of the consequences of Schwarz's failure to take the strong points of Communism seriously. Take, for instance, one of the Crusade's first major efforts, an anti-Communist rally held in the fall of 1961. A sequel to a week-long Southern California "school" of anti-Communism, the rally attracted 15,000 persons to the Hollywood Bowl for what actor George Murphy is reported to have praised as "the largest anti-Communist rally ever held anywhere in the world."

Among the prominent speakers were Representative Walter H. Judd (R) of Minnesota, Senator Thomas J. Dodd (D) of Connecticut, and C. D. Jackson, publisher of *Life* magazine. Jackson was there to apologize formally because on September 1, *Life* had called the coming rally "a new kind of revival meeting," and had observed that it served the "nonreligious ends of an outfit called the 'Christian Anti-Communism Crusade.'" That evening Jackson confessed that *Life* ". . . was wrong about Dr. Schwarz and is profoundly sorry." A full-page editorial that appeared in the magazine later declared that "Dr. Fred Schwarz is himself well-informed, and his Christian Anti-Communism Crusade attracts much respectable support." However, the editorial continued, ". . . it also attracts people who are too superheated to teach or learn anything."

This last sentence put the finger on what to many was one of the most disturbing aspects of the Hollywood Bowl rally. One member of the audience later spoke of his "continual amazement at the conduct of the fanatics and superpatriots in the audience," and expressed his "fear . . . at the growing signs of mob hate as the evening wore on: the longer, louder applause that followed each of the currently standard . . . phrases, like 'atheist creed bent on world domination' and 'subjugation of the freedom-loving peoples of the world under the yoke of Godless, Communist totalitarianism.'" The same observer also expressed disappointment ". . . that at this Christian Anti-Communism meeting none of the humanitarian tenets; indeed, none of any of the tenets of Christianity was discussed or even referred to obliquely by any of the speakers. . . ."

Then the Crusade moved on to Northern California for a rally in Oakland. A statement went out to the churches in the San Francisco Bay area, bearing, among others, the signatures of Methodist Bishop Donald Tippett; Episcopal Bishops Richard Norberg and James Pike; and Executive Secretary of the Northern California Baptist Convention Mack McCray, Jr. The statement agreed with the premise of the Crusade— *i.e.*, "that Americans need to be aware of the true nature of the Communist threat, as well as of their own American heritage," but went on to declare, "Experience in several communities has indicated that, in the wake of these schools, there has been a resurgence of attacks on churches, schools and councils of churches. While the crusade organization specifically denies any such intent, it is nevertheless a fact that the spread of the doctrines of the 'radical right' have had this effect elsewhere." Bishop Pike later observed that to the best of his knowledge not a single church, outside of the fundamentalist enclave, endorsed the school. The Crusade did succeed, all the same, in prompting some of the more orthodox churches to design and conduct their own programs on Christianity and Communism.

Later in the year the Crusade suffered its greatest financial loss to date—a total of $75,000 for preliminary organizational and advertising expenses, plus the cost of running a Madison Square Garden rally and a Greater New York School of Anti-Communism. According to the *New York Times*, Schwarz told five hundred guests at an August 1962 dinner meeting in New York City that businessmen who claimed opposition to Communism, but weren't willing to finance the fight against it, should "put their hands deep in their pockets and spend money before the Communists come and take it off them."

The advice was in keeping with one of Schwarz's basic contentions. "Christian money, American money," he says in one of his booklets, "should be invested in a vast education programme to preserve business, labour, the family, religion and America." He adds that Christians may expect to be "blessed beyond measure" for their support of an anti-Communist organization. (Which organization is not specified.) The work of anti-Communism should be regarded, he maintains, as "an investment" by American industry and business; it is, after all, the means for maintaining their whole business structure.

THE BASIS FOR AMERICAN FREEDOM

American freedom, according to Schwarz, "rests on an economic base." Free enterprise and capitalism—apparently in their present form—are commended to us as the roots of liberty.

That there is no inherent contradiction between free enterprise and liberty I have no doubt, but I am left a trifle uncomfortable when the Australian evangelist tells us, in a conversation which he quotes in his pamphlet *Communism: America's Mortal Enemy*, that "the freedom of the American citizen rests on an economic base." I am left uncomfortable simply because Schwarz has committed the same unhappy error that Karl Marx made a century ago: he has reduced the complex configurations of history to the single-cause theory of economics. To make freedom contingent on free enterprise is as absurd as to make it contingent on a fully communized system of production. We owe our free enterprise to American freedom—not the contrary.

American freedom is the product of a great many happenings and some historically audacious theories expressed in a document known to most Americans as the Constitution. But Schwarz somehow manages to disregard nearly two centuries of colonial history, to forget about the oppressive relationship that developed between the British crown and the colonies, and to ignore the remedy to that oppression which was drafted by Thomas Jefferson. Examine the list of grievances in the Declaration of Independence and you will find the particulars of the "absolute Tyranny" exercised by the ruling monarch; few of them are concerned with economic questions. Jefferson's words communicate, above all, the emerging nation's confidence in the notion that governments derive "their just powers from the consent of the governed." His is not the theorizing of an economic reformer. The revolution of 1776 was broadly concerned with liberty as it affected all dimensions of life.

Economic problems, without question, did much to hasten the breakdown of the Confederation and move the thirteen states toward a federal union. But the Constitution of the United States is far more than a remedy for economic ills. James Madison, and others among the fifty-five men who attended the Constitutional Convention, knew their history of governments well, and they sought to erect a new government, strong enough to act for the people, but sufficiently limited as to prevent an abrogation of their rights. The result, as every schoolboy knows, was a government divided into three branches, each independent of the others, coordinated with them, and yet checked by them. John Locke's radical notion that legislative power should rest with the "whole body of the people," was included in the very first words of the Preamble to the Constitution, "We the People of the United States . . ."

All this, and a great deal more, Fred Schwarz ignores. If he is at all aware of the history of American freedom he neglects to say so, leaving his reader with the untarnished and unqualified nonsense that an economic system has formed the basis for the personal freedoms of Americans.

It matters very little whether such explanations are from the left or from the right on the spectrum of ideas. It is of little significance whether the explanation is one peddled by the descendents of Karl Marx, or is another one served up by Fred Schwarz.

INTERNATIONAL ANTI-COMMUNISM

Despite Schwarz's failure to acknowledge the historical roots of American freedom, he is ready to declare that "history has given the United States the destiny of preserving freedom." Australia, he says, lives by the protection of the United States. When challenged by critics who maintain that he would have done well to have confined his anti-Communist activities to his native land, Schwarz is quick to remind them of the U.S. "destiny." Any contribution he can make to an understanding of the "pathology" of Communism, he believes, is best made within the boundaries of the "protectorate" state itself. "I'm always reminded," he says, "that another Australian, called Sister Kenny, came across, and most Americans didn't say to her, 'Aren't there people with poliomyelitis in Australia? Why don't you go home and treat them?' Most Americans," he adds, ". . . are very, very hospitable."

The operations of the Christian Anti-Communism Crusade are by no means limited to the United States, however. Out of the organization's Long Beach, California, headquarters comes an increasing quantity of literature aimed at the southern hemisphere.

In April of 1963 members and friends of the Crusade received an attractively printed flyer announcing, "The anti-Communist literature for Latin America project has the active cooperation of the United States Information Agency." Reproduced in the flyer were copies of correspondence between Schwarz and the U.S.I.A. office in Rio de Janeiro. In brief, it was a record of the U.S.I.A.s negotiation, on Schwarz's behalf, with a Brazilian publishing firm. The Crusade's June 1963 newsletter reiterated the cooperation of the U.S.I.A. in publishing a Portuguese edition of *You Can Trust the Com-*

munists and declared, "We now propose to place a copy of this book into the hands of every student in Brazil."

The Crusade ran into financial difficulties with its Spanish-language edition for distribution to University students in Mexico, however. Single-copy prices were too high in the Prentice-Hall paperback edition ($2.00 each), so the Crusade developed an illustrated magazine edition, variously estimated at costs of from sixteen to thirty cents per copy. In the summer of 1963 students began a pilgrimage throughout the whole of Mexico, distributing still another edition to the less well-educated segment of the population—this one, a twelve-page comic book entitled *If Communism Comes to Mexico.*

The first inside page of the anti-Communist comic portrays four workers with picks and shovels, supervised by a whip-cracking Communist wearing high field boots and dressed in a green field uniform with a buttonless, intern-type jacket. The caption proclaims, "We shall lose our liberty as has happened in Red China where people are not permitted to travel or to visit their acquaintances," and goes ahead to explain that the Communist Chinese may not choose their occupations, place of residence, or their hours of employment.

The following page shows four distraught-looking women gazing out of a prison window. A masculine female guard, her rifle over one shoulder and a hammer and sickle insignia on her chest, glowers at them. "Under the Communist system," says the caption, "men are separated from their families and are imprisoned. The women are also imprisoned in separate places. They take children from their parents and place them under the care and custody of the government. They permit the husband to visit his wife once a week for two hours, with the obligation of reporting to the government what they do. . . ."

Next is a picture of a priest being driven, at the point of a bayonet, through the streets. Two guards, with the familiar hammer and sickle emblazoned on red circles on the front of their coats, are in charge. One of them is whipping the *padre*. In the background the city mission may be seen, its doors and windows boarded over. The caption: "ALL THE CHURCHES WILL BE CLOSED. All priests . . . will be persecuted until they are incarcerated in concentration camps and . . . they can even be executed."

There follows a picture of a family of four, huddled together in prison. Looking on are the familiar Communist guards—one male, the other female. Both have whips, the female guard's apparently ready for immediate use. The explanation makes it clear that parents are permitted to visit their children in the Communist system—provided that they make no demonstration whatever of affection. They may not name their children, but must give them numbers; the children, of course, become the unthinking instruments of the state.

And so on. Another caption explains that a majority of Mexican citizens will lose their lives; another picture shows an attempted escape from Communist rule. The comic book concludes with Bible verses and an appeal to patriots to defend their country.

The booklet raises, in a moderately insistent fashion, a question that has troubled a good many persons. Despite its proclivity for concluding meetings, publications and anti-Communist "schools" with an appeal to faith—which sometimes turns out to be rather like what one critic called "a rally cry for Christ"—the question must be asked, is the Christian Anti-Communism Crusade *Christian?*

A QUAKER CRITIC AND THE WORDS OF JESUS

We have already seen that the Crusade devotes little time to presenting Christian doctrine. We have not as yet considered the Crusade's use of the word *Christian* as it applies to its approach to Communism.

J. Stuart Innerst, for years a Washington, D.C., staff member of the Friends' Committee on National Legislation, once raised the issue with Schwarz himself in the course of a Los Angeles radio program. Innerst is a quiet, soft-spoken person of particular sensitivity to questions of human misery and of unusual devotion to peace and social justice. He has, above all else, a deep confidence in the ability of all men to manifest goodness in their lives and in the capacity of all persons to see something of God in others.

"I put this question in a letter to Dr. Schwarz, but I never got an answer to it," said Mr. Innerst, "so I'd like to raise it now. I question the matter of using the term *Christianity* as descriptive of his Crusade when it preaches fear and hatred of the Communists.

"I don't find anything in the teaching of Jesus that warrants fear and hatred of other men. He himself lived under a totalitarian government that oppressed its people, slaughtered many of them and enslaved many others; and yet he taught men to love the enemy and he associated with the very subversives [of his day]—that is, with the tax collectors and the stooges of Rome.

"I am troubled by [the] idea of calling this a Christian movement, especially since it doesn't give credit to the good that Communism has actually done. Now, . . . I was in Russia for two weeks this summer, too short [a time] to be an expert, but I had a chance to see a great deal; and I lived for seven years in China before Communism came in. I know the conditions before and after because I have read both the critical and the favorable books.

"I hold no brief for Communism, but I wonder how [Schwarz] can justify the position that he takes in talking *only* about the evils in Communism. . . . I wonder what he makes, for example, of the rehabilitation of beggars in China, the rehabilitation of prostitutes in Russia, the elimination of illiteracy in both of these countries, the elevation of childhood and womanhood in China, and so on."

Schwarz spared no words in countering his Quaker critic. "That was a magnificent speech to eulogize what the Communists allegedly have done," he said, "but I wish I had time to answer this question with regard to Christianity. Our Christ took the whips and he drove the money changers out of the temple. He said, 'You serpents, you generation of vipers, how shall you escape the wrath to come?'

"To put up a straw man and then knock it down is an unworthy goal, and to say that we teach hatred and fear—why, in Christianity there has always been a place for fear. We've been told to fear God. . . . And in the Christian Anti-Communism Crusade we teach knowledge; we teach understanding; we do not teach hatred. That is a lie. That is a false accusation. That is unworthy of Christianity.

"What we do teach is that Communism is evil. It is Godless. And [as to] all these benefits, I could [discover] them by a visit to any well-kept penitentiary. . . ."

The reader will have to judge for himself whether the Crusade does, in fact, teach hate. Certainly neither the English *You Can Trust the Communists* nor the Spanish *If Communism Comes to Mexico* ever says explicitly, "Go, and hate the Communists." Neither do they urge one to love the Communists. If the Quaker contention that all men have something of the living God in them and that one may see that spark of divinity by acting and thinking in the spirit of love is pure foolishness, then Schwarz may be wholly right in his approach.

More than one image of Jesus is to be found in the New Testament, however. And one must choose in this world whether to follow the spirit of the prophet who drove out the money changers and denounced the Pharisees, or alternatively, to live in the spirit of one who said, "But I say to you, Do not resist one who is evil. But if any one strikes you on the right cheek, turn to him the other also. . . . You have heard that it was said, 'You shall love your neighbor and hate your enemy.' But I say to you, Love your enemies and pray for those who persecute you. . . ."

It may just be that neither, taken by itself, is a representative portrait of Jesus—or enough to suggest what it means to be a Christian. It may be that in this domain, as in all others, one must accept the ambiguity of life. Perhaps here too—even in shaping an image of Jesus—one cannot escape the shadow and the light, the subtle interplay of good and evil, and must accept for now, without further protestations, the knowledge that final judgments are impossible. Speaking for myself, I rather think that they are, and I suspect that ambiguity is nestled in close to the heart of human reality.

In application, this means that if the Christian anti-Communism Crusade continues to insist on calling itself Christian, it will no doubt find a multitude of reasons for doing so.

THE QUALITY OF CONCERN

It is perhaps the quality of the concern and action of the Crusade's supporters that most concerns its critics. Schwarz himself is sometimes embarrassed by the temper of his audience. I once attended a rally where a woman rose during the question-and-answer period to inquire about the possible Communist affiliation of Martin Luther King. Schwarz replied, "I know of no real evidence that he has any association with the Communist Party," and when the audience tittered at what many took to be only a qualified defense of King, he went on to deliver a short discourse on the damage to be done to the anti-Communist cause by unsupported allegations.

Earlier that same evening, Schwarz parodied those on the more extreme end of the right wing—such as the irresponsibles who referred to the Kennedy administration as "that nest

of traitors up there in Washington who are selling us down
the river." To Schwarz's discomfort the remark brought him
a solid return of applause—not for the parody, but for the
position he sought to criticize. He was quick to disengage
himself, but commented afterward, "You know, they *actually*
misunderstood what I was saying; they thought I meant it."

In general, the counsel of the faithful tends to be extrapo-
lated from wherever the evangelist stops. Thus, Schwarz's
generally reserved language is improved upon by a disciple
who declares in a booklet bearing the Crusade's imprint,
"Communism is a religion spawned in Hell by Satan himself
in his ruthless, relentless war against Christianity." Verbal
outbursts are likely to be even more intense when delivered
in person.

No man should be blamed simply for his disciples. Schwarz
is periodically embarrassed by what some of his have to say,
and notes that his opponents generally resort to quoting some
of his followers' more extreme statements. His own are less
sensational. He consistently refuses to play the demagogue.

Nor will Schwarz consent to forming a totalitarian organization in order to counter Communism. In an interview reported by the *New York Times* he is quoted as remarking,
"There is always the temptation, in fighting Communism, to
try to form a totalitarian organization modeled on Communism." Then he added, speaking specifically of the Birch
Society founder, Robert Welch, "Certainly, these people—
these dedicated anti-Communists—want a leader. . . . They
want to be led; they want me to lead them. But I won't do it.
If Bob Welch wants to do it he can; he's got a program of
action and a lot of ready solutions. But it's not my business."
Then came the punch line: "You know, I sometimes get the
notion he follows me around the country, signing up the
people after I've worked them up."

As I say, Schwarz should not be blamed for his followers.
He deserves our sympathy. And lest we begin believing that

there is any absolute correlation between a man and the movement he inspires, we should recall that Judas was one of the first to follow Jesus. All the same, the teachings of Jesus, considered over the long view, have tended to promote ethical behavior rather than inhibit it.

The Christian Anti-Communism Crusade will doubtless be best understood in terms of *its* long-range impact; for the time being, only preliminary judgments are possible. It would, of course, be helpful if we could outline the Crusade's objectives in any consideration of its long-term effect. Unfortunately, except insofar as education may be considered as an end in itself, neither Schwarz nor the Crusade gives us any hint of a tangible program. When asked, "How can we stop Communism?" Schwarz replies, "I wish I knew." He compares himself with the diagnostician who, though capable of naming a disease such as cancer, cannot prescribe a cure. One thing alone is now possible—education. A program for countering Communism should grow out of a study of the movement. We must, Schwarz believes, study Communism, learn the "laws of its being," and then begin to devise specific programs for given situations. Knowledge, he maintains, is the one certain way of discovering what Communism means to America and what we have to say to it.

I agree. There is only one difficulty. Education, as the Australian physician understands it, means *his kind of education*—none other. Indeed, he is quick to repudiate those centers of learning which might be most helpful in gaining a constructive understanding of Communism. An item in the Crusade's June 1963 newsletter declares, "The environment that conditions individuals to the acceptance of Communism is the college and university. An examination of the history of Communism will soon prove this." Again and again he asserts that a large majority of the Communist leadership is recruited on college and university campuses.

In his testimony before staff members of the House Committee on Un-American Activities, Schwarz said, "The ideology of communism is applied Godless materialism. The problem that perplexes many people is the overwhelming appeal that communism apparently exercises for the student mind." Just why students the world over should be consumed by this "overwhelming appeal" is not made clear, apart from the assertion that Communism offers the student a chance to participate in the "conquest of the world," and provides him with a program for changing human nature.

I have already said that I think Schwarz identifies the prime problem when he speaks of the Communist image of the man of the future. Communist philosophy does offer an appealing, but ultimately destructive, program for overhauling human nature. As to the students' desire to conquer the world? The argument, I submit, is fatuous, and until Schwarz brings forth some evidence indicating that students have a power drive, or a need to dominate not given to the rest of the population, I shall continue to dismiss the point as simple fantasy.

Now, what about the appeal of Communist idealism? It is no doubt real, but scarcely a live option, at least within our western universities. Given our culture's present attitude toward Communism, it would take a very neurotic, or a very angry student, indeed, to become a Communist. And even if he were to accept the Communist viewpoint, is there anything irreversible about the decision? I would hope that we have not become so academically calcified that the intellectual consideration of philosophical systems—no matter what they may be—is no longer possible. I would hope that we are still capable of permitting students the prerogative of free inquiry —that is, the right to inquire without the imposition of predetermined answers. I do not believe—not for a moment— that there is anything magical, or irresistibly alluring about a philosophical theory called Communism. And in any case, the man who has had some experience with the central ideas of that theory and then gone on beyond them is better able to deal with Communism realistically and effectively.

Given an open contest between the philosophical bases for western democracy and Communism, I have little doubt about the outcome. The truth will prevail. Some words of St. Paul speak to the question: "For we cannot do anything against the truth, but only for the truth."

My greatest objection to the Crusade's educational approach is that it is not education. It is indoctrination, and it is in terms of its commitment to that unhappy adjunct to education that the purposes of the Crusade must be judged.

Why the great emphasis on "education"? The Communist conquest is, Schwarz believes, taking place right now, at this very moment, and is due for completion in 1973. Schwarz gives no Communist source for this date, but is convinced that it is the Communist target for the completion of a program of infiltration, subversion and conspiracy, or perhaps even what he calls a "massive Pearl-Harbor-type attack."

1973 is the grim date for the end of freedom and the beginning of Communist world domination! If I believed that, I too would be busy with a crusade—at least as busy as Fred Schwarz. No more than he would I rely on the slow, difficult processes of free inquiry. There wouldn't be time to think. Action would mean everything.

Schwarz is entitled to his crusade, of course, and if he prods us into a more thoughtful consideration of the problems posed by Communism, totalitarianism and our own quiet acquiescence to the "good life," so much the better. We could not be prodded by a more genial, good-humored or sincere man.

I do regret that he has chosen to arrange so much of mankind in concentric circles with the Communists in the middle, the fellow travelers just outside, the sympathizers a little farther out, and the pseudoliberals at the outer rim (inhabiting "ivory cloisters of colleges and universities"), especially when he explains that the pseudoliberals on the outer rim are really caught up in the whole conspiracy. I also regret that Schwarz has bought the ready-packaged nonsense of those who look on the American clergy as a highly infiltrated pack of subversives. I am genuinely sorry that he has oversimplified Communism and undersold democracy, because I have a high regard for the American heritage and I doubt if his advice will do much to bring us to our senses. All the same, I am glad that we have Fred Schwarz. He makes life a great deal more interesting.

AND IN SUMMATION

Neither Fred Schwarz nor the Christian Anti-Communism Crusade are right wing in the strictest meaning of the term. Nor are they fundamentalist in the usual sense of the word. Schwarz's commitment to the right wing is qualified by a measure of good sense, a modicum of intellectual perception and an unwillingness to get involved publicly in naming names and denouncing particular instances of subversion. In terms of evangelical or fundamentalist (choose your word) Christianity, Schwarz's convictions are solid, but not very public. The Crusade does not function as a missionary enterprise.

Although no one has questioned the Crusade's anti-Communism, there are some who are doubtful about its use of the word *Christian* when speaking of itself. The doubt is not confined to doctrine, but spills over to the question of love and hate—the desirability of loving not only one's neighbors, subversive or otherwise, but even Communists. The counsel of Jesus on this matter, unfortunately, is not altogether clear.

Although Schwarz neglects Christian doctrine, he is nevertheless quick to take on atheism, liberalism and other assorted heresies. His fairness as a heresy hunter, however, is open to question, since he has a penchant for confusing the arguments with unsupported claims about the intimacy of the relationship between a state of godlessness and a Communist state. There is also some question about the depth of Schwarz's understanding of the history of American freedoms; his tendency seems to be to reduce them to a question of economics.

A good deal of the criticism directed at Schwarz and the Crusade follows from the temper of the crowds he attracts. Admittedly, individuals may sometimes be an embarrassment to both the Doctor and the Crusade; but it is something of a credit to him that he consistently shuns demagoguery and refuses to let his movement become an agency for counter-conspiracy. All the same, a group of prominent clergymen in the San Francisco area have observed that the Crusade's activities have been followed, in more than one community, by "a resurgence of attacks on churches, schools and councils of churches."

Schwarz's strongest asset is his understanding of the nature and consequences of a fundamental Communist assumption —*i.e.*, that human nature can be changed and that Communism is best equipped to change it. He rightly perceives this for the demonic distortion of humanitarian idealism that it is. Unfortunately for us all, the program of the Christian Anti-Communism Crusade is limited to education of the sort that is impossible to distinguish from indoctrination.

Doubtless, we will be hearing more from the Crusade. It has not had its full say yet, and since the date for Communist world domination is not far off, the Crusaders believe that there is much for them to do.

4 Christ-centered Americanism:
The Fundamentalist Approach

"CHRIST-CENTERED AMERICANISM," says the advertising message on postage-metered mail from the Christian Crusade in Tulsa, Oklahoma. Inside the envelope there may be an appeal for funds, a leaflet announcing a new book on Communist subversion, or a list of the organization's current selection of pamphlets. Whatever the contents of the mailing, they will reflect in some measure the ultraconservative political tone and the fundamentalist religious flavor of a movement that has been described by an Anti-Defamation League publication as "a million dollar a year organization that is one of the major forces on the radical right." Its founder and leader, labeled a "doomsday merchant on the far, far right" by the *Saturday Evening Post*, is the Rev. Billy James Hargis.

Hargis was born on August 3, 1925, in Texarkana, Texas. Following his graduation from Texarkana High School he enrolled in Ozark Bible College in Bentonville, Arkansas, a modest institution with some twenty students at the time, now located in Joplin, Missouri. Financial troubles cut short his formal education at Ozark, but he was able to attend summer classes at Burton College and Seminary in Manitou Springs, Colorado, in 1957 and 1958. He was ordained a minister in the Disciples of Christ denomination in 1943 at the age of eighteen.

Like many prominent individuals whose acceptance into the world of academic degrees postdates their success in the

world of practical affairs, Hargis received a Doctor of Divinity
Degree from Defender Seminary, Puerto Rico, in 1954. Burton College and Seminary awarded him a B.A. in 1956, and a
Bachelor of Theology in 1958, on the basis of a written thesis
he submitted to the school. In 1957 Belin Memorial University, then in Chillicothe, Missouri, conferred an honorary degree of Doctor of Laws on Hargis, and in 1961 Bob Jones
University of Greenville, South Carolina, also awarded him
an honorary Doctor of Laws.

The degree from Belin Memorial University has no doubt
been a source of embarrassment to Hargis, inasmuch as this
school has been listed as a "degree mill" by the U. S. Department of Health, Education and Welfare, an honor the school
shares with Burton College. By "degree mill," however, the
Department means nothing more sinister than "an organization that awards degrees without requiring its students to meet
educational standards for such degrees established and tradi-
tionally followed by reputable educational institutions." Despite the Department's opinion, the school has graduated a
good many students of fundamentalist persuasion over the
years, including, according to Hargis, a former Chief of
Chaplains.

Dr. Gaines M. Cook, executive secretary of the Convention
of Christian Churches (successor organization to the now
merged Disciples of Christ and the Christian Church), is
quoted as having this to say with regard to Hargis' one-time
affiliation with the Disciples of Christ: "Mr. Hargis' name
has not been listed since our 1958 Year Book was published,
inasmuch as he no longer serves a congregation connected with
the International Convention of Christian Churches, nor any
agency affiliated with us. We understand that he is now engaged in a private enterprise which has no connection whatsoever with the Christian Churches. . . ."

The growth of Christian Crusade has been one of the most
perplexing dimensions of the present-day coalition between

ultraconservative religion and politics. In 1954 Hargis was reaching about 20,000 readers and broadcasting over three or four radio stations, including two in Mexico. About that time he engaged "Pete" White, a public-relations adviser formerly with Oral Roberts. With White's counsel, the Crusade passed the one-million-dollar mark in its 1961 annual budget, gained more than 100,000 readers by 1962, and was broadcasting on more than two hundred radio stations and on at least a dozen television stations by 1963.

Hargis' personal salary is $12,000 per year, plus a generous expense allowance. The Crusade provides him with a $43,000 parsonage, domestic help, a custom-rigged Land Cruiser bus for his national tours, and two cars to assure the transportation of Mrs. Hargis and the Hargis children. His detractors are quick to point to the money to be made in the "anti-Communism and salvation line."

Most contributions to the Crusade are small—generally two to four dollars, according to "Pete" White—but the organization has its more affluent supporters as well. When it went national in October 1962, purchasing time on the Mutual Radio Network, the required $39,000 was raised in one session of the Crusade's third annual convention in Tulsa. The August 7, 1961, edition of the *New York Times* described Hargis' technique:

> . . . through alternate appeals to God and the 700 persons in his audience the evangelist began a prayer auction to raise the money.
>
> The 36-year-old Mr. Hargis spoke beneath a banner that read "For Christ! Against Communism!" He cried out:
>
> "I pray to God for one man to sponsor this program for six months. I know that man exists in the audience. Will he stand up?"
>
> No one stood up.
>
> "All right, then, we will divide this burden. I need four

men who will accept God's challenge and give $10,000 each to sponsor this program."

Two men stood up.

"Give us four, oh, God, who would give $5,000 each. Quickly! . . . $2,000?"

One man stood up.

"One thousand dollars?"

Three men stood up.

And so it went down from $500 through $100. At the end, seventy-nine men had pledged a total of $38,870—the exact amount needed.

The technique, with variations, is used wherever Billy James appears and a fund-raising job must be done.

Despite the apparent effectiveness of its fund-raising methods, the Crusade evidently has its share of financial trouble, even in the best of times. Twice in 1962 reports to Crusaders spoke of the necessity to cut budgets and expenses, and in the spring of 1963 Hargis himself complained about the Crusade's struggle for existence, stating that it had operated at a deficit for sixteen years.

THE WILES OF THE DEVIL

Doctor Hargis believes that he is fighting no simple worldly power. His fight is against Satan himself in his contemporary manifestation—Communism. Hargis is fond of quoting Ephesians 6:12 as his proof text: "For we wrestle not against flesh and blood, but against principalities, against powers, against the rulers of the darkness of this world, against spiritual wickedness in high places." Paul's advice to the early Christian community to "Put on the whole armor of God,

that ye may be able to stand against the wiles of the devil,"
is very sober counsel in Hargis' view.

The powers of evil may, according to Hargis, be manifest
in contemporary politicians. Such men are, as he puts it, "unknowingly tools in the hands of Satan." He has also warned
"that every minister who for any reason questions or attacks
the total inspiration of the Word of God, the Deity of Jesus
Christ, or the Hope of His second coming, is an instrument
of anti-Christ. . . ." Nevertheless, Christ will return and
vanquish evil. "Communism, the works of the devil, will be
destroyed," says Hargis. "Christ, the Great Destroyer, leads
His sheep. Sheep are not easily driven, but they follow a good
shepherd. Christ, the Good Shepherd, will lead America out
of danger, destroying the Satanic works of Communism, if
His sheep will believe and will follow." Therefore, Christians
must call on Christ and then, "in His Power and in His name,
go against Satanic Communism. He will save America," concludes Hargis, "through America's righteous people. He will
destroy Communism through Christian soldiers."

Offensive as the notion of "Christ the Destroyer" may be
to the sensitive Christian, such a portrait of Jesus is basic to
Hargis' theological system. He speaks eloquently of being
"washed in the Blood of the Lamb," and of receiving Christ
as King and Savior, who through the Holy Spirit guides the
faithful Crusader to an inevitable victory.

With equal eloquence, he keeps warning that many of the
nation's writers are aiding Communism, that radio, television,
and the press are systematically "brainwashing" the American
public, that churches are captive to Kremlin objectives, and
that Washington is full of "enemies of the United States."
In Hargis' own words, "Communism has infiltrated, subverted, perverted and sabotaged practically every phase of the
American way." Patriots, he says, should "stop aiding the
traitors!"

Hargis, the preacher, delivers his message to his audiences

in a one-to-five mix, giving them about ten minutes of fundamentalist Christian doctrine and fifty minutes of the "truth" about Communism. He is an energetic, attention-compelling speaker. As one observer put it following one of Hargis' appearances in Southern California, "Regardless of how trite or bromidic the comment . . . he can make it sound new and witty."

So convinced is Hargis that he is doing the will of God, so certain is he of his perception of reality, that all criticisms of the Christian Crusade, or of the right wing, are lumped together as the work of the Kremlin. As Hargis remarked in a June 1962 radio address, "The next time you hear some misguided dupe attack the anti-Communists, remember, they did not originate that attack. It came from Moscow. It bears the 'Made in Moscow' label. Beware of those who criticize the so-called ultra-right. Only those who criticize our common enemy—godless international Communism—should have our support, much less our ear."

UNMASKING THE DECEIVER

Hargis is probably most effective when he is exposing the specific work of the devil in the form of particular programs, persons, or organizations. Thus, in the pamphlet "Unmasking the Deceiver," he boldly declares, "Recent statements by race agitator Martin Luther King, Jr., clearly indicate that it is time to rip off his pious mask and reveal the real purpose and drive behind his anti-American activities. Though King has been sainted in many popular weekly magazines, his infamous alliance with Communist objectives and personalities has been kept a carefully guarded secret." If it appears that Hargis is hedging a bit about Martin Luther King's alleged political sympathies, it is only appearance. Hargis is perfectly willing to be blunt in his accusations. "King's Communist affiliations and acquaintances go back many years," he says, "and establish a clear pattern of Marxist affinity." The pamphlet concludes with an appeal for an immediate investigation of King and his activities, presumably by a Congressional committee.

Little wonder that when Hargis and retired General Edwin Walker went on a coast-to-coast joint tour called "Operation-Midnight Ride," NAACP pickets began to appear.[1] (Pro-Walker pickets in Los Angeles countered the NAACP demonstrators with a variety of signs, one of them reading, "Why doesn't Russia have a NAACP?") Hargis was quick to explain to his audiences that he had nothing against the NAACP, *but* the organization had initiated the attack and he is not one to avoid a fight. First of all, he told his hearers, the NAACP *does not* represent the Negroes of this country. Moreover, it has never had a colored president—or at least it hasn't had one in "a coon's age," as he told a Los Angeles audience. King's present influence over so large a portion of the American public, open and deceitful as it is, is something of a national disgrace in the view of Billy James Hargis.

When others made similar charges before the Senate Commerce Committee in July of 1963, Senator Monroney (chair-

[1] Hargis claims that he chose Walker for his "Operation-Midnight Ride" (inspired by Paul Revere's midnight ride which alerted his countrymen to "the enemy within and without") because "no man in our day . . . has paid a greater price to preserve freedom than Edwin Walker." Part of that price consisted of the former General's removal from his West German command following his attempt to exert political influence over members of the 24th Infantry Division; part was his self-imposed resignation from the Army, accompanied by the loss of more than $12,000 a year in retirement benefits; and part was his near martyrdom by a bullet fired from a high-powered rifle into his Dallas home on April 10, 1963. Walker views the "Midnight Ride" as the "most successful project" in the history of the Christian Crusade. Highlights of the tour included presentation of the keys to the city of Birmingham, Alabama, by the mayor, and the unanticipated (?) presence in the Atlanta, Georgia, audience of the parents of John Birch, an Army intelligence officer and missionary who was killed by Communist Chinese ten days after V-J day, now memorialized as the "first casualty of the cold war" by the John Birch Society which bears his name.

man of the committee) wrote to J. Edgar Hoover, asking if the F.B.I. had any information to support such charges. The reply was an unequivocal answer from Attorney General Robert Kennedy himself: "Based on all available information from the F.B.I. and other sources, we have no evidence that any of the top leaders of the major civil rights [organizations] are Communists, or Communist controlled. This is true as to Dr. Martin Luther King, Jr., about whom particular accusations were made, as well as other leaders." The Attorney General went on to say that Communist efforts to infiltrate and exploit civil rights organizations had been "remarkably unsuccessful."

DESTROYING AMERICA BY DEGREES

Even as Hargis sees the Communist conspiracy controlling the civil rights movement, so also he sees it as the moving force behind the United Nations. In an attractively printed pamphlet, closely modeled on the United Nations' own literature in terms of its cover design, he charges that the United Nations is "destroying America by degrees," and that it was ". . . conceived in subterfuge and was clearly the result of careful Kremlin planning." He goes on to present the now hackneyed charge that Alger Hiss was manipulated into a key position by the Kremlin so that he could mastermind the U. N. Charter in keeping with Soviet objectives. Such a charge is, of course, absurd, and the facts are not difficult to come by. Alger Hiss was indeed at the Dumbarton Oaks Conference where a draft of the Charter was prepared; and at San Francisco, where the final Charter was completed, he served as Secretary-General of the Conference. Unfortunately for U.N. critics, the job of Secretary-General of the San Francisco Conference had no relationship whatever to the later post in the U.N. which bears the same name. The San Francisco job consisted entirely of making administrative arrangements—scheduling meeting rooms, arranging for translators, and so on. Hiss was not even a delegate.

The United Nations Charter is the work of no single person, nor of any one nation. Various nations set up committees during World War II with the objective of hammering out preliminary proposals for a world organization. The Dumbarton Oaks Conference, held in Washington, D.C. from August to October of 1944, prepared a draft-outline of the proposals that served as a basis for discussion at the San Francisco Conference on International Organization, which convened on April 25, 1945. The eight hundred and fifty delegates from fifty different nations went over the Charter, phrase by phrase, in committees and in general session. Every section was passed, as required, by at least a two-thirds vote, and on June 25, 1945, the Charter of the United Nations was approved unanimously. It went into effect on October 24, 1945, with the ratification of the governments of China, France, Great Britain, the Soviet Union, the United States, and a majority of the other signatory states.

Now, I realize that this is a good deal more complicated than Doctor Hargis' Alger Hiss Conspiracy theory, and probably a whole lot less interesting. But it is one example of the sort of loose relationship Hargis maintains with the facts in his appraisal of the U.N., which concludes with the following:

> The United States pays approximately 33% of the cost of the United Nations. For this we are receiving an ever expanding Communist slave empire, the verbal propaganda invectives of the Kremlin and her stooges, the ultimate loss of national sovereignty and the Communist-dominated slave camps which will accompany our surrender. It is only common sense then to unite with free nations who have a common purpose and face a common enemy.

At least Hargis is accurate on one point. The United States does pay approximately 33% of the regular budget of the U.N.—which figures out to be an annual cost to each United States citizen of about one dollar and sixteen cents.

THE PATRIOTS CONVENE

The most exciting aspect of the Christian Crusade is its continuing schedule of schools and conventions. An Anti-Communism Leadership School, held in Tulsa in 1962, included in its faculty such notables as Gordan Scherer, member of the House Committee on Un-American Activities, John Rousselot, then a U. S. Congressman from California, retired Major General Charles A. Willoughby, Salt Lake City Mayor J. Bracken Lee, and Myers Lowman, director of Circuit Riders, Inc.

The fifth annual national convention of Christian Crusade, held in Oklahoma City, August 2–4, 1963, advertised in its advance publicity: "12 famed patriots to speak," and gave Birch Society founder Robert Welch top billing. Other patriots on the program included the Rev. Charles Poling of the Committee of Christian Laymen in Phoenix, Dr. Bob Jones, founder of Bob Jones University, conservative news commentator Fulton Lewis, Jr., and General Edwin Walker. Even Mrs. (Betty Jane) Hargis helped to promote the convention by way of a letter to friends of the Crusade.

Those who made it to the convention heard attacks on the Kennedy family, the State Department, the NAACP, liberals, Communist dupes, Communists, the U.N., the Supreme Court, civil rights legislation, Dwight D. Eisenhower, Alger Hiss, and Harvard University.

Although the convention speakers did not indulge in electioneering for the 1964 presidential primaries, Donald

Janson stated in the *New York Times* that "there seemed
no doubt that Senator Goldwater was solidly the political favorite of the crusade's leaders and delegates. There were
shouts of approval when Mr. Hargis, calling the roll of the 33
states represented, came to Arizona and remarked: 'We're ex-
pecting great things from your state in the days ahead.'"
The silence of the speakers was by conscious intent. Hargis,
according to Janson's account, had told the speakers "not to
praise the Senator because 'we don't want to hurt him' in his
Presidential aspirations." Large portraits of the Arizona Senator hung in the balcony of the hall, however, and gave it the
appearance of a campaign headquarters. Reflecting the mood
of the convention, the Rev. Charles Poling of Phoenix picked
up a Goldwater button, but put it away remarking, "I don't
want to be a kiss of death."

Mr. Welch's address, which avoided current political questions, was said to have "set the keynote of the convention."
There can be little doubt that he was the convention's largest
attraction. But even the presence of Robert Welch was not
enough to attract more than 500 people, and on the last evening of the convention Hargis disclosed an even more distressing truth to those present: the Christian Crusade was in
serious financial trouble. This was no pep talk put together
to raise additional funds. Income had dropped so precipi-
tously as to require cutting the fifty-person staff almost in
half. Those remaining had taken a ten percent salary cut. The
mailing list for the Crusade's monthly magazine had been
reduced nearly 50% by eliminating those who had stopped
contributing. The headquarters building had been sold and the
Crusade was reduced to renting space from the new owner.
Hargis attributed the Crusade's financial troubles to "liberal
smears" and to the increasing competition offered by rival
organizations. The growth of the John Birch Society had undermined the Crusade's position, he admitted.

In an effort to regain some of the losses, the founder of the

Crusade staged a prayer-type fund-raising campaign on the spot and came up with $18,000 in tax-deductible contributions—scarcely enough to cover the Crusade's losses, but a substantial beginning toward the underwriting of the organization's new "anti-Communist university" in Manitou Springs, Colorado.

Four two-week sessions had been held at the "university" just preceding the convention. The setting for the school was an old resort hotel, purchased almost entirely by a Pasadena, California, family and given to the Crusade. April plans had called for a minimal "university" attendance of 600, but according to an account published in the *New York Times*, total attendance numbered 116 youths, and most of them were on "scholarships."

The hotel provided an ideal place for the Crusade to retrench its forces for the next assault. Renamed the "Summit," and uncomfortably suggestive of the abortive Eisenhower-Khrushchev summit talks which had been heartily opposed by the right wing, the hotel was seen by the founder of Christian Crusade as the proper site for "summit conferences in the years ahead that will help change the course of America and help save our beloved country. . . ."

A TWENTIETH-CENTURY REFORMATION

Compared with the Rev. Carl McIntire, Hargis is no more than an upstart. In one of McIntire's letters to listeners he spells out some of the dangers facing America in 1963 with the polish of a practiced observer: "Gus Hall, the leading Communist spokesman in the United States, presents his praise of Pope John XXIII's encyclical in the Communist *Worker* . . . ; also, Khrushchev's praise, and President Kennedy's approval. Things are shaping up so rapidly. The Communists want us to trust them and the Pope says disarmament must rest on 'mutual trust alone.' President Kennedy also has learned from the Pope."

Mr. McIntire is a fearless fundamentalist reformer, intent on exposing the threats posed to freedom by Communism, Roman Catholicism and the "Modernism" of the National and World Councils of Churches. Not so very many years ago he was saying that Catholicism was the greatest threat then facing the American public. Today, he has subordinated Roman Catholicism to Communism in his hierarchy of evils. Sometimes, as in the quotation above, he manages to take on Communism and Catholicism at the same time.

Carl McIntire was born in Ypsilanti, Michigan, on May 17, 1906. He received a B.A. from Park College in Parkville, Missouri, in 1927, and entered Princeton Theological Seminary in preparation for the Presbyterian ministry. When one of the Princeton faculty members withdrew to found Westminster Seminary in Chestnut Hill, Pennsylvania—a school with a decidedly conservative orientation compared to Princeton's—McIntire followed and took his theological degree at Westminster in 1931. In 1950, the Toronto Baptist Seminary awarded him an honorary Doctor of Divinity degree.

Following his ordination into the Presbyterian ministry, McIntire became active in a growing protest movement working against the liberalization of the Presbyterian Church in the U.S.A. The activities of the protest movement proved to be disruptive, and in 1934 the General Assembly voted decisively to abolish the Independent Board of Presbyterian Foreign Missions that the dissident group had established. The action only increased the ardor of the members of the protest group, however, and in 1936 the Presbyterian Church in the U.S.A. brought them to trial. Although charged originally with six counts, the Synod found McIntire guilty of three: namely, "Disapproval, defiance, and acts in contravention of the government and discipline of the Presbyterian

Church in the U.S.A.; not being zealous and faithful in maintaining the peace of the Church; [and] violation of his ordination vows." Notably, none of the three counts involved doctrinal issues. All were concerned with McIntire's deportment as a Christian minister within the Presbyterian Church in the U.S.A. The denomination did what any organization jealous of its structural integrity must do. It took dissident behavior seriously, and distinguishing behavior from belief, it took its stand. The result in this instance was that Carl McIntire was formally deposed from the Presbyterian ministry.

McIntire's Collingswood, New Jersey, congregation, long fundamentalist in its outlook, stood behind its deposed minister, and when a legal battle developed over the parish property, the overwhelming majority of the church walked out of its Gothic building to a vacant lot where a tent was put up. Later a frame structure was erected; it is still the congregation's place of worship.

Since his expulsion from the Presbyterian Church in the U.S.A., McIntire has established his own denomination—the Bible Presbyterian Church, Inc. The latest membership figures available are for 1959 and list the denomination as having a total of 5956 members in 69 member churches,[2] the largest of which is doubtless McIntire's own Collingswood congregation with approximately 1600 members. In 1941 the Bible Presbyterians and a denomination calling itself the Bible Protestant Church met in New York City to found the American Council of Christian Churches. The new organization firmly repudiated ecumenicity—*i.e.*, interdenominational cooperation on both a local and worldwide basis—and declared in the course of the preamble to its constitution a firm commitment to the following:

[2] See Frank S. Mead, *Handbook of Denominations in the United States* (New York: Abingdon Press, 1961), p. 242.

. . . the full truthfulness, inerrancy, and authority of
the Bible, which is the Word of God; the holiness and love
of the one sovereign God, Father, Son, and Holy Spirit; the
true deity and sinless humanity of our Lord Jesus Christ,
His virgin birth, His atoning death, "the just for the unjust," His bodily resurrection, His glorious coming again;
salvation by grace through faith alone; the oneness in Christ
of those He has redeemed with His own precious blood;
and the maintenance in the visible church of purity of life
and doctrine.

Although accurate statistics are difficult to come by, the
American Council of Christian Churches is said to have approximately 300,000 members in fourteen affiliated fundamentalist denominations.[3] Its activities are many, ranging
from missionary work to such projects as hard-hitting exposure campaigns aimed at State Department cooperation with
NCC exchange programs involving clergymen from behind
the Iron Curtain. The ACCC's heaviest fire is directed toward the National Council of Churches, an organization it
regards as utterly beyond redemption.

In 1948 McIntire was instrumental in the founding of the
International Council of Christian Churches in Amsterdam,
just a few days before the founding of the World Council of
Churches in the same city. Despite the fact that the ICCC
was founded first, credit for the notion of a world organization
of Christian churches must go to the founders of the World

[3] Membership statistics are those cited by Louis Cassels in *Look* magazine
(April 24, 1962) in an article entitled, "The Rightist Crisis in Our Churches."
Mr. Cassels' figures may be correct, but if so, they are difficult to confirm.
The number of member denominations of the ACCC changes frequently,
and membership statistics are not readily (if at all) available for many of
them. Critics of the ACCC claim that the organization's own membership
figures, which are generally within the 300,000 range cited by Cassels,
are greatly exaggerated. In any case, a dispute over membership claims and
leadership is reported to have caused a rupture within the ACCC at a St.
Louis, Missouri, meeting in the spring of 1956, an indication that the
ACCC may have had its own difficulties in arriving at a responsible estimate
of its numerical strength.

Council. The McIntire group came to Amsterdam in protest. Said to represent sixty-one Protestant bodies from twenty-nine countries, the ICCC is nonetheless relatively small. (Claims to large membership are sometimes made by the ICCC leadership, but to date the organization has been unwilling to make public any materials confirming its claims.) Its chief activity —or so leaders of the World Council of Churches see it— seems to be the harassment of meetings conducted by or under the auspices of the World Council.

The Bible Presbyterian Church, the American Council of Christian Churches and the International Council of Christian Churches are all part of a "Twentieth-Century Reformation," inspired and carried forward by Carl McIntire. The object of the reformation is simple: to return the church to fundamental Christian beliefs and purge it of sinister influences.

THE RADIO MINISTRY

Although McIntire writes and publishes his own Christian anti-Communist tracts and publishes a weekly paper called *The Christian Beacon,* his most effective medium is plainly a five-day-a-week radio program broadcast over almost six hundred stations in North America and one shortwave station beamed at Europe and the Soviet satellite nations. His newsletter to listeners regularly appeals for more funds—$1000 per station—to build the total still larger. Generally paid for at the regular religious program rates, McIntire's programs are a continuing irritant to the National Council of Churches and its member denominations. Sporadic attempts are made to get the Twentieth-Century Reformation Hour off the air in this community or that, but most attempts are unsuccessful simply because the programs are on paid time. Station managers rightly insist that there is no reason why they should replace a paying program with a public-service program, and the complaining churches are seldom ready to dip into their treasuries in order to offset the effect of the Twentieth-Century Reformation Hour message.

In January of 1963 McIntire came under heavier fire than that leveled at him by local parsons and church officials, however. On January 17 the *New York Times* radio and television critic, Jack Gould, reported that shortwave station WINB in Red Lion, Pennsylvania, was being investigated by the Federal Communications Commission. The investigation, which centered around a complaint lodged with the F.C.C. by the United States Information Agency, was concerned with the "international distribution of McIntire's views" over WINB. U.S.I.A. monitors had made recordings of McIntire's broadcasts and were distressed lest his opinions be confused with official United States policy. Of particular concern were his attacks on the United Nations.

Newton Minnow, then chairman of the Federal Communications Commission, acknowledged a paucity of clear-cut policy lines on the question, but stated that such stations were expected to reflect the American point of view on matters of political import. The difficulty for the U.S.I.A., and for its "Voice of America," was not complicated. Most shortwave stations are government-owned, and listeners tend automatically to associate viewpoints expressed on shortwave broadcasts with the country of origin.

McIntire responded indignantly to the very notion of the investigation. "This is serious. It involves freedom of speech and also monopoly by the government," he said, and then added, "How our broadcast could possibly produce any confusion in regard to American policy it is difficult to comprehend. For anyone who listens to our program . . . hears our emphasis upon God, the Bible, the Ten Commandments, righteousness, the Devil, and our militant opposition and exposure of the Communist conspiracy. . . ." He took the opportunity to expose U.S.I.A. discrimination in its broadcasting policy, which allegedly limits "Voice of America" broadcasts of religious services to Roman Catholic churches, churches in NCC member denominations, etc. McIntire made it clear that the ACCC had protested against the U.S.I.A.s policy, but protests notwithstanding, no member of the ACCC had ever been invited to participate in a shortwave broadcast under U.S.I.A. auspices.

McIntire appealed to his listeners to get protests off to their congressmen and the F.C.C. The replies that listeners received, some of which were quoted in McIntire's periodic letter, were not encouraging. One was from F.C.C. Legal Assistant Joel Rosenbloom and said, in essence, that in light of the limited number of shortwave frequencies and growing government needs, there was strong sentiment in Washington for reducing the number of frequency allocations available to private broadcasters; and further, that it was clear, in any case, that there could be little or no increase in the number of frequencies then allocated. Mr. Rosenbloom observed that, with the shortage in broadcast allocations in mind, the F.C.C. had always pursued a policy of assigning frequencies to broadcasters who would use them "to the best advantage of the United States." But the whole subject, said Rosenbloom, was being re-examined.

McIntire was furious. "So it seems clear that it is our 20th Century Reformation Hour that they are after," he said. "Our 'right-wing' 'fundamentalist' broadcasts now are not in the best interests of the present administration!!"

Speaking for myself, unacceptable as I may find most of Carl McIntire's views, I cannot help feeling that his anger was justified in this instance. Although one may scarcely argue that the framers of the Constitution could have anticipated the invention of the radio, they nevertheless spoke clearly on the question of freedom of communication in the First

Amendment, dealing with the means of communication then in existence—freedom of speech and of the press. The development of mass communication has, without question, complicated the matter of granting unqualified freedom, but it has in no sense limited the desirability of doing so. Granted that the airways are a public trust and that they must be administered in a fashion calculated to ensure order, the question of which ideas are to be explored on the airways, apart from questions of slander or efforts to start an insurrection, is no business of the government. Granted that the F.C.C. has a responsibility to encourage quality programming and a duty to curb false advertising, I can imagine no rationale consistent with the ideals of American freedom that would support the right of the Commission to judge which ideas may be broadcast and which may not.

The Commission apparently accepts such a view with regard to McIntire's programs aired on the broadcast band. They reach only a North American audience. The trans-Atlantic coverage is open to question because the program content is not consistent with government policy.

I will concede that the viewpoints of Carl McIntire might well be an embarrassment to the administration—particularly so, since he reflects in many ways the Marxist image of the aggressive defender of capitalism, addicted to a very literal sort of religion—but any government that proposes to guarantee the freedom of ideas and their expression must be prepared to live with all kinds of ideas and all manner of expressions. It cannot pick and choose.

It is of little help to argue that the F.C.C. must investigate all complaints, regardless of motive. The fact stands that the U.S.I.A., an official government agency, initiated the inquiry. McIntire has a good case when he contends that his freedom to disseminate his religiopolitical viewpoint is potentially threatened. All the same, he is not alone in his predicament. The F.C.C. is playing no favorites in its scrutiny of nonconformity on the airways. On January 16, 1963, the *New York Times* announced that the Commission was holding up licenses on three listener-supported F.M. radio stations operated by the Pacifica Foundation, pending the completion of an investigation then being conducted by the Senate Internal Security Subcommittee. Pacifica, it seemed, had been broadcasting a full range of programs in music, drama, public affairs, and children's programs, including in its public affairs broadcasts such diverse types as official spokesmen for the Communist Party (announced as such) and official spokesmen for the John Birch Society (also announced as such). The unanswered questions behind both investigations: Is the First Amendment to be taken seriously by those who are charged with administering our airways? And may members of the listening audience be trusted to make up their own minds about the truth?[4]

DISSENT CONFOUNDED AND APPLAUDED

The American Council of Christian Churches is sometimes an effective protest movement, but not always. In March of 1963 four Russian churchmen visited Austin, Texas, during the annual assembly of the Texas Council of Churches. Ministers of several ACCC churches in the area were determined to let the public know that there was subversion loose in the land. After an unsuccessful attempt to get the First Presbyterian Church to rescind its offer of hospitality to the Council

[4] After more than a year of deliberation the F.C.C. clarified its position with regard to Pacifica. On January 22, 1964, the Commission granted an initial license to KPFK in Los Angeles, and renewals to KPFA in Berkeley and WBAI in New York. In the course of an extensive "Memorandum Opinion and Order" the Commission declared, "We recognize that . . . provocative programming . . . may offend some listeners. But this does not mean that those offended have the right, through the Commission's licensing power, to rule such programming off the airwaves."

of Churches, the ACCC pastors staged an airport picket-line protest and two anti-Communist rallies, the first to be held on the afternoon of the Russians' arrival, the second, a statewide affair, to be held the following evening at the ballroom of a local hotel. Advertisements were run in Austin papers announcing the rallies, and leaflets were passed out. One leaflet pictured a Russian Orthodox priest walking from the "Kremlin Spy Center" across a "gulf of godlessness" toward the open arms of a figure identified as the National Council of Churches.

The Russian delegates, four of them in all, were expected to arrive at 6:45 P.M. on Sunday afternoon. A large delegation of pickets were present at the scheduled hour, but there were no Russians to protest. The plane was late. Word of the delay had been passed along to students and faculty members at the state university and local seminaries, and when the plane did arrive, around midnight, hundreds of people were on hand to welcome the delegates. But by then no more than a few stalwart pickets were left to protest. Cheers and applause greeted the Russian clerics as they emerged from the plane.

On Monday evening the protest rally brought out fewer than one hundred persons. As Harold Kilpatrick, executive director of the Texas Council of Churches, remarked in his account of the affair, which appeared in the *Christian Century*, "The dissidents of the ACCC . . . learned that a protest movement can backfire—hard."

Not all ACCC protests end so dismally for the organization, or so happily for the National Council, however, particularly when Carl McIntire's personal dynamism is directly involved. In the spring of 1963 the religious programming on the local radio station (WCME) in Brunswick, Maine, consisted of the following: 1) selected Bible readings prepared by the American Bible Society, 2) Father Keller's "Thought for the Day," 3) two nondenominational (Christian) hymns, and 4) the "Twentieth-Century Reformation Hour." Local clergymen and the area Council of Churches, feeling that the mainstream of Protestantism had been slighted, protested, and a small controversy developed. Efforts were made to get McIntire's program off the air, or to broaden the spectrum of the station's religious programming. (The station manager indicated that time was available to any Christian denomination, or other religion, at the regular rate, which McIntire was paying.)

McIntire announced that he would hold a rally in Brunswick, but found that no public meeting place was available to him. He settled for a gymnasium in the nearby town of Wiscasset, population 1700. Not long before he appeared in Wiscasset the Brunswick *Record* leveled its heaviest editorial fire on McIntire. It compared his message with those offered by McCarthy and Robert Welch. It called him a "witch hunter" and accused him of playing the martyr before the Brunswick area Council of Churches in order to gain the sympathy, and the attendance, of the local citizenry. From his followers he gets money, the paper observed, and he "makes no bones about asking for it." The paper went on to say that the rally would be a "well engineered affair with the possibility of failure reduced to nearly zero." Despite the build-up, the *Record* pictured McIntire as destined for oblivion, and it manfully concluded, "This newspaper considers it fortunate that he has chosen this area as an arena, because now he has become subject to the very exposures which will topple his empire of extremity."

Were the down-Mainers taken in? They were. One thousand to twelve hundred persons attended McIntire's "Freedom Rally" on July 12, a number of them sitting outside the gymnasium listening to the goings-on inside over loudspeakers. McIntire, genial, cordial, and with all the perfected oratorical skill of the well-done platform speaker, told the audience that there is "no such thing in Russia as religious liberty" (which was probably news to no one). He took on

Communist ideology and attacked the National and World
Councils of Churches, and toward the end of his ninety-
minute talk moved into a rousing finale of gospel preaching that brought the *amens* rolling forward.

The audience that evening was, for the most part, Baptist
in affiliation, although there was a sprinkling of Methodists,
Episcopalians, Pentecostals and Congregationalists present.
Even a few Roman Catholics were reported to have been
present. The evening netted the Twentieth-Century Reformation Hour two new radio stations. "Maine," said McIntire,
"had never seen anything like this." No doubt he was right.

THE GOSPEL OF FREE ENTERPRISE

McIntire's successes also include the purchase and promotion of a 333-room hotel-type conference center at Cape May
on the Atlantic seaboard, the founding of Faith Theological
Seminary in Elkins Park, Pennsylvania, and active leadership
roles with Shelton College, Ringwood, New Jersey, and Highland College, Pasadena, California.

Highland College boasts that it is part of "the growing
'Twentieth-Century Reformation,'" and includes among its
purposes "college training of the highest academic standards,"
and the presentation of "the Biblical basis for the free enterprise system and the profit motive. . . ."

Robert Kofahl, President of Highland College and a militant supporter of the ACCC, not only believes that free
enterprise is the most appropriate economic system for the
United States, but that it is "established by the Ten Commandments and the teaching of Jesus Christ and His apostles." Other facets of Dr. Kofahl's academic outlook include
the notion that the theory of evolution is a fraud (which he

proves in a six-page tract) and the conviction that "Modernism" and Marxism were brought to America by young seminary professors who had studied in Europe and had been subverted in their thinking by German advocates of higher criticism. The Modernism-Marxism mixture, thus prepared, apparently was strong enough to open the way "for Communist agents to infiltrate and to use the churches to promote the aims of the Communist world conspiracy." With such ideals behind it, Highland College has been turning out Twentieth-Century Reformers at a steady pace.

Formulas for identifying free enterprise with the Ten Commandments and the gospel are not without their value for the Twentieth-Century Reformation movement. "This nation is in the most serious condition it has ever been," says Carl McIntire in one of his letters. "Never before in history have we faced such peril. We must act today. If you can send a contribution at the present time, in any amount, please do so." McIntire's financial pitches are mild, though, compared with the tribute paid by his listeners. One wrote, "My money is so slow accumulating that I sold a U. S. Bond so that I could send you the money needed for my new station." Another wrote, "I am behind you 100% and contribute to your valuable program regularly. I am an old retired Methodist minister. Thoroughly disgusted with the leaders of the church." And a lady from South Carolina wrote, "I am an old lady of 96 years old. I am sending you all of my savings Daddy left to me. I got it out of the bank today." It wasn't McIntire's fault that the savings proved to be two $500 Confederate bills. All the same, it worked out all right. The "Widow's Mite Fund," as McIntire called it, soon bulged with contributions from those who felt the pathos of the situation.

I have only two questions about the Twentieth-Century Reformation movement's approach to economic philosophy and fund raising. First, is it truly honest to identify *any economic system,* including free enterprise, with the Ten Com-

mandments and the gospel? (As appropriate as I feel the free
enterprise system is to America, I seem to recall something
about a golden calf and the idolatry involved in raising worldly
things to a level approaching the ultimate commitment normally reserved for deity.) And second, is it altogether honest
to appeal for funds for one's cause in the name of a self-
proclaimed, impending disaster? I suppose that the answer to
the second question is *yes*, provided that one actually believes
in the imminence of the disaster, and Carl McIntire plainly
does. "We are witnessing the destruction of a great and free
Republic," he says, "and our downfall will be internal and
the Communists will not have too much difficulty in taking
us over." I have little doubt that any man that pessimistic
about the moral fiber of America is entitled to go after money
to prevent the collapse of everything. Still, I can't help feeling
that the republic is going to stay put for quite some time to
come.

THE PATRIOTS COMPARED

Obviously, Billy James Hargis and Carl McIntire have a
great deal in common, but for all their similarities, the
Reverends Hargis and McIntire are very different persons.
Hargis, a relatively young man, is something of a newcomer
to the anti-Communist scene. McIntire is a veteran of many
campaigns not only against Communism, but against Roman
Catholicism as well. Moreover, the two men have different
styles of promotion. Hargis takes advantage of the techniques
offered by the modern-day publicity agent. McIntire sticks to
the tested techniques of sending public letters to the faithful,
and making evangelistic appeals for funds on the air. It may
be that McIntire is more sensitive than his younger colleague
to the potential for exploitation latent in commercially pack-

aged anti-Communist Christian patriotism, finds such exploitation ethically objectionable, and so keeps it to a minimum. He may also be aware of the ephemeral nature of some public-relations campaigns and is wary of building his reformation on uncertain ground. Then, too, it may simply be that he has never thought much about the matter.

The two preachers' similarities strongly outweigh their differences, though. Both are extremely capable speakers with genuine talent for saying what an audience enjoys hearing most. They know how to size up a crowd and how to handle it. Both are highly sensitive to the mood of carping discontent to be found among pseudoconservatives and are quick to relate political dissatisfactions to religious solutions.

Both Hargis and McIntire take their doctrine seriously, and although McIntire's statements are generally somewhat more guarded and a great deal more sophisticated than Hargis', the two men seem to agree on the essentials of the faith: a hard-rock fundamentalism that gets down to the literal truths of the Word of God, the essential machinery of salvation to be found in faith, and the premillennial return of Christ. Moreover, a binary interpretation of reality pervades everything. There is God and there is Satan. One must make his choice.

To a large extent both men represent the faith of the right-wing segment of an emerging fundamentalist minority in the United States, a group convinced that it not only has the answers to the questions of human meaning on this planet, but also an understanding of how best to counter threats to faith and to freedom. The mentality of this group is such that historical development is reduced to conspiratorial agreements made by the emissaries of Hades. They feel that they have, therefore, an obligation to enter into a counterconspiracy of righteousness.

The most noteworthy thing about Hargis, McIntire and their followers, it seems to me, is simply that they are altogether convinced that they, and they alone, have found the truth. They have the answers, and any alternatives offered by others are thought to be one piece with the value system invented by Satan. Something is either right or it is wrong. There can be no ambiguity about this life. The righteous see clearly what is true.

Somehow I keep thinking back to the words of a rabbi from Nazareth who spoke of those who in his day built "the tombs of the prophets" and decorated the "monuments for good men of the past." "If we had lived in the times of our ancestors," said the tomb builders, "we should never have joined in the killing of the prophets." The rabbi spoke with the words of a prophet: "Yes, 'your ancestors,'—that shows you to be sons indeed of those who murdered the prophets. Go ahead then, and finish off what your ancestors tried to do!"

I think of those words of Jesus and I recall a fundamentalist preacher standing in the Shrine Auditorium of Los Angeles telling of the great losses suffered by the revolutionary fathers of our nation. I recall the preacher's eloquent testimony for those men, his deep dismay over the price they paid, and I think of his great tribute to their stature, his declarations of unending loyalty to them. I think of that and it occurs to me that the ways of men may not have changed so very much in nineteen centuries. The prophets are still murdered by one generation and praised by the next. And those who do the praising of past prophets must necessarily deny those who dare to speak now. At least I imagine that it may be so, that that is the way things are.

"Alas for you, you hypocritical scribes and Pharisees!" said Jesus. "You are like whitewashed tombs, which look fine on the outside but inside are full of dead men's bones and all kinds of rottenness. For you appear like good men on the outside—but inside you are a mass of pretense. . . ."

Jesus had little love for the descendants of those who murdered the prophets. Or was it that he had little sentimentality? But he left them their humanity in what he said. He continued to communicate with them, while repudiating what they were with a holy anger. Perhaps that is the deepest kind of love: to be honestly angry with a man without rejecting the man himself, to speak one's anger toward a man at the moment when the fire brushes one's lips and to do so without forgetting that the man is there all the while.

Jesus mourned for Jerusalem, the city of those who were "a mass of pretense," the city that stoned "the messengers sent to her." There was compassion in his anger, for he longed to gather the children of that city even "as a hen gathers her brood under her wings." Jerusalem would have none of it, and the rabbi turned his thoughts to things eternal.

Perhaps these thoughts, these images, apply even in the present day.

5 Enter the Birch Society, and Founder

THE PURPOSE OF the John Birch Society is as commendable as the purpose of any organization I can think of. What is more, it probably comes as close to being universally acceptable as any short statement of objectives ever drafted. It is simply "to promote less government, more responsibility, and a better world." Those words appear on page 162 of the *Blue Book*, the official handbook of the John Birch Society, written by its founder, Robert Welch.

There are, of course, a power-hungry few who see government as something more than a necessary liability for putting human affairs into order. There are others who would just as soon forget about responsibility. And there are, to be sure, some unfortunates in this world whose psyches are so arranged as to cause them to want to see the world slip downward into nothingness, or disappear with one colossal bang. The rest of us, which is more than likely the bulk of humanity, are right in step with Robert Welch. So far as the purpose of the John Birch Society goes, we are Birchers all.

The John Birch Society is, in fact, a rather inclusive organization. It has no economic or political requirements. Any man able to come up with twenty-four dollars per year, or any woman able to pay half that amount may be a member. A Democrat may join, or a Republican. It matters not what your religion is. Only troublemakers and Communists are excluded.

In point of fact, the Society rather prides itself on its diversity. In a footnote to the 1961 printing of the *Blue Book*

Robert Welch mentions that the organization has two all-Negro chapters, as well as several chapters (in the North) where Caucasians and Negroes meet together. The same may, of course, be said for Republicans and Democrats.

Not long before he lost his congressional seat to a Democrat and became a full-time, paid staff member for the Birch Society, California Republican John Rousselot made a statement in the *Congressional Record* which indicates the diversity of religious belief within the Society. "With a very few exceptions," said Rousselot, "the members of the John Birch Society are deeply religious people. . . . Our hope is to make better Catholics, better Protestants, better Jews—or better Moslems—out of those who belong to the society."

Rousselot, a Christian Scientist, went on to contrast the Birch Society's "onward and upward forever" philosophy with Communist objectives, which he and other Birchers believe are just the opposite of what the Birch Society has in mind. The Communists, said Rousselot, intend ". . . to drive their slaves and themselves along . . . [a] downward direction, to the Satanic debasement of both man and his universe." Rousselot further stated that the Society believes Communism to be wholly incompatible with all religion, "contemptuous of all morality and . . . intrinsically evil. . . . We believe that the continued coexistence of Communism and a Christian-style civilization on one planet is impossible. The struggle between them must end with one completely triumphant and the other completely destroyed. We intend to do our part, therefore, to halt, weaken, rout, and eventually to bury, the whole international Communist conspiracy."

In short, the attitude of the John Birch Society toward Communism is, "We will bury you."

METHODS FOR THE BURIAL

How does the Society intend to bury Communism? By
legitimate means for the most part. In common with many
organizations in the United States the John Birch Society
provides public speakers on behalf of its cause, encourages
radio and television commentators to take a more forthright
position, organizes letter-writing campaigns, publishes and
distributes literature, etc. It sees itself primarily as an educational organization, and is chartered as such under the laws of
the Commonwealth of Massachusetts.

Some of its methods, however, are difficult to reconcile with
the traditions of a free society. Take, for instance, its counsel
to heckle speakers suspected of being pro-Communist in their
viewpoints (see Chapter II). Or consider its policy of "shocking the American people." In the view of Robert Welch
the United States is already predominantly Communist.
At this very moment the Communists are carrying out a
master program for the merger of the United States and the
Soviet Union. Many of our most venerable foundations have
long been secretly working under a "directive" to convert the
U.S. into a Socialist nation before a Communist police-state
rule is imposed. Welch even quotes the "directive" (without
indicating where it may be found) as saying that the final
objective is "so to change the economic and political structure
of the United States that it can be comfortably merged with
Soviet Russia."

Now obviously not everyone is aware of the plight we are
in as a result of the perfidy of our foundations, much less
aware of the extent to which the Communists, according to
Welch, have brazenly moved into every phase of American
life. Hence, people should be shocked into a realization of

what is going on in institutions and communities that have been infiltrated by Communist influences, and this can best be done by way of exposure.

Welch observes that since a Birch Society committee for exposure would not have the power of subpoena granted to Congressional investigating committees (nor the freedom from libel), its job would be difficult indeed. All the same, it could be done. The evidence could be gathered on suspected Communists, and if it were impossible to prove Communist Party membership, then pro-Communist activity could be proved. Through paid advertisements in nationally distributed magazines the Communists and their sympathizers could be exposed. The advertisements would not come right out and say that the men in question were Communists or Communist sympathizers, of course. They would ask questions—leading questions moving toward inescapable conclusions. Such a technique would be "mean and dirty," Welch admits, but, we gather, the true Communist-fighter must sometimes be willing to suspend ethical judgment.

Notably lacking from Welch's *Blue Book* counsel is any cautionary directive urging members of the Birch exposure committee to seek objective evidence corroborating their private judgment as to who is a Communist. It is enough to make the judgment, confirm it for oneself, collect the "evidence," and then spring the advertisement on the public.

Welch's counsel, reduced to plain language, is nothing less than the advocacy of a vigilante group. It brings to mind the sober words of J. Edgar Hoover in the February 1962 issue of the *American Bar Association Journal*. "Today," said Hoover, "far too many self-styled experts on communism are plying the highways of America, giving erroneous and distorted information. This causes hysteria, false alarms, misplaced apprehension by many of our citizens. We need enlightenment about communism—but this information must be factual, accurate and not tailored to echo personal idio-syncrasies."

The very notion that a vigilante committee is necessary in our country is, of course, a manifestation of an outrageous disregard for American legal traditions. It is a woeful con-fession of a loss of faith in the ability of the courts to perform their rightful function, a base admission that the possibility of justice is being forsaken by the Society. Since the inception of our nation, we have held that conspirators and traitors should be publicly charged, judged and sentenced. Welch ap-pears to have forgotten that if he ever knew it. Hence his advice to the Birch Society: "Start Shocking the American People," and his plan for setting up a committee for exposure.

Even so, his advice ends in an absurdity. He makes so much of the Communist conspiracy and involves so many persons in it that, once it is exposed, there will be precious few people left to shock. As he wrote in an official Birch Society publica-tion in February 1961, "Communist influences are now in al-most complete control of our Federal Government. These same influences are very powerful in the top echelons of our educational system, our labor-union organizations, many of our religious organizations, and of almost every important segment of our national life. Insidiously but rapidly the Communists are now reaching the tentacles of their conspir-acy downward through the whole social, economic, and political pyramid."

So who is left to shock? Only the Birch Society members, I suppose, and they already "know." An absurd dilemma!

Fortunately for all of us, Welch's vision of the tentacles of conspiracy misses the mark. Unfortunately for most of us, the exposure committees remain, ready to make their "disclo-sures" whenever possible.

Another Birch Society technique outside the best American traditions of fair play may be found on page 86 of the *Blue Book*, where Welch proposes the formation of various front organizations and then goes on to observe that the Communists have been "far smarter" than the "conservative side," having been wise enough never to set up an organization to promote Communism as such.

A summary of the position is not difficult: Adopt Communist methods for gaining your objectives. Why? Because they work. Pretend to be someone or something you're not if it will advance the anti-Communist cause. Act a little. Pretend. Fool the Communists—and the public—by organizing fronts to attack the Communists—or persons, institutions and movements which you think may be giving aid to or comforting the Communists.

With such a blatant willingness to keep up with the Communists, I wonder how the Birchers can live with themselves, and I once said as much to John Rousselot in the course of a West Coast radio program. Rousselot, who was then still a U. S. Representative, but an acknowledged member of the Birch Society, responded to my criticism with candor. "I think you may have a good point," he said. "Bob Welch is a rugged businessman and I think he tends to use harsh language. Why? Because he has become very concerned over a period of eleven years as he traveled around the world, and other places [*sic!*], seeing the kind of things that were happening. And I think he does use harsh language that . . . you and I wouldn't."

When we returned briefly to what, for many persons, are the more objectionable tenets of the Society later in the program, Rousselot punctuated his earlier observation with the comment, "Maybe it's just the harsh language you object to."

That, without question, is the best defense of the Birch Society's more antidemocratic methods I have heard. Still, it is not enough simply to reduce the issue to a matter of semantics. Robert Welch may be a poor writer, although it would be hard to develop an argument to prove it. Judging by his felicity and close attention to definitions in the *Blue Book* alone, he uses the English language tolerably well. Even were we to assume that Welch chooses his words badly, this much must stand: Birch Society members read what Welch says, not what he intends to say. They read the *Blue Book* as it is printed, harsh words and all. Should they have personal propensities for discrediting public speakers by meeting-packing-tactics (harassment), should they have a hankering to organize an exposure committee (vigilante group), should they want to promote a Birch Society objective by organizing a front group (like the Communists), they have the counsel to do so. Robert Welch, "wittingly or unwittingly," to use a favorite right-wing phrase, has given them the go-ahead. At this late hour no amount of prettying up his language—which has *not* been done to date—will repair the damage already done to personal reputations, constitutional traditions and institutional integrity in America.

THE GREAT CONSPIRACY

Welch's appraisal of the Communist influence is open to constant modification. Each year he and the Society publish a scoreboard of the Communist control of governments around the world. In 1958 Welch "conservatively" estimated that the Soviet Union was 100% Communist-controlled, which probably startled no one. It may have surprised some of our Canadian neighbors, however, to learn that they were 20–40% Communist-controlled, and it may have startled our friends in Norway to discover that they were 40–60% Communist-controlled—still "conservatively" estimated. By 1963 Welch's *American Opinion* magazine saw Canada as 50–70% Communist, Norway as 50–70%, and the United States, 50–70%. (The Soviet Union was still ranked at 100%.) A footnote to the U.S. figure indicated that, "This year some of our readers will think it [the percentage] too low." The figure hadn't gone up since 1961, and while it might seem at first obvious (to any trained observer) that the conspiracy has made great strides since then, "a more careful consideration will show that our enemies are neither more numerous nor more powerful than they were in 1961. They have merely become far more brazen and open in their operations."

Cynics thought they saw another reason for the restraint suddenly shown by the Birch Society magazine. At the rate it was using up percentages, it was clear that it would soon have worked itself out of a job. In a few years the magazine would still be in business, but in the midst of a Soviet state. Even Robert Welch knew better than that.

The cynics were wrong as usual, however; and Welch, as usual, was sure of himself. He did not shrink from the possibility of a Red America. Bravely, *American Opinion* voiced its horrible prediction: "The Conspiracy has become more brazen because it is in desperate haste. The enemies of mankind know that they must win total victory within the next two years or face total defeat."

Welch himself had become a little brazen by 1963. Long besieged by attacks on his "confidential letter to friends" called *The Politician*, he finally published the three-hundred-and-some-page document, complete with footnotes and index. Strangely, however, the copyright page bore the legend, ". . . no portion of this book may be reproduced . . . without written permission . . ." The letter had suddenly become a book.

The dedication page contains a quotation from Daniel Webster: "There is nothing so powerful as truth, and often nothing so strange." What follows is strange all right. Powerful too, although the "truth" depends upon one's mental framework.

Before saying anything about the book, or rather letter, I should acknowledge the burden of the Prologue, a tediously long affair filled with the tribulations of the author, including a blow-by-blow account of the (Communist-motivated) attack on the John Birch Society. The burden is this: no one, living or dead, has the slightest responsibility for the letter, except for Robert Welch. (The point seems to me a little trivial, since I cannot imagine why anyone in his right mind would want to claim responsibility.) Further, says Welch, he is solely responsible for printing and distributing the letter. All the same, my copy came by way of Poor Richard's Book Shop in Los Angeles, an outlet responsible for the distribution of a good many pages of Birch Society literature.

To paraphrase an observation made by Alan Westin, Associate Professor of Public Law and Government at Columbia, *The Politician* is to the Birch Society what Leninist dogma is to Communist fronts in the Western nations. It is the final truth, taken quite seriously by the Founder and the inner circle, but too powerful as yet for the masses.[1] Thus, Welch is at some pains to disengage the Birch Society, as an organization, from direct involvement with *The Politician*.

The message of *The Politician* is simple: almost everyone in government is either a Communist, or working closely with Communists. It turns out that the Eisenhower brothers, Dwight and Milton, are the worst of a rotten bunch. George Marshall, to quote Welch, was "a conscious, deliberate, dedicated agent of the Soviet conspiracy [page 15]." F.D.R. was guilty of "deliberate treason" (page 13) and was directly controlled by Communists in nearly everything he did (page 62). Truman moved along comfortably, if passively, under Communist domination (page 279). Eisenhower, who was groomed for the Presidency by a secret, top-level "strategy board" of Communists (page 61), was maneuvered into Re-

[1] See Alan F. Westin, "The John Birch Society: 'Radical Right' and 'Extreme Left' in the Political Context of Post World War II" (1962). From *The Radical Right*, edited by Daniel Bell (Garden City: Doubleday & Company, Inc., 1963), pp. 201 ff.

publican ranks and became the most effective spokesman for Communism in the United States. As Welch puts it, Eisenhower ". . . has been sympathetic to ultimate Communist aims, realistically and even mercilessly willing to help them achieve their goals, knowingly receiving and abiding by Communist orders, and consciously serving the Communist conspiracy, for all of his adult life [page 278]."[2]

Welch also claims that Eisenhower may be guilty of "deliberate treason [page 279]." His brother, Milton, is described in an earlier edition of *The Politician* as "Dwight Eisenhower's superior and boss within the Communist Party," but in the 1963 edition Milton is mentioned merely as his brother's "superior and boss within the whole Leftwing Establishment [page 222]." The late John Foster Dulles is described even in the 1963 edition as "a Communist agent who always has had one clearly defined role to play; namely, always to say the right things and always to do the wrong ones [page 223]."

And so on, and on and on, through a monotonous labyrinth of conspiracy. Even the prettying up of the language in the later editions does little for *The Politician*. The frantic tone is endemic, the hysteria chronic.

Stated alone, the conclusions of *The Politician* are an amusing grotesquerie, a plainly ludicrous work of the imagination. When coupled to the rich fantasy world of the book as a whole they become something else. So tightly drawn is Welch's imaginative structure, so carefully correlated with numerous strands of reality (each pegged down by a footnote), so uncompromising is Welch's own belief in what he is saying that the reader is almost unavoidably drawn into his

---

[2] An earlier edition of *The Politician* reads, "But my firm belief that Dwight Eisenhower is a dedicated, conscious agent of the Communist conspiracy is based on an accumulation of detailed evidence so extensive and so palpable that it seems to me to put this conviction beyond any reasonable doubt." Obviously, Welch has eliminated some of the "harsh language" in the later editions of his letter, but the message is unchanged in content.

thought system. The facts, taken from a host of sources—
Newsweek, U. S. News and World Report, State Department
bulletins, *New Republic, Reader's Digest,* personal conversa-
tions, correspondence, etc.—come alive with new meanings
never before suspected. Each part of the system is carefully
related to every other. The author states his willingness to
guarantee the veracity of his account. He is plainly an open-
minded man, eager to be chastened and corrected by his
readers should they discover imperfections in his thought
system.

The book reminds me somewhat of a "scientific" treatise I
once read which purported to solve the mysteries of the creation of the earth. An impressive document it was, heavily
laden with footnotes, learned in its use of ancient literary and
religious texts, internally consistent. The author, who sported
several doctorates, was intensely serious about his theories. All
in all it was a fairly convincing piece of work, so long as you
kept your eyes on the page in front of you and firmly rejected hypotheses more commonly accepted by the world of
science. While browsing through the bookstore in the Harvard Coop in Cambridge, Massachusetts, a few years ago, I
happened to notice that the book was properly shelved
under the heading "science fiction." The author's only intent
had been to write the truth.

Just so, Welch quotes George Washington at the beginning
of *The Politician* as saying, "Truth will ultimately prevail
where there is pains taken to bring it to light." I must hand it
to Robert Welch. He is at pains to bring us truth. He is an
inveterate collector of data, and he combines his facts in an
outwardly impressive system. His unspoken premise troubles
me, however. It is the notion that the Communist conspirators, of whom there are a great many, are incredibly intelligent, and unlike other men, are capable of making history run
just so. They have been around, hauling and manipulating
people and institutions, taking all of us in, for longer than

most men suspect. And they are not far from achieving their objective—the domination of the world.

That premise frightens me. I am thankful that it is so plainly false.

THE FOUNDER

Who is the man behind *The Politician?* Robert Welch is somewhat cautious about making the details of his biography public, but this much at least is known. He was born on December 1, 1899, in Chowan County, North Carolina. The family line sprang from one Miles Welch, a 1720 immigrant from Wales. Robert was educated at the University of North Carolina, the U. S. Naval Academy, and the Harvard Law School where he spent two years. He moved to Boston in 1919. He is married and is the father of two sons.

Prior to his retirement, Welch served as vice-president of the Welch Candy Company, and although his business life was an active one, he found time to serve on the board of the National Association of Manufacturers. He has also served as a director of a bank and as a member of the boards of several business corporations. During two of his seven years on the N.A.M. board he acted as chairman of the organization's Educational Advisory Committee.

Active in community affairs, Welch has worked with the Belmont, Massachusetts, School Committee and has lectured widely on the evils of Socialism. Already the author of several books, including *May God Forgive Us* and *The Life of John Birch,* Welch retired from the candy business in 1957 in order to bring the truth about Communism to the American public.

On December 9, 1958, he met with eleven fellow businessmen at an Indianapolis, Indiana, hotel to found the John Birch Society, which he named for a World War II U. S.

Army intelligence officer and Baptist missionary. Welch claims that Birch was the first casualty in World War III. The *Blue Book*, called the "Koran" of the John Birch Society by the *New Yorker*, is a nearly verbatim transcript of the two-day-long lecture which Welch delivered to the eleven disciples in Indianapolis. From the beginning, the *Blue Book* has been the undisputed text of the organization.

Because of the "imminent and horrible" danger of the "physical enslavement of the whole world," including the U.S., there was no time for dawdling in Indianapolis. Welch laid out his plan with precision. He recognized that it constituted an ambitious undertaking, but envisioned the project as *the* means for enabling true patriots to fight the Communist conspiracy in all spheres of American life—labor unions, classrooms, community organizations, government, churches and other religious organizations.

Just so that his disciples wouldn't think that he was "entirely crazy" (his words), he told them that he was quite aware of the demands made by his projection of complex organizational plans. The building of the John Birch Society, in all of its many dimensions, would require the erection of an organizational scaffolding of great strength. In a 166-word sentence that must have left the disciples stunned and gasping, he explained how he would begin this task of organizing, and led on into a ten-point list of things planned for the future.

We have already considered three items on his agenda of plans—harassment of public speakers who are identified with the "enemy," exposure by citizens' groups, and the organization of front groups. The other seven ranged from the establishment of Christian-Science-type reading rooms with the writings of Robert Welch (and others) available, to swinging the Society's weight into the political scales of the United States and setting up an anti-Communist Internationale.

Eventually, the Birch Society was to become a world-encompassing movement.

What was needed in all this was a boss, and Welch had one in mind. "The John Birch Society will operate under completely authoritative control at all levels," he said, and then added, ". . . it is imperative that all the strength we can muster be subject to smoothly functioning direction from the top." That "smoothly functioning direction" was, of course, to come from Robert H. W. Welch, Jr., the Founder of the John Birch Society.

With a capital *F* Founder to run it, the Birch Society was to be a "monolithic body." An organization in the republican mode would have been too open to infiltration from sinister sources. Besides, human-type squabbles could more easily be settled when one man had the final word. A democratic organization was out of the question. Democracy, no matter where encountered, is, in Welch's judgment, "merely a deceptive phrase, a weapon of demagoguery, and a perennial fraud."

Those who were to join the John Birch Society during its early years would do so because they would believe in Robert Welch and his leadership, said Robert Welch. Those who would cease "to feel the necessary degree of loyalty" could resign. And if they didn't resign they would be put out.[3]

Welch seemed to realize that the eleven men who were gathered in Indianapolis might have other ideas about the best leader for such an operation, but he put it to them squarely that, "under the pressure of time and the exigencies of our need," there was no other choice. And that settled that. The John Birch Society was founded and ready to go to work. As the *New Yorker* put it, "The Birch creed should . . . tickle the pants off any Russian official in his right mind, for its essence is unilateral disarmament through permitted obsoles-

[3] In practice, Welch has used his power of excommunication infrequently.

cence, a breakup of federal authority, and a withdrawal from the international field."

In fact, one of the most sobering aspects of the Birch Society program is the way in which it parallels Communist notions in some important respects. Let me offer a few examples: Get the U.N. out of the U.S. and the U.S. out of the U.N., says the John Birch Society; move the U.N. to Austria and denigrate its executive function with a troika, says the U.S.S.R. Stop spending money on arms and arms development, says the John Birch Society; unilateral and uninspected disarmament is an honorable goal for the peace-loving nation, claims the Soviet Union. John Birchers would like nothing better than to have us drop all foreign aid. So would the Russians.

I do not mean to suggest, as some people have, that the John Birch Society is a Communist front. Belief alone, as the Birch Society is slow to learn, is not enough to define a man, or a group.[4] One thing is clear, however. The Communist Party could have done little better had it set out to create a custom-made foil for its views. The John Birch Society personifies the stereotyped reactionary. It represents the uses of American freedom at its worst, and threatens to make a dirty joke of considered, responsible criticism of Communism.

The mentality that enables the members of the Birch brigade to see Communists everywhere is a frightful aberration for a good many reasons, not the most trifling of which is that it is debilitating. It saps the believer of his true

4 In a May 23, 1961, session with "Meet the Press," Lawrence Spivack asked Welch if many of the John Birch Society's objectives were not, in fact, the same as those of the Communists. Welch responded with the ingenious, if not ingenuous, comment, "Our people have probably made more showings of [the film] 'Operation Abolition' than all other groups put together." Whether he realized it or not, he had stuck his finger into the mechanism of a working principle he has consistently refused to acknowledge: one must look at the activities of a group, as well as its beliefs, in appraising its place in the scheme of things.

strength and diverts the nation into a game of patriots and
traitors in which no one—absolutely no one—is to be trusted.
If taken seriously, this ugly mental set could, as A. J. Lieb-
ling once put it, "be more destructive than the nerve gas that
. . . paralyzes the will to resist. Only this gas, instead of
being carried over our borders by ICB missiles, is a native
product. . . ." Perhaps that is why the April 8, 1961, issue of
the national Catholic weekly *Ave Maria* cited the John Birch
Society as "a dangerously unchristian movement," and Senator
Stephen Young, a Protestant who attends both Episcopal and
Unitarian churches, wrote in the *Saturday Evening Post*,
". . . the John Birch Society, in my opinion [is] the most
dangerous organization in the United States today." Perhaps
that is why the leading journal of Protestant opinion, *The
Christian Century*, declared on April 12, 1961, with regard
to the John Birch Society and its methods, "Americans have
to take a stand. Civilization collapsed under the Nazis because
millions of Germans refused to be the first to say No."

Fortunately, a great many Americans *are* saying No, and
meaning it.

COMMUNISTS IN THE CLERGY

"The man who has given the widest circulation to the
charge of 'Communists in the clergy' is Robert Welch," wrote
United Press Correspondent Louis Cassels in the April 24,
1962, issue of *Look* magazine. Cassels quoted Welch as
claiming that "the largest single body of Communists in
America is in our Protestant clergy."

Usually, Welch declares that there are about 7000 Red
clergymen in American Protestant churches, although he
sometimes pushes the number to as high as three percent of
all U. S. Protestant clerics, or about 7200. Welch's most

detailed charges appear in *The Politician*, where he cites
Circuit Rider Myers Lowman as his authority (see Chapter
I). "Lowman published, not long ago," says Welch, "a
list of 2109 ministers, of the Methodist denomination alone,
who are either Communists or fellow travelers. He says his
forthcoming lists for several other denominations are much
larger—the Unitarian list, somewhat naturally, being relatively
the worst of all. Bundy . . . states categorically that . . . the
percentage of Communists and Communist sympathizers
among the Protestant clergy is twice as large as it is among
educators."

The "Bundy" referred to is Edgar C. Bundy of the Church
League of America, who is a major in the Air Force Reserve.
Although he is reported never to have served as minister of
a church, he is an ordained Southern Baptist minister. According to a report released by the National Council of the
Protestant Episcopal Church, Bundy sparked an American
Legion attack in Illinois on the Girl Scouts for trafficking in
subversive propaganda a few years ago, and drafted a resolution
on the same topic which was passed by the Legion at its
National Convention in 1954. In 1955 he drafted a resolution
calling UNESCO (United Nations Educational, Scientific,
and Cultural Organization) subversive. It too was passed by
the Legion convention, which met that year in Miami. In
1956 Bundy turned from fighting the Girl Scouts and
UNESCO to leading the Church League of America.

The Church League has been around, under one name or
another, since 1937, and has, in its own view, "awakened
thousands of Christian laymen over the nation to those
subversive forces which have penetrated both the religious and
educational fields." In his book *Collectivism in the Churches*
Bundy claims to give an account of the destruction of American liberty by the promoters of the social gospel who, in his
judgment, do the work of Socialists, Communists and their
fellow travelers. Like others in the fundamentalist, anti-

Communist line, Bundy feels that it is sufficient to point an accusing finger. If a man can't "prove" his innocence on Bundy's terms, he's guilty.

The attitude fits into Welch's view of things nicely. In the *Blue Book* he declares that there are those within the ranks of the American clergy who "actually use their pulpits to preach outright Communism, often in very thin disguise if any. . . ." He tells his readers that such ministers are not true believers in the Christian teachings they profess, but have converted Christianity into a social gospel indistinguishable from the welfare-state measures offered by Socialist politicians. Welch does not confine his criticism to Protestantism, however. He is truly ecumenical. Also included are Catholics, Jews, Muslims and Buddhists.

On October 9, 1961, he is reported to have told a Garden City, Long Island, audience that one half of one percent of the Roman Catholic priests in the United States were Communists or "Comsymps." That figured out to 273 "Comsymp" priests, a figure which left more than a few Roman Catholic prelates uneasy—but about Welch, not the priesthood. The Boston *Pilot*, official newspaper of the archdiocese of Boston, challenged Welch to name the offending priests. The paper agreed to print all names and evidence. Mr. Welch responded by writing to the editor of the *Pilot*, Monsignor Francis J. Lally, stating that the figure was "simply pulled out of a hat as a complete guess and without any substantiation even being claimed."

Similar challenges to produce his evidence or hush have come from Protestant church officials, including Methodist Bishops in Indiana and California. Welch thus far has produced not one single item of evidence, but continues to make public charges. He does, however, now commonly confine himself to attacking Protestant clergymen, who have no single authorized voice of defense. As Father John F. Cronin, speaking for the National Catholic Welfare Conference, once wrote, "If the disseminators of such charges were asked to list fifty living Protestant ordained ministers who *at any time* belonged to the Communist Party, they could not do so without committing libel. They would be hard pressed to name 200 living clergy who are or have been Communist sympathizers in the correct use of the term [emphasis supplied]."

Not all Birch Society partisans are as bold in their denunciations of the clergy as is the Founder. In a November 14, 1961, speech, the then Representative John Rousselot attacked the churches with exemplary finesse. The speech, taken as a whole, was a tribute to Rousselot's ability to build on the emotional preconceptions of a crowd, saying always that which suggested what everyone knew to be so, but never quite saying *what* was so.

He dealt with the churches after a long, mid-speech pause, when he began: "Well, other areas where we see this [Communist] attack beginning—in our churches!

"And in saying this I don't mean to say for a minute that there are thousands of Communists in church work. There aren't."

Then what's the problem, I asked myself. It turned out to be the familiar story. The *few* had gained influence and control, or as Rousselot put it, "They are able, through these other groups, to influence a great number of people.

"Now if you don't see. . . ."

Rousselot became tentative—use your imagination here. "Now if you don't see in certain areas of activity, in so-called social action work of certain churches [unspecified] the kind of activity that I think we begin to have to take an interest in—"

He raised his voice quizzically—then went on.

"Let me give you an example," he said, (and again the disclaimer) "and I'm *not* saying that the Presbyterian Church is Communistic. . . ."

He went on to quote a 1961 resolution of the Presbyterian General Assembly on the "national purpose" of the United States, in which the denomination expressed concern about the health of the body politic (no special option of the Presbyterians).

"It questioned," quoted Rousselot, source unnamed, "the adequacy of the Declaration of Independence and Constitution of the United States, framed more than a century and a half ago by a youthful, small, isolated and relatively homogeneous nation to direct a vast and heterogeneous populace with [the] new problems of a great world power. The statement suggested that the principles of the Founding Fathers, though admirable as statements of basic objectives, provide insufficient guidance among the tangled issues which confront us today."

End of quote. But of what? Rousselot didn't say. My first impression was that he was quoting the resolution. My second thought was that it was a press account—in which case we should have ignored it, since Rousselot told the audience a few minutes later that the American press had been taken over by journalists from Columbia and Harvard. Many of them are even "former members of the secret Fabian Society at Harvard University," he said, and singled out Walter Lippmann for special attack.

Whatever the source of the quotation, be it a paraphrase of the resolution, a misrepresentation by the press, a direct quote from the document itself, the question was raised: Why was Rousselot quoting it?

"You see this is the beginning of a movement," he said in a confidential tone, "to downgrade the Constitution."

Quickly his voice leaped more than an octave. "Why? Why is this important?"

The awful truth was about to be revealed. "Because built into this Constitution legally is the right that you and I have to the freedoms that we enjoy. We are legally given license to have freedom [*sic*]."

Now, if I follow Rousselot's reasoning (?) correctly, he meant to tell us that the Presbyterians, or rather the few people in social action groups who control the Presbyterians, are 1) joining the right wing in questioning the health of the body politic, 2) passing, perhaps unaware of what they are doing, a resolution whose first effect is to downgrade the Constitution of the United States, and 3) participating in a drive to deprive us all of our freedom.

Is that what Rousselot said? I see no alternative.

There was an unanswered question, however. *Who* was responsible for getting the Presbyterians to behave in such an unseemly fashion? The ubiquitous *few*, I suppose, who happen to be Communists.

The daisy chain is complete. The Presbyterians are clearly understood to be doing the work of the Communists. But did Rousselot say so? He said no such thing, and he can quote himself to you to prove it.

Other unanswered questions: Just what did the resolution behind the unidentified quotation say? And what did a 3500-word report from a special committee on national purpose, which provided the background for the resolution, say? Was it a sinister sequel to the *Communist Manifesto?* Did it propose a series of collectivist governmental reforms? Or did it perhaps say something that people living in the twentieth century should hear? You must draw your own meanings. Believe whatever you wish.

I must confess that the account, as Rousselot gave it, sounded fairly sinister, and even shorn of all its shoddy logic, I found that it caused me to wonder what the Presbyterians *could* have been up to in questioning our Constitution. Speaking personally, I feel strongly that the document is a trustworthy and adequate guide, although I admit that we must do a good deal of interpreting, living in the twentieth century as we do. I make no claim to the discovery of a new revelation in this. It is merely my ground for puzzlement and curiosity over what the Presbyterians might have had to say on the matter. Alas, I shall probably never know, and neither will anyone else who heard John Rousselot on the topic. All I was able to learn from his exposition of the text was that the Presbyterians, unknowingly, played into the hands of a sinister few.

Why all this attention to a relatively minor attack from a former Representative, now an organization man for the Birch Society? I have two reasons. First, the attack is fully representative of the more subtle charges brought against the churches, and as such, deserves detailed analysis. Second, the greatest danger from the John Birch Society comes not, in my judgment, from the plainly absurd fulminations of Robert Welch. He is too direct in his denunciations ever to become a demagogue. The greatest danger comes from the Welch apostles who display an ability with a crowd, before a microphone or in front of a television camera, quite unknown to the Founder himself.

John Rousselot is the leading representative of an emerging type—the John Birch Society's professional organization men, a group of paid patriots, flanked by an increasing number of volunteers—20,000 in California alone as of June, 1962. This is the professional push behind the movement that now threatens democracy from the legislative hall to the church pew.

THE THEOLOGY OF THE FOUNDER

Disagreements notwithstanding, Robert Welch and I agree emphatically on at least one thing. Ralph Waldo Emerson is the most profound American who ever lived. Emerson, more

than any other American up to the present day, was in touch
with things deep and elemental. He knew the reaches of the
human spirit, the interior realities, the drift of the universe.
Conversant with the European ancestry of our nation, he was
an interpreter of ideas who knew what the Continent had to
say to our land, but possessed the genius to discover what was
uniquely our own. He was able to perceive where the divine
and the worldly met in human personality, and although it
was heresy to do so, he voiced his perceptions.

Emerson was a Unitarian clergyman before he turned to
lecturing and writing. He created no cult and built no sect
of Emersonians, but he set a conversation going among religious liberals in America that shaped much of the Unitarian
movement in the second half of the nineteenth century.

It is from the nineteenth-century tradition of religious liberalism—not all of it Emersonian by any means, but liberal
still and in the spirit of Emerson—that Robert Welch speaks.
There are some major exceptions in his thought, but it is fair
to say that although he does not belong to a liberal church,
he is, in the main, a religious liberal *as the term was defined
in the nineteenth century.* He begins the *Blue Book* with an
acknowledgment of his debt to Emerson. His commitment to
nineteenth-century liberalism emerges as one reads on. He
quotes often and with appreciation the great nineteenth-
century religious liberals—Daniel Webster, James Russell
Lowell, Julia Ward Howe and others.

Welch's theology is liberal, and it is universalistic. That is
to say, he looks for the common denominators of all world
religions as they may be expressed in the humanitarian goals
of societies which encourage tolerance and personal integrity.
He does not believe that one may describe the mystery of
God, but he is certain that there is purposefulness in life
which moves upward with a kind of inner direction. I am not
sure that Welch would care to assent to a summary of Unitarian beliefs common to the nineteenth century which reads,

"We believe in the fatherhood of God, the brotherhood of man, the leadership of Jesus, salvation by character and the progress of mankind onward and upward forever," but the statement comes close to the spirit of his faith, if not the letter. Judging by his writings, his major disagreement would be with the importance accorded in the affirmation to the place of Jesus.

Welch likes Tennyson's words, "Yet I doubt not through the ages one increasing purpose runs," and he makes them the touchstone of his belief. He sees man's purpose, which is but a reflection of cosmic purpose, as the product of the same evolutionary forces that produced man. Man is what nature has made of him. The laws of the universe are to be taken seriously, says Welch, but one must not assume that there is any finality to our present understanding of how things are. If the Creator of life and existence permits man to continue on this planet, the scientific laws we now know will pale against the greater insights man will someday gain. Even as we look back at the mistaken literal belief in the Biblical account of creation cherished by our ancestors, so men will look back one day at our present beliefs and theories, and see them for what they are—literalistic and egocentric. Just as we see that the religious views of our forebears made God into a being that was somewhat less than God by reducing him to the human scale of the world as it was then understood, so also will man see someday how limited are our most profound conceptions. Man moves upward in his thought, says Welch, who is fond of summarizing his belief with a line from the poet Harry Kemp: "Thou hast put an upward reach in the heart of man."

Welch's universalist beliefs become clear when he speaks of the common basic values advocated by the religions of the world: prohibitions against theft, murder and bodily harm, concepts of charity, and so on. The qualities found universally in religion, Welch would have us note, are precisely those with which evolution has gradually endowed the species of man. The difference between man and his hairy quadruped ancestors, in terms of ethical perception, is a function of evolutionary development. No magical formulas or supernatural explanations are needed to explain man's better qualities. They are one with nature.

Welch admits that he broke with the strictures of his Baptist upbringing while he was still a young man, but hastens to point out that the spirit of his fundamentalist background proved meaningful to him even when he parted with the more formal aspects of the religion. The Southern Baptists had a kind of appreciation for life and its direction that was wholesome and right. It was the doctrine that was unacceptable to Welch, and it could be put aside. What was left was the humane heritage of brotherhood, loyalty and morality. That heritage was, after all, his birthright. His ancestry was filled with farmers and Baptist preachers.

He tells of his Sunday School attendance in a country Baptist church as a small boy. The church had a great chart hanging on one of the walls, of the sort that was common to the fundamentalist churches of the era. It began with creation in 4004 B.C. and traced the development of man down through the Biblical stages of history. Even today Welch has a deep appreciation for the people who invented that chart, as well as for those persons who still believe in such literalistic mythology. He gently rebukes any efforts they may make to impose their pious literalism on others, however, and insists that there is a syncretistic faith of breadth in which they can share. In that fashion both the rationalists and fundamentalists may be united by a common confidence in the roots of morality, leaving to each man the details of his faith. Welch believes that his universalistic ideals would be equally acceptable to the Baptist missionary and army officer John Birch, to the deist Thomas Jefferson (whom Welch wrongly calls an agnostic), and to the Roman Catholic Hillaire Belloc.

The basic principle of his faith, to which he returns repeatedly, is the "upward reach" that he sees in man. He conceives of his faith as "a basis and a beginning of renewed dedication to a dream of man's future." He correctly observes that his theology has a very direct and practical bearing on the problems of this world. His idealism is seen clearly in the generalized goal of the John Birch Society—"to promote less government, more responsibility and a better world."

It is no accident that Welch's best friend among the clergy of the United States is probably James W. Fifield, Jr., minister of the First Congregational Church of Los Angeles. Fifield is probably one of the most theologically liberal and at the same time politically conservative ministers in the continuing Congregational movement (consisting of those churches and/or ministers who are out of sympathy with the Congregational Christian—Evangelical and Reformed merger of 1957).

Fifield says reading the Bible is "like eating fish—we take the bones out to enjoy the meat. All parts are not of equal value." Unlike his fundamentalist colleagues, he is quite willing to state, "The men who chronicled and canonized the Bible were subject to human error and limitation." As though anticipating the criticism of those on his theological right, he quips, "Some of those who can best quote the Bible least understand it."

He is no less outspoken on the doctrine of God. "To believe in God is to seek to do His will," says Fifield. He commits what must be heresy in the view of more conservative clerics by observing that many people who say they believe in God are, in fact, "unconscious atheists," while many atheists do God's will daily and so may be classified as "unconscious theists." As long ago as 1936 Fifield wrote, "I once thought God a human-formed and human-limited Being with a long beard. . . . I recall thinking that one had to believe in the Virgin Birth, Inerrant Bible, Physical Resurrection and Second Coming of our Lord to be a Christian. . . . But in all these thoughts and convictions, I was wrong. . . ."

On the political side, Fifield admits that even as he gave up belief in the virgin birth and a physical resurrection, so also he gave up a benighted patriotism which led him to believe that his country was incapable of wrong. Today he knows *much* better.

Frequently host to Robert Welch's Los Angeles visits, Fifield and his church keep a full program of reconsidered patriotism under way. As the 1959 Lenten manual for the church proclaimed, it is ultimately "Christ or Communism, victory or slavery." The Freedom Club at First Congregational Church backs the John Birch Society in a fashion that would have astounded John Birch himself.

The Fifields of the country are rare. Welch must rely on the universalistic character of his theology to pull in the fundamentalist anti-Communists, who if aware of his theology, invariably grant him the right to be guilty of theological heresy in the light of his unqualified doctrinal rectitude in politics.

The point they doubtless miss is that Welch's political views, which entail an absolute division between good and evil, are the product of his theology. His nineteenth-century religious liberalism has no adequate doctrine of evil. Indeed, it has no doctrine of evil at all, and so he must invent one or live with phantoms. Even as evil was never seriously reckoned with by nineteenth-century Unitarianism—Emerson called it "merely privative, not absolute . . . like cold, which is the privation of heat."—so Welch ignores it completely in developing his theological system. It is all onward and upward forever, which was a tolerably sensible view in the nineteenth century. A sane man could get by with it fairly well then. In the twentieth century the same notion is, of course, sheer madness. The escalator of human destiny is not, after all, moving irreversibly up. In fact, humanity seems not to have been riding an escalator at all. The illusion could be maintained well enough during the nineteenth century to convince some men of its certitude, despite periodic evidences to the contrary. The Civil War, to name the greatest evidence, came close to being a catastrophe for a good many religious liberals of the day, but they warded off the information the great war brought them.

No man could have lived through the first fifty years of the present century, however, without discovering the dreadful meaning of two world wars, a Hitler, an Auschwitz, a Bergen-Belsen, Hiroshima, radioactive fallout, the hydrogen bomb, Stalin and Mao Tse-tung. They all speak of evil, and any theology that ducks it is certain ruin to its proponent.

Hence Welch's troubles. In the midst of evil, he ignores its religious meaning (*i.e.*, its theology). When he encounters evil firsthand, in the guise of Soviet aggression, he creates a monster. What he failed to provide for in his religion he makes up for in his politics in one colossal overcompensation. He gets into trouble by becoming jammed into the same corridor with his fundamentalist friends on the far right. They make a place for evil, but provide it with the throne of a lesser deity. They carve the universe up into the province of the good God and the bad god, and call the bad god *Satan*. All men must work for one God or the other. If you are not with us you are against us.

Welch leaves room in the universe for God alone, who is understood to be wholly good, and then has no room for evil. When evil hits him it demolishes his theology and he has but one recourse: to hate it. Hate it not with the passion of radicalized anger, which is proper for evil, but with a consuming hatred that knows no bounds.

What is wrong with Welch's theology? Like fundamentalism, it has no place for an authentic doctrine of man. It has no capacity to absorb the complex assaults of reality. Man is an unfallen angel for Welch. When he sees a particular man in whom there is evil—such as Khrushchev—he makes of that man a devil. As a devil, the man receives the whole complement of anger normally spent on one's fellows and on one's self.

Welch has no adequate theology, no interpretive framework capable of making sense of twentieth-century complexities. What is missing in theory must be made up for in the immediacy of concrete persons and events. He manages to keep the anxiety of radical negativity out of his religion, but it exacts its revenge. An all-good, all-benevolent, universalistic, upward-reaching, inclusive theology prepares the way for self-righteousness. The evil which is unaccounted for in theory suddenly becomes everywhere present. Unallowed for, it must be destroyed. Wherever it appears it must be eliminated. "Somewhere there seems to be some demonic group or power . . . which seeks to make hatred and not love the rule of life," says Welch in a television address. The group is then identified and the attack is mounted.

It is regrettable that Welch manages to borrow from Emerson's one great failure, but ignores his insights. Welch joins the Concord sage in forgetting about evil, but when it comes to Emerson's deep appreciation for individualism as self-reliance, as the manifestation of indwelling Reason, and as the way to a near-identity with the structure of reality, Welch fails us and comes forward with a trifling egocentrism labeled "more responsibility." When it comes to Emerson's considered appraisal of the encumbrances placed on men by social machinery and government—devalued by him because they inhibit spontaneity and therefore true selfhood—Welch is content to argue for "less government" and against Socialism. Emerson called for an inflamed individualism, argued for an equality of rights and succeeded in inspiring men, such as Theodore Parker, to wrestle with the epoch's most angry social problems. Welch argues blandly for "a better world," and denounces social legislation, offering nothing in its stead.

Welch's greatest offense to his mentor, however, is in his appraisal of democracy. Democracy for Welch is "merely a deceptive phrase, a weapon of demagoguery, and a perennial fraud." Emerson, in his essay on *Politics*, speaks of democracy as a necessary corollary of equal rights:

> Of persons, all have equal rights, in virtue of being identical in nature. This interest, of course, with its whole power demands a democracy.

Emerson takes it for granted that an equality in rights follows from an identity in nature, and so *demands a democracy*. For him democracy is an essential prerequisite to selfhood. It is close to the center of truth.

Would that Welch had bothered to read Emerson as well as praise him!

SANTA BARBARA: A SHORT CASE STUDY IN THE CONTROL OF BIRCHISM

What happens when the Birch Society moves into a community and begins to implement its program? How may a community defend itself against a breakdown of trust and confidence in democratic processes? In terms of the Birch Society and its work, Santa Barbara, California, was among the first cities in America to find out.

The site of two colleges, home of the Center for the Study of Democratic Institutions, a haven for retired persons, and a center for numerous burgeoning small research and electronics industries, Santa Barbara has not been noted for political squabbles. Late in 1960 the Santa Barbara *News-Press* began to print some letters to the editor that were out of the ordinary for the community. Consisting for the most part of violent, reactionary attacks aimed at school officials, the local library board, church leaders, the university faculty, and the Center for the Study of Democratic Institutions, they reflected more than a random relationship to one another.

In January of 1961 Granville Knight, a local physician of some national prominence, approached the Santa Barbara *News-Press* and suggested that the paper run a story on a new national society on whose board he served. A young Norwegian reporter named Hans Engh, now a U.S. citizen, was assigned to the story.

Mr. Engh was no hack writer. The more he learned the more he wanted to know, and he soon began interviewing as many local members of the organization as he could find. Dr. Knight became alarmed and requested that the paper forget about the whole thing. By this time Engh knew that he had a story of some note, and continued his research. He turned the story in to the paper, and it was run as two articles, both of them factual, devoid of editorial content. Birch activities continued to expand.

Attacks in Santa Barbara were now no longer confined to the letters column of the local paper, and a number of prominent citizens became concerned. A group consisting of, among others, the Chancellor of the University of California in Santa Barbara, the President of City College, representatives from the public schools, staff members of the Center for the Study of Democratic Institutions and the managing editor of the *News-Press* met privately to discuss the problem. They decided to see what effect Engh's articles, and future *News-Press* publicity, might have before taking any action.

On February 19, 1961, the Rev. John Crane, minister of the Unitarian Society of Santa Barbara, and a member of the group which had met to discuss the Birch problem, delivered one of the first sermons preached in America on the John

Birch Society.[5] He began by quoting several of the more out-
landish statements from the *Blue Book*. He went on to an
analysis of Welch's views, reviewed his organizational approach, and concluded with an appraisal of the Society, together with suggestions on how his congregation might best
relate to Society members when they encountered them.

Robert Welch, said Crane, "is convinced that it is his mission to save the world from the ravages of Communism. He
will go to any lengths to achieve this mission. He openly
confesses that he will even use the very methods of the Communists to defeat them. He means business." Crane observed
that such movements as the Birch Society "crop up from
time to time. . . . It's a great pity," he said. "It means that
good men must turn themselves to the task of containing the
eruption." Crane remarked that there were, no doubt, "many
good, earnest people in the John Birch Society," some of
whom could well be friends of members of the congregation.
"We ought to be as patient as we can, realizing that [they]
are doing what they feel they must do," he said, and then
concluded his sermon with these words:

> Don't condemn them. Don't threaten them. Let them
> talk about their views. Question them closely. Sometimes
> just hearing their own words spoken in the presence of
> someone who is calm and rational will help them to feel
> their absurdity.
> Be patient. Be firm. This too will pass, if we are alert
> and watchful.

Then on February 26 the Santa Barbara *News-Press* opened
its heaviest editorial fire on the Birch Society, and reprinted
in toto Mr. Crane's sermon, commending it to its readers as
a "well-reasoned" appraisal of the Society and its objectives.

[5] So far as I have been able to discover, the Rev. Robert Lehman, another Southern California Unitarian, was the first to devote an entire sermon
to the Society.

Thomas M. Storke, the eighty-five-year-old publisher of the paper, began that Sunday edition with a front-page statement and an editorial that were later to win him a Pulitzer Prize. The publisher had lived in Santa Barbara since the "west was west and men were men," the paper reminded its readers. He had grown up with the community, and had lived in times when men who bandied the word "traitor" about carelessly were "made to answer. . . . He lived when men were considered cowards when they hid behind their women's skirts and clothed their identity through anonymity," said the paper, alluding to the Birch Society's policy of keeping membership lists secret. While agreeing with the Birch Society that Communism must be vigorously opposed, Storke voiced his opinions of the Society and its program:

> The *News-Press* condemns the destructive campaign of hate and vilification that the John Birch Society is waging against national leaders who deserve our respect and confidence.
>
> . . . .
>
> The *News-Press* condemns the tactics that have brought anonymous telephone calls of denunciation to Santa Barbarans in recent weeks from members of the John Birch Society or their sympathizers. Among the victims of such cowardly diatribes have been educational leaders, including faculty members of the University of California at Santa Barbara, and even ministers of the Gospel.
>
> . . . .
>
> The *News-Press* challenges members of the society to come into the open and admit membership . . . [and] the responsible local leaders of the society to make themselves known, . . . to tell their fellow citizens exactly what they are up to and specifically what program they have in mind for Santa Barbara.
>
> The John Birch Society already has done a grave dis-

service to Santa Barbara by arousing suspicions and mutual distrust among men of good will. . . . The *News-Press* challenges [society members]: Come up from underground.

Storke concluded his editorial by urging the Birchers to sue the paper if they thought that they had in any way been libeled. No suits were forthcoming.

One can only imagine what the reaction of the Birchers was. Other Santa Barbara residents sighed in relief and began again to breathe fresh air. The Birchers and their activities, as John Crane later observed, "had been a vague, ominous, menacing presence that few dared talk about." Once the whole matter was out in the open, sanity came ebbing in. As Storke put it in an article in the *New York Times Magazine*, "Air the ideas of the radical extremists, and you will find in a hurry, as we did in Santa Barbara, that the moderates—conservative and liberal—are in control. That knowledge makes all the difference in the world to the church and school leaders and others who have been under attack." The hard-hitting publisher concluded his account of the *News-Press* encounter with Birchism by observing, "I have learned that you can't kill a rat with a feather duster."

In the fall of 1961 the Birch Society picked UNICEF (United Nations International Children's Emergency Fund) as one of its primary targets, and voiced opposition to the notion of children taking up Halloween collections. Santa Barbarans knew by this time the origin of such attacks, and promptly doubled their gifts to the U.N. organization.

From that point on, the mysterious John Birch Society was no longer so sinister a force in Santa Barbara. Its hold on the community had been broken. Its members had been forced, at least partially, into the open.

By the spring of 1963 there was still the need for an occasional community conference to deal with outcroppings of distrust in Santa Barbara. A convocation held in May of that year, at the Center for the Study of Democratic Institutions, addressed itself to right-wing attacks on the United Nations. Judging by comments from representatives of the local chapter of the American Association for the United Nations, its impact was all that they had hoped for.

The Birchers are still around in Santa Barbara, still busy writing letters and holding meetings. But people are no longer afraid to speak out against them. Residents say that they are not at all sure what the outcome would have been had the *News-Press* failed to take its forceful stand. There is little question that the newspaper turned the drift of events, but the turning point could not have been reached without thoughtful public support.

THE SOCIETY AND ITS CRITICS

Santa Barbara was largely successful in its attempt to arrest the growth and development of Birchism. Quite early in the game it forced the Society and its membership to come into the open and work within the accepted rules of a democratic society. Not every community has been so fortunate. In many areas Birch attacks continue to grow and still constitute an ominous, poorly understood threat for those who have yet to acquaint themselves with the Society, its objectives, and above all, its methods.

In some areas, and among some members, the Society has taken on the colors of an almost apocalyptic, quasi-religious movement. Members may be told by a Society professional of the impending disasters faced by the nation. The Communist take-over may be described in hushed tones, but with graphic language. The day in which the news media will cease merely voicing its subtle propaganda, will stop slanting the

news, and will actually announce its identification with the
Communist apparatus is within sight. Travel, even between
local communities, will be sharply restricted. Water supplies
will be cut off. Libraries, colleges and public schools will
openly begin to teach Marxist dogma. Communists in government will show their true colors in a bloodless *coup*. And
all this, it is said in some places, will come to pass even before
this generation has passed away.

When the last moment arrives, Birch Society chapters
across the country will be ready, and it may just be that even
at this late hour the organization can still stop the headlong
rush into subservience to the Communist foe. In fact, the
Society *must do so*, and Robert Welch is altogether convinced that it can. Tyranny will be overthrown and the Birch
Society will prepare the way for the revolution. "We are not
beginning any revolution, nor even a counterrevolution, *in
any technical sense*," says Welch in the *Blue Book* (emphasis
supplied). "While we are opposing a conspiracy we are not
ourselves making use of conspiratorial methods. Yet our
determination to overthrow an entrenched tyranny is the very
stuff out of which revolutions are made."

Just what is Welch talking about? It is clear that he sees a
revolution in the offing, and yet he says that the Birch Society
is not making use of conspiratorial methods; it is providing
the "determination" for a revolution. Is Mr. Welch advocating revolution, preparing the ground for revolution, seeking to
create an emotional climate for revolution, or what? Perhaps
none of these alternatives. Perhaps all of them. He is not at all
clear about what he means. He leaves us confused about his
intent.

Considering the Birch Society's image of the clear and
present danger to our nation from Communism, it is not
surprising that both the Founder and a great many members
find within themselves an intensity of dedication and a purposefulness perhaps unequaled among religious and political

organizations on the modern American scene. Consider John
Rousselot's remarks before the California Republican Assembly in the fall of 1961:

> I am being threatened by godless Communism. I must
> defend myself or submit to slavery.
>
> I know that the Communist leaders plan to slaughter
> sixty million of us. And they do! They lay out the people
> they plan to execute when they take this country—the
> police, the F.B.I., certain government officials. It's laid
> down. It's a program. They aren't kidding—they mean to
> do it!

A great deal of determination and an impressive measure of
dedication may come from such beliefs.

Perhaps it is the dedication of Birch Society members that
has enabled the organization to show a substantial growth
record since its founding in 1959. The Society is still far from
its goal of one million members, and it is difficult to know
how much it has grown since, in 1961, the *Christian Science
Monitor* estimated its membership as "close to 100,000."
(Other estimates in 1962 and 1963 put the figure closer to
60,000.) Although many members freely acknowledge their
membership, the Society keeps its membership lists secret.
Finances too are kept secret, even from the membership, as
a matter of official policy; but an Anti-Defamation League
report published late in 1961 indicates that "the annual dues
received by the John Birch Society headquarters in Belmont,
Massachusetts, would appear to be a minimum of $1,200,000
a year, and in all probability more." The additional funds
referred to come from $1000 life memberships. By the fall
of 1963 Birch Society leaders were speaking of the organization's "$8000-per-day income"—nearly $3,000,000 per year.
Whatever the exact amount, it is clear that the Birch Society
has a budget of substantial size—large enough to finance an

extensive professional staff, both in Belmont and in the field. The Society is getting things done.

Its effectiveness has no doubt been largely responsible for both the denunciation and the praise that have been showered on the Society and its Founder, sometimes from somewhat unlikely sources. Gus Hall, Secretary of the Communist Party in the United States, has claimed a sharp rise in party membership and credited it to publicity given to Communism by right-wing extremist groups. All the same, the party has launched a flaming attack on the right wing, perhaps because martyrdom can pay off well, but more likely because the ultra-right so closely resembles Lenin's image of bourgeois capitalism. It thus provides the modern Communist with a ready-made formula for interpretation. Then too, a verbal salvo aimed at an Eisenhower-type Communist may have accidentally hit an authentic Communist.

Some of the heaviest attacks on the Birch Society have come from conservatives, however. On Sunday, March 12, 1961, Otis Chandler, publisher of the conservative *Los Angeles Times*, declared in a front-page editorial that "if the John Birchers follow the program of their leader, they will bring our institutions into question exactly as the Communists try to do." Subversion, said Chandler, "whether of the left or the right, is still subversion."

At the 1962 meeting of the California Republican Assembly in Berkeley, Senate minority whip Thomas Kuchel told those gathered, "I think I was the first member of Congress who arose to denounce the John Birch Society's so-called tenets." He went on to add, "I have said that anyone who followed the society's tenets, whether a member or not, is not qualified for public office."

If Kuchel was the first to take on the Birch Society in Congress, Democratic Senator Stephen Young was not far behind. In April, 1961, he told the Senate that the John Birch Society and other organizations like it were "as serious a threat

to our security and way of life as internal Communism."
Democratic Senator Thomas Dodd of Connecticut and others
called for a Congressional investigation of the group and its
leaders.[6]

Perhaps the most outspoken criticism of the Society came
from former Vice-president Richard Nixon, who stated in an
April 1, 1962, interview in the *Los Angeles Times*, "There is
no place in the Republican Party for the John Birch Society
or members of the John Birch Society who, by the very act
of becoming members, have agreed to accept the dictatorship
of Robert Welch, who has declared that Dwight Eisenhower
is a conscious agent of the Communist Party."

In their book *The Far Right* Donald Janson and Bernard
Eismann indicate that even Senator Barry Goldwater has had
some reservations about the Society's membership and some
harsh words about its leadership. They quote him as having
said sometime in 1962:

> Conservatives must beat off the idiots that are always
> attracted to a movement in its beginnings. The idiots are
> being drawn toward the conservative movement now just
> as they were attracted to liberalism in the 1930s. There are
> always people who will go off on a tangent if they don't
> think their ideas are being carried out to the letter. I mean
> any group that goes to extremes. I'm a member of the
> American Legion and I can remember when it practiced
> some of the things we object to in the John Birch Society.
> My chief objection to the John Birch Society is its leader.
> He is intemperate and unwise. I wish he would step out
> so the fine, responsible people who are members could
> take charge.

---

[6] Such an investigation was carried out by the California State Senate
Fact-Finding Subcommittee on Un-American Activities in 1963. The Subcommittee's report probably indicated as much about its own understanding of
democratic processes as about the Birch Society, however. From the Committee's point of view the organization was difficult to criticize.

Conservative leaders opposed to Welch's leadership have continued to grow in number: William Loeb, publisher of the conservative Manchester, New Hampshire, *Union Leader;* Russell Kirk, the perceptive conservative pundit; Walter Judd, former missionary and U. S. Congressman from Minnesota, who met defeat in 1962. William Buckley's journal of responsible conservative opinion, *National Review,* in a June 13, 1962, editorial, called for Welch's resignation. Most conservatives, however, endorsed the idea of the Society while calling for the removal of its Founder, apparently feeling that once Mr. Welch's influence was gone, the more extremist aspects of the organization could be rooted out.

Even George Lincoln Rockwell, Commander of the American Nazi Party, has endorsed the Society while criticizing its Founder. When asked his opinion of the Society, Rockwell told San Gabriel, California, newsman Tony Potter, "I would go so far as to say that the man who would relieve me if I am killed . . . is now one of the top men of the John Birch Society, unknown to Mr. Welch." Rockwell also made it clear that he regarded members of the Birch Society as potential members of his party. "When they've had all they can stand," he said, ". . . the Welch people will be Nazis."

From the far left to the farthest out on the far right, then, the appraisal of the leadership of the John Birch Society has been largely negative. The radical left and the radical right have united in endorsing the Society itself, however, but for very different reasons.

"IT CAN'T HAPPEN IN AMERICA"

Many of Welch's critics, from those on the extreme left through those in the balanced middle to those on the extreme right, forget one thing. The John Birch Society **is** what Welch is. He is the architect for the organization, the inspiration for its founding, the theorist of its structure and strategy. As Emerson once wrote, "An institution is the lengthened shadow of one man." And so it is. No organization ever reflected more accurately the truth of Emerson's insight. No attempt to banish Robert Welch can be successful because his ideas live in the structure of the body he built—the John Birch Society. Do away with the man Welch and you still have the Society, shot through with his political theories, his theology, his methods of operation, and his way of encountering the world.

From Welch's own perspective, he provided well for his continuation as leader. He would be difficult to depose. There is no way in which the members of his "monolithic organization" may vote to put him out. It is unlikely that the governing council will seek to do so. Birch Society members well know that although the Founder's personal views may sometimes be embarrassing to the organization, he is still its greatest asset.

So long as Welch is able to dream of new conspiracies and see Communists or Comsymps in public or private places, the Society will do well to keep him on as Leader. He has a marvelously fertile mind and a great capability in organizational matters. Moreover, he is able to point out a new conspiracy and build his organization almost with one breath—even at those times when conspiracies are difficult to come by. He is seldom conventional.

Take, for instance, his approach to growing racial tensions and civil rights demonstrations during the summer of 1963. The civil rights campaign, according to Welch, was part of a Communist plot to establish a "Soviet Negro Republic" in the southeastern part of the United States. The July-August bulletin of the Society, which was in the form of an open letter to Nelson Rockefeller, inquired about the Governor's reaction to the idea of Martin Luther King as President of the new republic with its capital in Atlanta. Society members were advised that this latest unmasking of a Soviet plot should inspire them to put their whole strength into the movement to impeach Chief Justice Earl Warren.

The same issue of the Society's bulletin outlined a $250,000 promotional program and solicited contributions for it. One idea included a special category of contributors, an inner financial circle, so to speak, called the "Century Club." Members of the "Club" would each be expected to contribute $100 a month.

Let me repeat my earlier observation. Robert Welch has an exceedingly fertile mind and genuine talent as an organizer. More than that, he has the ability, the almost unique ability, to appeal to the deeper and darker regions of the human mind, to those regions where we manufacture our devils. We all have them. The proof lies in the appeal of men like Welch. He reaches down into the very depths of men and discovers there the archetypes of evil. He dresses those archetypes in the garb of real persons . . . here . . . now—tangible persons of flesh and blood, who may be hated with an unholy passion too terrible to turn toward oneself. It would destroy the man who did.

The Founder and Leader of the John Birch Society has the rare capacity to make men believe that the things they hate are never of themselves, but are, in fact, the very essence of evil. He has the ability to endow his Society with all the power of the unconscious mind projected outward. Were Welch deposed, that great driving force, present from infancy in all mass movements, which the John Birch Society now possesses, might well be lost. Were it lost, the image of the all-pervasive evil of Communism would vanish like a vapor. The body of the John Birch Society would begin to rot.

When Robert Welch passes from the scene or grows faint-hearted, as all men must, what then? Given his ability to build his images solidly into his organization, he can relinquish his post without great fear for the Society's future. Nor will he, the Founder, need to be sainted by his followers. His memorial will be the Society he built.

The Birch Society will do well to keep in mind Mr. Welch's counsel concerning his successor. More than likely he will know who may best pursue his work. The Society will one day be ready for a younger man, a man with the sensitivity to share the Founder's image of the world and with the same ability to shape people into an organizational body; but this man must be a Leader with a special quality not possessed by the Society's Founder. He must be a brilliant and convincing speaker, charismatic in his bearing, a man who can sense the longings and frustrations that people carry with them from day to day, who can express all the petty angers and all the great ones, a man who knows enough to discover how others may sometimes despise themselves inwardly. Such a man can take the hatreds that men harbor, fling them out against the great screen of humanity and leave the one who hates feeling purged and self-possessed with all the sentiment of righteousness.

We need only project today's developments a few short years into the future to see that what "can't happen in America" can indeed happen, given only a large measure of fortuity. The demon *Communism* serves well as a vehicle in the present day. The holy word of patriotism, no matter how warped and cut off from its original meaning, can continue to sanctify the Cause, whatever it becomes. When enough Americans *truly believe,* we can stop worrying about preserving our liberties and begin to recite the holy litanies of those who speak of liberty, but fail to court its practice.

I do not believe that such a day is near. I do not believe that its coming is a probability in our land. I do believe that it is a possibility, however, and I know that possibilities must be reckoned with for what they are. Those who take liberty seriously dare not trifle with the improbable. It must be openly examined and honestly assessed.

Freedom is best preserved by its practice. No danger, present or future, real or imagined, can be so great as to justify its sacrifice. We may preserve our freedom from the encroachments of those who find it vulgar or untenable by first insisting that they be permitted to retain it for themselves. In this land even the least deserving may be free. The force of arms may not be tolerated, but the force of ideas must be.

If we are truly sensitive, the John Birch Society and its like can tell us much about ourselves. It can remind us that there are always men willing to sacrifice freedom in the name of freedom, men willing to establish the Great Protectorate, to play the part of the benevolent despot. We have only to relax the maintenance of justice and of liberty. We have only to neglect the cultivation of freedom, and the self-appointed guardians of our persons will take over. Already, they have discovered that the Supreme Court of this land is the key to our stability as a free nation. The attack on the court has therefore been relentless. "Impeach the Chief Justice and reform the Court," we are told. The brooding corollary is never voiced: "We will tell you how to be free," it says. "We will instruct you in how to use your liberty."

The heritage of 1776 is ours to lose but once. We may hand it over to the new inquisitors, and they will cherish it for us and entomb it. We may then forget it.

Liberty, as Jefferson wrote in the year 1796, is a "boisterous sea." "Timid men," he said, "prefer the calm of despotism."

6   Target: The National Council
of Churches

TREASON IS A FAVORITE word on the far right. In all serious-ness, it has been applied to a great many persons and in-stitutions in America, including the Chief Justice of the Supreme Court, several former Presidents of the United States, and the National Council of the Churches of Christ in the United States of America. This chapter is concerned with charges leveled against the National Council of Churches by those who believe that this largest interdenominational or-ganization in the United States is a grave threat to our national security and a shocking example of Christian apostasy.

The NCC has been charged with such varied activities as promoting obscene literature, helping to engineer the 1958 Cuban revolution, and supporting Communists and Commu-nism. Representative of anti-NCC sentiment on the far right is a forty-eight-page pamphlet by Billy James Hargis entitled *The National Council of Churches Indicts Itself on 50 Counts of Treason to God and Country!* (The exclamation point belongs to Hargis.) His fifty-count indictment includes such subheadings as "National Council Leaders Go Behind Iron Curtain," "National Council of Churches to Blame For Socialist Trend in United States Today," and "World Govern-ment of Left-wing Clergymen Means World Slavery." Hargis' sources range from Edgar C. Bundy to Carl McIntire and include no fewer than eight references attributed to himself, together with three to his *Christian Crusade* magazine. Using his information as it stands, without any attempt to check its accuracy, I discovered that only eleven (22%) of his "50 counts of treason" were related to the policies, program or activities of the National Council of Churches. The others were concerned with member denominations (10%), National Council affiliates (4%), individuals connected with the NCC who spoke for themselves, but not for the NCC (22%), individuals in no way connected with the NCC (16%), the Federal Council of Churches, an interdenominational organization predating the NCC (6%), and the World Council of Churches, which is unconnected with the NCC (12%). The remaining "counts of treason" involved short summaries of the charges made by persons other than Hargis and presented no new material (4%), and charges entirely irrelevant to the whole matter (4%). One of the two irrelevant counts is worth quoting in full:

> The work of unbelievers in Protestant theological seminaries was brought to light during 1961 in a news report. In part, this news dispatch informed readers that Protestant ministers-to-be reveals that more than half regard as myth the virgin birth of Christ and His physical ascendancy into Heaven. The poll was conducted by Louis Harris and Associates and published in Redbook magazine. [*sic.*]

Just what that has to do with treason on the part of the National Council of Churches Hargis leaves to the reader to puzzle out for himself. But let us examine some of the more substantial charges in Dr. Hargis' fifty counts of treason against "God and Country." His ninth count deals with NCC aid to Yugoslavia. More assistance went to that Communist nation, says Hargis, than to any other country. The inference, of course, is that the NCC is aiding Communism. But what are the facts? Through its Church World Service division, and in cooperation with Lutheran World Relief, the NCC has given aid to the Yugoslav needy. In 1960 alone shipments totaled 216,195,000 pounds of clothing and foodstuffs, representing a total cost of $15,000, including the salary of a full-time American representative. In a country where the annual per capita income is less than $300, the NCC aid meant minimal clothing for children and adults, and a diet above the level of minimal subsistence. Church leaders reported that children participating in the NCC-financed school lunch program responded with an increased learning capacity, reflecting their improved physical condition. The aid, whether in the form of food, clothing, or drugs, was distributed in containers indicating their NCC origin by the Red Cross, without regard to race, religion, or political belief. The sole consideration was the need of the individual. By including a yearly reduction in the amount of aid, the program placed an increasing responsibility on the recipient nation.

A principle that may often make good sense with regard to armaments given to governments is extended by Hargis to the basic needs of the people themselves. Just as U.S. foreign aid is condemned *in toto* by those on the far right, so also is private aid assailed—even when it is to provide for the relief of hungry or poorly clad persons who have the misfortune to live in a Communist state.

Another of Dr. Hargis' accounts of treason to God involves the virgin birth of Jesus,[1] which he believes the NCC repudiates. His entire argument rests on the rendering of Isaiah 7:14, which has been interpreted by many Christians as predicting the coming of Christ. The King James Version of the passage reads, "Behold, a virgin shall conceive, and bear a son, and shall call his name Immanuel," in conformity with Matthew 1:23, which speaks of the fulfillment of a prophecy declaring, "Behold, a Virgin shall be with child, and shall bring forth a son. . . ." The NCC authorized the publication

[1] Hargis fails to specify which counts of "treason to God and Country" apply to God and which to country, but we may fairly assume that this question involves treason only to God.

of the Revised Standard Version of the Bible—the work of a committee of thirty-two scholars—in 1951. The Revised Standard Version drops the word *virgin* from the passage in Isaiah and substitutes the words *young woman*. A footnote indicates that *virgin* is an alternate reading. The change in the wording of the passage is based on the simple fact that *young woman* is the correct translation of the Hebrew *almah*. Had Isaiah wished to say *virgin* he would doubtless have used the word *betulah*.[2]

The exact words of ancient texts, together with their precise meanings, apparently is of no concern to Hargis. He prefers the King James Version of the Bible to any other, and he is particularly unhappy with the Revised Standard Version, which he mistakenly calls the "National Council Bible." The cumulative efforts of all the Biblical scholars who have lived since the 1611 King James translation was completed, and the greater accuracy made possible through the discovery of texts unknown to the translators of that Version, mean nothing. Any tampering with the wording of the holy King James Version by the NCC is said to be treasonous.

Hargis also thinks that there is something treasonous about copyrighting the Revised Standard Version, contending that it enables the NCC to control the use of the Bible. The King James Version, he observes, "is not copyrighted by anyone." Hargis is wrong in both contentions—as usual. The NCC copyrighted the RSV not as a sinister move to assure the organization complete control of the Bible (in that version), but simply to protect the integrity of the text. The King James Version is similarly copyrighted in Great Britain.

---

[2] The Hebrew *almah* excludes the possibility of virginity no more than does the English translation *young woman*. Hence, the reader who is concerned with the prophetic significance of Isaiah 7:14 may read prophecy into the passage if he wishes to do so. Isaiah says nothing, however, to indicate that this is what he had in mind. The whole argument of those who see the passage as a prophecy of the virgin birth of Jesus must rest on passages from the first chapter of Matthew.

Hargis also charges that the NCC has been exploiting the RSV commercially, merchandising the scriptures for profit as it were. He neglects to say that royalties derived from the RSV go not into the NCC general fund, but are used by the Division of Christian Education for specific projects related to Bible teaching and the use of the RSV—scarcely commercial ventures by ordinary standards.

Dr. Hargis' most comprehensive charge, however, involves a guilt-by-association ploy, which seeks to discredit the RSV by throwing tarbrushes at its translators. According to Hargis, eight of those on the translation committee had affiliations with Communist fronts and one translator was active in no less than fifteen Communist or Communist-front organizations. Not only that. The translation committee "actually included . . . a Jew," says Hargis, who then observes that Jews do not accept the divinity of Christ, and concludes that this singular fact helps to explain the "unitarian emphasis" which he sees in the RSV. When we get down to cases we quickly discover that the alleged Communist-front affiliations of the translators are either nonexistent, or stem from the World War II period when the U.S. and the U.S.S.R. were allies and a great many responsible persons belonged to organizations concerned with Soviet-American friendship.

NAMES AND IMAGES FOR THE NCC

Hargis, unlike some of his colleagues on the right, admits that the Christian Crusade "does not know positively that any members of the National Council of Churches are members of the Communist party," but claims that he is concerned about a far more serious problem in the NCC, which he identifies as the "activities of 'fellow-travelers,' sympathizers and gullible dupes . . . who . . . promote and work for many primary objectives of the communist conspiracy."

Calling interdenominational organizations names is nothing new. It is, in fact, something of a tradition among fundamentalists. Before the National Council of Churches was formed, the chief target was the Federal Council of Churches, and the names were a good deal more venomous than they are today. More original too. Some of the denunciations in Carl McIntire's *Christian Beacon* fairly crackled with vindictive originality. Take the following, written for the *Beacon* by the southern evangelist, J. Harold Smith, and quoted by Ralph Lord Roy in *Apostles of Discord:*

> You cannot destroy the pollution of leprosy by clothing its victims in purple and fine linen. It is impossible to drown the stench of the Federal Council under the flood-tides of philosophical perfume sprayed on by certain preachers. The Federal Council is not a penknife, it is a guillotine to behead every "faithful preacher." It is a demoniac vulture sitting upon the pinnacles of our churches waiting to devour their carcasses. The Federal Council is an internal cancer, gnawing at Divinity's vitals.

Now that's what I call colorful writing. Full of fire and enthusiasm, brimming with passion. It has just about everything but sense.

J. Harold Smith was capable of even more sulfuric utterances, however. Witness this appraisal of the Federal Council, also cited by Roy, originally quoted in the August 1949 issue of *Harper's Magazine:*

> The Federal Council of Churches of the Anti-Christ would make prostitutes out of your daughters and libertines of your sons. This is the dirty, hellish gang of sex-mad devils that some of the Knoxville preachers are falling over themselves to defend. Leave this atheistic, communistic, Bible-

ridiculing, blood-despising, name-calling, sex-manacled gang of green-eyed monsters and hell-bound devils before God's judgment is poured out on them.

You don't read many accounts like that one these days, and more's the pity. It had style. In its place we must be content with the more placid fulminations of the likes of Carl McIntire, whose denunciations make the National Council appear like a knitting society in comparison to Smith's appraisal of the Federal Council. Consider, for instance, McIntire's eyewitness account of the machinations of one organization that plans to enslave us all:

In New Delhi I saw and witnessed a worldwide force, organized, efficient, driving, with great resources of finance behind it, which is determined to reshape the churches and unite them in one great world organization which will have the power to enforce its decisions over them.

McIntire's distress involves, of course, the World Council of Churches rather than the National Council, but he considers the World Council as merely an extension of the evil NCC, which he regards with no less hostility.

One of McIntire's prime concerns over the nefarious work of the National Council is this: the NCC has been doing its best to reach some kind of understanding with Christians behind the Iron Curtain, and so far as McIntire is concerned, anyone behind the Iron Curtain is a Communist. Or, at the very least, anyone the Communists permit to come out from behind the Iron Curtain is a Communist. Which amounts to pretty much the same thing.

In a February 1963 newsletter to his radio listeners, McIntire began with the personally penned message, "The Russians are coming!!" Which is pretty frightening, of course, until one discovers that the "Russians" are only Russian Orthodox priests.

McIntire assails the NCC sponsorship of the priests—whom

he calls "spies, secret-police agents and Khrushchev propagandists"—and adds, "What a spectacle, Christian churches paying for their own destruction and the destruction of their land as the Communists engage in . . . subtle psychological warfare to win the cold war." He announces that the McIntire forces will be "following" these guests of the National Council of Churches and holding "great mass meetings and protests." (See Chapter IV for an account of a protest that flopped.)

One particularly obnoxious publication that has been around since the days of the Federal Council of Churches, but has been updated to make the NCC the main object of its attack, is a tract published by the American Council of Christian Laymen. It is entitled "How Red is the National Council of Churches?" and consists mainly of an interminable list of NCC leaders and their alleged affiliations with Communist-front organizations. (First listed is the American Civil Liberties Union, an organization which is, in no sense, a Communist front. The ACLU ousted Communists from its national board in 1940, and since that time has refused membership to all persons whose devotion to civil liberties is qualified in any way by commitment to a totalitarian organization, including Fascist and Communist groups, and the Ku Klux Klan.[3]) In the course of two of its six crowded pages, the pamphlet concludes, among other things, that the NCC promotes Socialism, has many Communist preachers in its ranks and even more fellow travelers, and that some NCC funds come from a variety of Jewish and "other non-Christian or anti-Christian groups." While making this pitch to anti-Semitic readers, the tract urges all Christians to get their churches to stop contributing to the NCC.

[3] No less an anti-Communist than Senator Thomas Dodd has given his endorsement to the ACLU by remarking, in the course of a hearing held by the Senate Internal Security Subcommittee on January 10, 1963, "I think very highly of the American Civil Liberties Union."

THE RESPECTABLE CHRISTIANS OPEN FIRE

Not all of the attacks on the NCC have come from the Biblical fundamentalists. In Redondo Beach, California, a number of laymen, calling themselves the *Episcopalians for Christ*, organized a group advocating a kind of ecclesiastical fundamentalism which included the promotion of the "true faith," to be found only within the Episcopal communion, great emphasis on the importance of strict doctrinal interpretations of the virgin birth of Christ, the holy trinity, and apostolic succession. Most important to the group, perhaps, was its stress on the supreme authority of the Bishop. The interdenominational NCC together with its social pronouncements was, of course, singled out as particularly offensive to the true Christian.

In Phoenix, the Committee of Christian Laymen[4] has, from its inception, devoted its major attention to the NCC. In all probability, the Committee's influence has been greatest among Presbyterians, but it has not been confined to that one denomination, by any means.

The writings of the retired Presbyterian minister, Charles Poling, figure prominently in the Committee's selection of literature on the Council. "It is frightening," writes Poling, "to see the drift toward a World Church—to be known . . . as the Holy Protestant Catholic Church. . . . A world government, a world church, one third of this world based on slavery, socialism or Communism!"

The local Committees of Christian Laymen repeatedly attack the NCC with such sweeping phrases as, "We . . . feel that The National Council of Churches is being used as a

[4] See Chapter II for an account of the activities of the Committee.

means of bringing about a Socialist economy in the United States; also, it is promoting the one-world, one-church idea in complete disregard of our country's welfare." On another occasion, a local Committee may declare that informed laymen are "just commencing to wake up," and to begin to recognize "many of the Socialistic, and what many consider un-American, positions taken by the National Council. . . ."

The work of the Committee of Christian Laymen and its sister organizations sometimes pays off. In January of 1961 All Saints' Episcopal Church in Phoenix adopted a resolution at its annual meeting condemning the NCC for its involvement in social issues, and filed an official protest with the Bishop of the diocese. In May of that year the Sessions of six prominent Presbyterian churches on the West Coast adopted anti-NCC resolutions. A group of anti-NCC Episcopalians came close to running up a majority vote, at an annual diocesan convention in Texas, for a resolution calling on the Episcopal Church to secede from the Council.

In Shreveport, Louisiana, the vestry of St. Mark's Episcopal Church passed a resolution petitioning the Bishop of Louisiana to "take such steps as may be necessary and expedient" to cause the Episcopal Church to withdraw from the NCC. The resolution was the result of a report turned in by a special vestry committee, appointed to look into the NCC. Later published and widely distributed as an attractively printed booklet, the report has become one of the most influential documents on the far right.

A carefully written and apparently well-researched study, it clearly presents the value judgments of its authors, together with the evidence on which they base their conclusions. The report is virtually free from theories of conspiracy, notions of intrigue and mudslinging for the sake of slinging mud. The facts selected by the committee go a great distance toward making its case, but I would not want to second the committee's self-appraisal, printed in the preface to the report, which indicates that its approach was "neither prejudiced nor provincial." The committee's arguments are not faultless, but neither are they irrelevant or stupid. Indeed, were one to accept the premises of the committee and admit no evidence apart from that provided by the report, the committee's conclusions would be inescapable. Unlike much of the literature produced by the Christian ultras, the report of the St. Mark's vestry committee on the National Council of Churches is painstakingly careful in its effort to be fair. For that reason, it deserves careful analysis.

THE VESTRY REPORT

The Shreveport reports begins by admitting that the NCC may have done some good things from time to time, but states that the organization performs no useful functions not already a part of the Episcopal Church. Major charges, in summary form, include: 1) the contention that the NCC speaks without warrant in the name of its constituent denominations, 2) the accusation that the NCC, though not Communist itself, nevertheless aids the "Communist conspiracy," 3) the thesis that the Council is "dominated by a hard core of professionals, some of whom have never done pastoral work," 4) the contention that the NCC should not lobby with the Federal government, and 5) the conviction that the NCC made a bad mistake in compiling and distributing a reading list called "The Negro American."

But let us examine these charges in some detail, together with some of the premises behind them.

The National Council as a Representative Assembly: First, there is the matter of NCC pronouncements. The Shreveport vestry committee objects to the notion that the NCC is speaking for its thirty-four constituent denominations and their thirty-nine million members on issues of social importance. The NCC, says the report, "has become a national and even international propaganda machine in controversial political issues. . . ." Since Protestantism has no single voice, the NCC cannot presume to speak in the name of not only Protestantism in general, but for the Orthodox communions as well. There are many Protestant and Orthodox viewpoints, the argument goes, and no workable system of membership polling could possibly establish a Protestant-Orthodox consensus. Yet, says the vestry committee, the NCC speaks in the name of the majority of Protestant and Orthodox communions *as though* such a consensus had been achieved.

The premise behind the committee's position, of course, is the notion that no organization—particularly an interdenominational body—has a right to speak for individual Christians on matters of social concern. Therefore, the NCC should avoid involving itself in issues on which specific stands might sometimes violate individual Christian consciences.

The premise from which the NCC speaks is just the contrary. In the judgment of its General Board, the churches have a continuing responsibility to speak on social issues. In the words of a resolution adopted by the Board in December, 1958:

> What has often been said must be said again. The Christian churches of the United States and their councils not only have the right but also the duty to study and comment upon issues, no matter how controversial, in the realm of politics, economics, and social affairs, in view of their common faith in Jesus Christ as both Lord and Savior. For all matters of concern for human beings are matters of concern to the churches and the churches' Lord. . . .

J. Irwin Miller, past president of the NCC, is even more specific in his appraisal of the responsibility of the churches. "The care of the sick, feeding of the hungry, liberation of the oppressed, justice and mercy for everyone, have always been proper concerns of the religious man," he says, and then adds, "If the Church does not speak on such matters, I do not know who will. . . . I think all of us need such a voice."[5]

How does the NCC speak on social issues? Quite simply —through a representative system. The Council is governed by a 700-member General Assembly which meets once every three years. The pronouncements, resolutions, and other actions of the Assembly reflect the thinking of the delegates from the thirty-three denominations represented. No more than that is claimed. No more is possible. The General Assembly of the NCC is a *representative* body, just as is the 270-member General Board, which meets three times a year and determines policy between meetings of the General Assembly.

An individual, or a member denomination, may, of course, maintain that the NCC does not represent their opinions on particular questions. The right of dissent is assumed by the NCC. More than that—the Council encourages a loyal opposition to develop and to voice its objections. It fully recognizes the fact that its pronouncements carry only the authority of moral persuasion.

The National Council and Social Justice: When it comes to the question of the NCC's alleged promotion of Communism, the writers of the St. Mark's report are burdened by another premise. They willingly confess that they know of "no instance where any responsible person has accused the . . . [NCC] of being Communist, a Communist front, or of having any of its executive or administrative posts manned by a Communist." But they assume that any pronouncement

[5] J. Irwin Miller, a prominent layman in the Disciples of Christ denomination, is Chairman of the Boards of the Cummins Engine Company, the Irwin Bank and Trust Company (both in Columbus, Ohio) and the Union Starch and Refining Company (Granite City, Illinois). He has served the NCC since it was founded in 1950, and was its first lay president. The statement quoted above is from a letter dated March 1, 1961.

urging further understanding of the Communist-block nations, calling for heightened sensitivity to abuses of governmental power (a privilege reserved for the right wing) or the exploitation of the underprivileged is, by definition, aiding Communism.

The premise? Communism advocates certain reforms; therefore, anyone else who advocates those same reforms is aiding Communism. The premise completely misses the point, of course, that a good and honorable objective remains what it is regardless of who supports it. A noble purpose is not defiled merely because the ignoble choose to identify themselves with it.

Particularly troubling to the Shreveport vestry committee was a "Message to the Churches" issued at the conclusion of a November, 1958, World Study Conference held in Cleveland, Ohio, by the NCC's Department of International Affairs. The report, which was concerned with the status of the diplomatic recognition of Communist China, included the observation that "while the rights of the people of Taiwan and of Korea should be safeguarded, steps should be taken toward the inclusion of the People's Republic of China in the United Nations and for its recognition by our government." Such recognition, said the message, "does not imply approval." The message went on to point out that continued isolation of Communist China promoted a false image of the U.S. on the part of the Chinese and, at the same time, prevented Americans from knowing the facts about China. The statement, the NCC made clear, spoke only for the Cleveland Conference and not for the National Council as a whole.

Also of concern to the vestry committee was a statement adopted unanimously by the General Board in February 1961 on the motion picture "Operation Abolition." The film, which was produced commercially from films subpoenaed by the House Committee on Un-American Activities, purports to be an accurate account of the "Communist-inspired riots" protesting the May 1960 H.C.U.A. hearings in San Francisco. After viewing the picture and hearing a report based on an intensive investigation conducted by the Division of Christian Life and Work, the General Board decided that the filmed account might not be as honest as its producers claimed.[6] In subdued language (the *Washington Post* called the film "a propaganda movie" that "makes a dirty joke out of the Congressional investigating power") the Board concluded that churches would do well not to screen the film until all the facts were known. Specifically, some of the Board's questions were as follows:

> What evidence, admissible in a court of law, links the Communists and alleged Communists named in the film with the students leading or participating in the demonstration?
>
> What is the legal status of the film subpoenaed by the Committee and now being sold by a private profit-making firm?
>
> Are there errors of fact and interpretation included in the film as presently distributed?
>
> What is the responsibility of the House Committee on Un-American Activities, and of the House of Representatives itself, in respect to this film and the charges made in it against students and other citizens?

To put the matter briefly, the General Board of the National Council said, in effect, "There is serious doubt about the veracity of 'Operation Abolition.' If you care about truth, wait until the facts are in before you show the film."

The St. Mark's vestry committee was distressed too about

[6] Although the film carried no credits indicating who the producer actually was, it was narrated by Fulton Lewis, III. The then Representative John Rousselot, speaking at Knott's Berry Farm, California, in November of 1961, indicated that "Operation Abolition" was ". . . a film done by the Congress of the United States." Whether other members of Congress, particularly members of the H.C.U.A., would claim as much is an open question.

the NCC stand on the McCarran-Walter Act (called simply the "McCarran Act" by the vestry committee). Repeal of the act, observed the committee, would enable the Communists "to bring more spies into this country."

In December of 1959 the NCC General Board *had* called for a revision of immigration policies on a nondiscriminatory basis, and reminded the churches that "both major political parties incorporated demands for . . . such changes in their party platforms in 1956." Campaign promises had not been fulfilled, said the resolution, and it was time that Congress acted. The Board statement was in line with an earlier resolution, passed by the General Assembly, that called for a revision of the national origins quota system and for an end to immigration policies that discriminated on the basis of race, color, or sex.

As with the study conference's recommendation on the recognition of Communist China and the General Board's cautionary counsel on "Operation Abolition," the NCC's advocacy of immigration policies more in keeping with American ideals was seen by the Shreveport vestry committee as aiding the "Communist conspiracy."

The National Lay Committee: Let us turn now to the vestry committee's concern over the "hard core of professionals" in the NCC. In the committee's judgment, this group of ambitious men see themselves as the creators of a superchurch and, as such, are dedicated to destroying lay initiative in the NCC.

The Lay Committee, which was formed at the time the National Council was founded in 1950, was, according to the vestry committee report, deliberately disbanded in 1955. Why? Because, says the committee, the NCC professionals were "obviously . . . unable to tolerate a dissonant voice in the form of independent laity."

Again, the vestry committee and the NCC have begun with different premises. Whereas the vestry committee sees an independent committee of laymen, representative of neither the General Assembly nor the General Board, but exercising a veto power over Board decisions, as a power-balancing asset, the General Board holds that such an arrangement would thwart the desires of the democratic majority. In its own defense, the NCC points out that the Lay Committee was formed in 1950 as a financial advisory group and was subsequently invited to continue "in a planning capacity to help the Board formulate plans for the 'more complete integration of laymen into . . . the National Council.'" The Committee soon began to regard itself as a "superlegislative body" rather than as a creature of the Board, however, and in 1955 its charter was permitted to lapse.

J. Howard Pew, the former chairman of the Lay Committee, sees the situation differently. Feeling strongly that the church should keep to itself and not meddle with the affairs of the world, he upbraids the NCC for passing resolutions which, in his view, "frequently coincide with the Communist objectives." On December 15, 1955, Pew issued a report strongly critical of the NCC Board's stand on the Lay Committee. Although the report had no official standing with the National Council, it nevertheless gained the approval of 115 out of the 168 Lay Committee members who received the document. In 1959 the 316-page report was reprinted by Mr. Pew and, according to a statement issued by the NCC's Office of Public Interpretation, "was repeatedly referred to by a radio commentator [unnamed] noted for his attacks on the Protestant clergy, the Protestant denominations, and the National Council. . . ."

Basing its opinion, to a large extent, on the Pew report, the Shreveport committee concludes that the NCC "felt it must do away with the Lay Committee so that it could profess unanimity of opinion, and so that the professionals could in fact dominate the . . . [NCC]."

The point at issue between the St. Mark's vestry committee and the NCC is plainly one of governmental theory. The NCC believes that the will of a representative majority should prevail. The vestry committee proposes a continuing oligarchy of the elite, capable of stopping action on any issue that causes it displeasure.

As Thomas Jefferson once wrote, "Men by their constitution are naturally divided into two parties." To the two parties he applied the appellations of "aristocrats and democrats." The sentiments of the NCC, at least in theory, are with those of the small *d* democratic persuasion.

The Washington Office: The vestry committee's contention that it is "wrong for the . . . [NCC] to carry out lobbying activities with the Federal government at all. . . ." also brings basic assumptions into conflict, although the NCC hedges a bit in describing its role in the matter.

The NCC does maintain a Washington, D.C. office, but claims that it is an informational outlet, specifically prohibited by the office's Statement of Purpose from engaging in lobbying activities.[7] According to the Council, the only functions of the office are to disseminate factual information on pending legislation of interest to churches, inform government about the churches, and inform the general public and nongovernment organizations about the churches and the NCC.

In the strictest sense, such a description of the office's responsibility probably does exclude lobbying, but at the same time, the wording of the Statement of Purpose indicates that the office is to be a good deal more than a tract society. Its purpose, according to the official Board action, is "to serve the National Council and its member churches . . . by *indicating proper channels for contacts in Washington* and fur-

---

[7] The Statement of Purpose for the Washington Office, adopted by the General Board in 1951 and revised in 1953, includes the statement: "The Washington Office is not to engage in efforts to influence legislation."

nishing facilities *for effecting such contacts* when desired
. . . [emphasis supplied]."

Such words seem to me to mean something very close to
lobbying, and I must confess that I fail to see the point of
having the Washington Office at all if the NCC anticipates
no tangible effects following from its work. When the Washington Office "informs government" about the churches, it is
not, I submit, functioning merely on church matters unrelated
to legislation, about which an occasional congressman may
become interested.

On this issue the St. Mark's vestry committee is at least
partially correct. Judging by the evidence, the NCC's Washington Office *is* interested in communicating the ethical judgments of concerned Christians to legislators who must often
make up their minds on issues freighted with ethical and
moral implications. This is as it should be. Were the churches
unconcerned with the outcome of the debates on Capitol Hill
there could be little defense of their ethical lethargy. To indicate, as docs the NCC, that its Washington operation is
a low-pressure affair, functioning without attempts to coerce,
bribe, or cajole legislators, is simply to say that the Office
seeks to conduct its affairs in a Christian manner.

Again, we see that basic assumptions are in conflict. The
writers of the St. Mark's report assume that the church should
remain aloof and unconcerned with the worldliness of the
legislative hall. The National Council believes that the will
of God may be made manifest there as well as in the churches,
and that for the churches to remain silent when matters of
ethical and moral concern are involved would be for them to
abdicate their witness to their Lord and Savior.

The American Negro—A Reading List: Finally, the St.
Mark's committee takes on an NCC reading list called "The
Negro American," and argues that the NCC displayed in-
competence in compiling and distributing the list. A number
of authors whose names appear on the list have been active

in Communist-front organizations, and some apparently have been Communists. At one time or another more than one of the authors has turned out writings of an obscene, blasphemous, or mediocre character.

What does the NCC say to these charges? First, it acknowledges that the bibliography was prepared in 1957 by its Department of Racial and Cultural Relations. Second, it states that only about 3000 copies were distributed over a period of three years. And third, it observes that the list is now out of print and claims that there are no plans to reprint it.

The Rev. Roy G. Ross, General Secretary of the NCC, wrote on December 15, 1960, to a correspondent in Tennessee that he was "very much embarrassed by the fact that this book list was issued," and added that he felt that it was "very unwise and inappropriate," reflecting a "lack of wisdom" on the part of the department.

Since the list is out of print I have had no opportunity to examine it. But taking the examples of authors and their works cited by the list's critics, the list would seem to me to be indefensible—if only from the standpoint that it is not representative of the best literature available on the plight and the stature of the American Negro. It is difficult to imagine what criteria could have been used in making the selections, or what the compiler thought listing some of the works might accomplish either for race relations or the NCC. In a dimension of American life which desperately needs the illumination of human understanding in order for the Negro to achieve the freedom which is his right, it is regrettable that the Council's Department of Racial and Cultural Relations involved itself in such folly.

All the same, the publication of one admittedly indefensible list, mailed on request to no more than 3000 persons, and now out of print, is scarcely enough to call into question the integrity of the whole National Council of Churches.

A Summary of Conclusions: What conclusions may we

draw from the Shreveport vestry committee's report? The most obvious one, I suppose, is that the NCC is not infallible —a virtue that it never claimed for itself, anyway. Less obvious, and more important, is the fact that the NCC and its opponents begin with different premises. To recapitulate, the vestry committee believes that the NCC has no business speaking for the Protestant and Orthodox communions in the United States; the NCC maintains that it has precisely the right of any representative body to speak—no more, no less. The vestry committee believes that all NCC actions that parallel Communist objectives brand the Council as a friend of Communism; the NCC believes that a moral course of action cannot be turned into an immoral one simply by the Communists saying that they favor it. The committee feels that the NCC is controlled by an ambitious group of professionals and it would have the Council invest an autonomous Lay Committee with a veto power over all Board actions; the Council prefers a representative system of decision-making not subject to the veto of a committee which would not be responsible to the democratic majority. The Shreveport report contends that the NCC should not lobby in Washington; the NCC claims that it is not engaging in lobbying as such, but that it has a responsibility to speak from the Christian perspective on ethical questions raised by pending legislation.

The deepest conflict involves the question of the churches' social responsibility. The NCC believes that both the churches and the Council have not only a right, but a weighty responsibility to speak the word of ethical wisdom in the world of secular concern. Religion, the Council assumes, permeates all dimensions of life or it is not truly religion. For the Council, the God of creation is also Lord of creation, or he is not God. Men and their institutions, which are but two aspects of one creation, must be molded by humanitarian concerns stemming from an acknowledgment of Jesus Christ as Divine Lord and Savior.

The value system held by the Shreveport vestry committee is just as coherent as the NCC's, but it begins at a different point. For the vestry committee, politics is politics, and religion, religion. The church should concern itself only with the redemption of men. It is enough that individual Christians in public life may be called upon to give evidence of their faith. You cannot coerce society. You cannot reform culture by legislating out of a pious concern.

So far as I can see, these premises and their corollary beliefs are wholly antithetical. They admit no possibility of reconciliation. And they go to the very root of *the* crucial conflict over what it means to be a Christian in our culture. The final question posed by the conflict is this: *Does the gospel have any direct relevance to man as a social being, to society and its structures?* For my own part, I find that the humanitarian commitment of the National Council speaks to me of true religion.

THE AIR FORCE MANUAL SCANDAL

The heaviest fire aimed at the NCC to date has come from the United States Air Force. On January 4, 1960, an official training manual bearing the legend "Student Text" was issued for the training of noncommissioned officers in the Air Force Reserve. Its charges were multitudinous. "Communist fellow travelers and sympathizers have successfully infiltrated our churches," it said, and then added, as though the point were in some way obscure, "There appears to be overwhelming evidence of Communist antireligious activity in the United States through the infiltration of fellow travelers into churches and educational institutions."

The firepower of the Air Force was then turned on the NCC and the RSV Bible. "The National Council of Churches of Christ in the U.S.A. officially sponsored the Revised Standard Version of the Bible," said the manual. "Of the 95 persons who served in this project, 30 have been affiliated with pro-Communist fronts, projects, and publications."

The NCC was far from happy with the Air Force appraisal and said so. James W. Wine, Associate General Secretary of the NCC, took his complaint straight to the Secretary of Defense, Thomas S. Gates, Jr., saying that he regarded the manual as "an example of irresponsibility at its worst." Gates agreed and replied, "I am very glad you came direct to us and can only express my very deep regret over the entire incident. I assure you that the unfortunate contents of the manual in no way reflect the attitude of the Air Force or the Department of Defense toward the National Council of Churches."

The manual was quickly withdrawn, but controversy was not avoided. The *New York Times* observed with characteristic restraint that "something is wrong in our defense organization when this kind of venomous nonsense can be put out at Government expense." The *New York Herald Tribune* declared that the Air Force had the duty to make known who wrote its manual.

The principal author was one Homer H. Hyde, a Baptist and a civilian, whose comprehensive research program on Communism and religion involved going to his local minister and asking him what he knew. The minister, in turn, suggested that Hyde write to Billy James Hargis. Hyde did.

Hargis sent him two of his own pamphlets, together with one from the Circuit Riders entitled *30 of the 95 Men Who Gave us the Revised Standard Version of the Bible*. These three tracts provided the data for Hyde's one-man attack in the name of the U. S. Air Force—an attack that badly embarrassed the defense department and delighted NCC critics from Carl McIntire to Fulton Lewis, Jr.

Donald Jackson, Congressman from California, and Francis Walter, chairman of the House Committee on Un-American Activities, valiantly defended the manual, but most of Congress was as outraged as was the Secretary of Defense. John F. Kennedy, then a Senator, called the manual "shocking" and "an unwarranted slur on the Protestant ministry in general and the National Council of Churches in particular."

Moved by its many concerned readers to look into the whole matter, the conservative, evangelical magazine *Eternity* assigned Contributing Editor Walter R. Martin to do a thorough and "objective investigation." Martin was, in the magazine's words, told "to get the facts. If the NCC was at fault, he should say so; if the Air Force Manual was wrong, that also should be acknowledged."

Martin discovered that the manual was wrong, of course, and *Eternity's* Editor-in-Chief, Donald Grey Barnhouse, declared in the September 1960 issue of the magazine, "The manual was only one more step on the part of a determined group of ultra-fundamentalists to discredit the National Council of Churches, if not on theological, then on political grounds. Other examples of their ways of working are not wanting."

Despite such conclusions on the part of responsible persons ranging from liberal to fundamentalist in their religious viewpoints, the manual continues to turn up as a new disclosure to be quoted in letters-to-the-editor columns. It is still distributed, in photocopy form, by those on the far right. The fact that it was promptly withdrawn and apologized for by the Air Force fails to dismay those who find its conclusions to their liking. It serves their purposes well enough, despite its sordid history.

THE SOPHISTICATES
AND THE NONSOPHISTICATES

As a minister in a denomination that is not affiliated with the National Council of Churches, I often find myself amazed by the intensity of the hostility directed against the Council from those on the far right. More than once I have felt a conversation between myself and an ultraconservative freeze solid the moment that he discovered I was a minister, only to thaw minutes later when he found out that the Unitarian Universalist Association is not affiliated with the NCC.[8]

Why the intense feelings against the NCC on the part of ultraconservatives? There are several reasons, I believe. But first, it may be well to note that criticism of the NCC is almost wholly Protestant in origin. I know of no significant Jewish, Roman Catholic, or other religious dissent to the work of the National Council.

Within Protestantism, the criticism is divided between the nonsophisticated and the sophisticated. The nonsophisticates, who are largely the Biblical fundamentalists, are offended first

[8] The Unitarian Universalist Association is excluded from membership in the National Council by a phrase in the Preamble to the NCC Constitution which defines the organization as a manifestation of "oneness in Jesus Christ as Divine Lord and Savior." As a noncreedal denomination, the Unitarian Universalist Association could not assent to such a proposition for individual Unitarian Universalists, each of whom is free to define the content of his own belief—indeed, responsible for developing his own religious philosophy. In any case, the vast majority of Unitarian Universalists do not believe that Jesus of Nazareth is a "Divine Lord and Savior," but prefer to describe him as a moral leader and teacher of unexcelled greatness, as one who in his life and teachings made the divine more nearly manifest to man, or as one of the great prophets of humanity. Despite this basic difference in belief and the absence of any affiliation with the NCC on the part of the Unitarian Universalist Association, it is probably fair to say that most individual members of the denomination are sympathetic with the humanitarian work of the NCC.

in terms of doctrine. They believe that the NCC is denigrating scripture in its simple affirmation of "Jesus Christ as Divine Lord and Savior." That, they say, is not enough. They would see the Council acknowledge a whole series of Biblically derived points of doctrine, ranging from the virgin birth to the bodily resurrection. The failure of the NCC to take sides theologically is, in their view, inexcusable and makes the Council guilty of heresy. From heresy they go on to differences in social values. Their attack is as intemperate as it is illogical and crude.

The sophisticates, on the other hand, although highly skeptical about ecumenical efforts, are primarily distraught over the NCC's view of social responsibility. Whereas the NCC sees itself and its member denominations in the traditional roles of "comforting the afflicted and afflicting the comfortable"—as obligated to make ethics and morality real in life—the sophisticates firmly believe that the world may be changed only by the transformation of individuals *qua* individuals. Social institutions are best left alone. The sophisticates, unlike their far-right counterparts of more simple bearing, wage a campaign that is at once logical, coherent, and sometimes decorous.

Other factors are involved in the present-day bombardment of the National Council of Churches, of course. First, there is the question of money. The NCC has been remarkably successful in its fund-raising efforts. Its annual budget, which is generally in the $12–15 million range, is derived primarily from member denominations (61%), gifts from individuals, foundations, etc. (12%), and sales of Council materials (26%). The money goes to finance activities ranging from evangelism and teaching missions to social-welfare programs.

The expenditure of such sums is not without its effect, and critics of the NCC's purposes tend to see the Council's effectiveness as the workings of a colossus. Moreover, the sheer size of the NCC's professional staff, which by 1962 numbered over 180 executives and around 500 office workers, is formidable. No doubt it is frightening to those who see size alone as threatening, and worrisome to many others who are acquainted with the progress of organizational malaise as it is described by Professor Parkinson.[9]

Most of the NCC's work would probably go unnoticed and unchallenged were it not for the organization's solid commitment to social justice. It is this aspect of the Council's work that consistently draws the heaviest fire. As Methodist Bishop Gerald Kennedy once expressed the difficulty, "In a kind of desperation we get afraid of change of any kind. Frightened churchmen sometimes foolishly attack the National Council . . . because it dares to speak a prophetic word now and then."

How does the NCC feel about the charges hurled at it? The Rev. Dean Kelley, a Methodist and head of the Council's Department of Religious Liberty, once summed it up this way: "The NCC makes its pronouncements out of feelings of responsibility to millions of church people [some of whom] have no other organized voice. . . . The criticism [we hear] is one good evidence we're getting through and speaking to real problems." The counsel of Jesus, "Woe unto you, when all men shall speak well of you!" is, to Mr. Kelley's way of thinking, sound advice.

Although unalterably opposed to Communism,[10] the Na-

---

[9] The NCC is not unaware of the danger it faces from creeping internal bureaucracies. As one member of its executive staff acknowledged, "There is a problem [in the Council] as with all large organizations, in its becoming fairly remote and losing touch with the grass roots." He admitted that much of the day-to-day decision-making is done by the staff, but added that there is a continuing and conscientious effort made to hold to the policies "laid down by the Board."

[10] On May 19, 1953, the General Board spelled out its opposition to Communism in a typically unambiguous fashion: "No body of people is more concerned to combat Communism than the church groups of our country. If any Communists are carrying on their subversive work under the guise of serving the church, all who have responsibility for leadership in the church should insist that such deception be exposed. The National Council of Churches is and always has been unalterably opposed to Communism. . . ."

tional Council of Churches has managed to make its positions clear without launching an I'm-more-anti-Communist-than-you-are campaign. It has kept its objective straight—"to manifest oneness in Jesus Christ as Divine Lord and Savior." It has not hesitated to follow in the footsteps of one who suffered even the agonies of crucifixion for his love of God and man.

7   One Nation Under God

"AMERICA'S CHRISTIANITY is challenged. . . . If we do not awaken and do something about the atheists and Communists who are trying to have us conform to their disbelief in our God, we are in real trouble," wrote a correspondent to a local newspaper in the summer of 1963.

Her complaint was voiced soon after the U. S. Supreme Court handed down its decision holding that Bible readings and the recitation of the Lord's Prayer in public schools are unconstitutional. She went on to articulate the opinions of many who identify themselves with right-wing fundamentalism.

"Our country has always been a Christian country," she said. "Why have we never lost a war? Because God is on our side. How can any one question the validity of the virgin birth of Christ? . . .

"Awake, all true Americans, and let us preserve our Christian country."

Whatever the religious and political affiliations of the lady who wrote that letter, it is a graphic summary of the convictions held by a significant number of American Christians who have adopted a sort of nationalist religion of piety and patriotism.

To hear the proponents of the faith talk, one would think that the United States is the favored child of God, guided constantly by the promptings of pious Christians who read their Bibles and believe their doctrines without blemish of doubt or misgiving. The Bible, they insist, is always right—

and so is the United States. Unlike Lincoln, who maintained that we should ascertain first of all whether we are on the side of God, the new Christian patriots declare that our side is God's side. We begin there, by definition. If prayers are to be offered they will not be for guidance, but rather for the further sanctification of the cause or for the revelation of some new stratagem to use against the dread enemies of the new national religion—Christian Americanism.

The first proposition promoted by the new breed of Christian nationalists is that this is a Christian nation and always has been—since Plymouth Rock. If you ask them in what sense our nation is Christian you are being impertinent, perhaps blasphemous, possibly unpatriotic. All the same, the question needs asking.

In what sense *is* the United States a Christian nation? Certainly not in terms of the religious affiliation of the colonists. Only a minority were church members. By the time of the American revolution the best estimates are that church membership was limited to about four percent of the population.[1]

The Founding Fathers had no illusions that they were founding a Christian nation. Many of them were only marginally identified with Christianity, at best. Jefferson, Franklin, Paine and Madison were deists, advocates of a religious philosophy that included belief in a divine Creator, but dismissed most orthodox Christian beliefs as so much fantasy. John Adams was a member of the first church in America to take formal action to identify itself with the liberals.[2] As a young man he intended to study for the ministry, but discovered what, in his words, was "such a spirit of dogmatism and bigotry in clergy and laity" that he gave up the no-

[1] See Leo Pfeffer, *Church, State and Freedom* (Boston: Beacon Press, 1953), p. 85, for a review of the place of the unchurched at the time of the founding of the republic.

[2] Organized in 1639, the church is now the United First Parish (Unitarian) in Quincy, Massachusetts.

tion. His doctrinal views were enough to have placed him outside the limits of conventional Christianity, and it is doubtful whether his Calvinist contemporaries thought of him as a Christian. Washington, though an Episcopalian in affiliation, would be difficult to classify in terms of belief. He has been quoted, however, as having remarked that America could not formally be called a Christian country.

We cannot claim to be a Christian nation in terms of an established religion. The first words of the Bill of Rights—"Congress shall make no law respecting an establishment of religion. . . ."—prohibit just that.

Nor can we, even by the most persistent argumentation, convince ourselves that we have behaved consistently as a Christian nation in the past, or that we do so today. The words we use may be Christian. Our deeds are not. As Willard Sperry, the late Dean of the Harvard Divinity School, put it in his perceptive study *Religion in America:*

> There is . . . an unresolved contradiction at the heart of American religion. The old sombre theological words are still said, but daily life is conducted on another assumption. This contradiction is, of course, met wherever the modern world exists, but it is most perversely present in the land where the record thus far seems to have given the lie to ancient creeds.[3]

In two senses only may we call the United States a Christian nation. First, of the 63.4 percent of the estimated population of the United States who claim some religious affiliation, the vast majority call themselves Christian. They may be Methodists, Presbyterians, Mennonites, Roman Catholics, Disciples, Jehovah's Witnesses, Bible Presbyterians, Two-Seed-in-the-Spirit Predestinarian Baptists, or one of the

[3] Willard L. Sperry, *Religion In America* (Boston: Beacon Press, 1963), p. 15.

more than two hundred other denominations, but they all call themselves Christian. Christianity, in one form or another, is the majority faith of the present.

Second, we are by history and inheritance a Christian nation. The colonies, from Anglican Virginia to Pilgrim and Puritan New England, were Christian in their founding. New England was conceived by the Puritans as the proper site for a "due order of government, both civil and ecclesiastical," in which, to quote the church historian, Conrad Wright, church and state were to be "close and compact, but not compounded." The Virginia colonists arrived with business interests in mind, but availed themselves of the opportunity to found a Christian commonwealth with the Church of England as the established church. Maryland, founded primarily as a commercial venture, was Roman Catholic, but extended tolerance to other Christian groups. Pennsylvania, both a commercial enterprise and the "Holy Experiment" of the Quakers, was broadly tolerant. The Middle Atlantic colonies supported a variety of faiths, tolerances and intolerances. Only Baptist Rhode Island kept the church and the government strictly separated and maintained toleration as an ideal.

Insofar as the existence of a variety of Christian faiths could make the North American continent Christian, prerevolutionary America was a Christian land. A consensus was missing, however, and beliefs which were normative in Massachusetts could get a man banished from Virginia. Conventional opinions in Rhode Island were heresy throughout New England. Ideas which were commonplace in Philadelphia could get a person executed in Boston—and did.

It was against this polyglot religious background that our Founding Fathers labored to devise a means for insuring religious stability, if not harmony, in the new republic. The final outcome of their labors—in the form of the First Amendment—was, of course, no part of the Constitution as it was first drafted, although the Constitution did provide that "no religious Test shall ever be required as a Qualification to any Office or public Trust under the United States."

THE FIRST AMENDMENT
AND FREEDOM OF RELIGION

The framing of the First Amendment was no fortuitous event. A combination of some insistent historical conditions and some persuasive ideas informed the precision of its language:

> Congress shall make no law respecting an establishment of religion, or prohibiting the free exercise thereof; or abridging the freedom of speech, or of the press; or the right of the people peaceably to assemble, and to petition the government for a redress of grievances.

Behind the religious clauses of the First Amendment is a balanced accommodation to the practical realities of the time of its drafting, and an acceptance of rationalist idealism. But let us examine the background for the First Amendment's guarantee of freedom of religion in America in some detail.

a) *Religious Diversity and the Rival Establishments:* The multitude of "true faiths" in America at the close of the eighteenth century gave the drafters of the Constitution at least one compelling reason for choosing no single church as a national religion. Each contending sect was too convinced of its own authenticity to be denied. To establish one as the national religion would have been to repudiate the others. The expedient thing was to declare the government neutral in matters of religion.

Only two established churches in prerevolutionary America might have seriously contended for the place of a national church—the Congregational in New England and the Episcopal in Virginia. Each was so thoroughly out of sympathy with the other that a coalition would have been unthinkable; neither was sufficiently powerful, by itself, to have swayed the makers of the Constitution. It is one of the subtle ironies of history that the two oldest establishments in America managed, in effect, to cancel each other out, and in doing so, provided one of the most powerful arguments for religious pluralism.

Practical considerations aside, the diversity of sects in colonial America was thought of, by many, as desirable in its own right. Thus Madison is quoted as saying:

> Security for civil rights must be the same as for religious rights; it consists in the one case of a multiplicity of interests and in the other of a multiplicity of sects.

b) *The Founding Fathers and the Shaping of the Social Contract:* The Continental Congress encompassed as pious a group of delegates as any one legislative body might hope to boast of. Its legislative acts were sprinkled liberally with a Christian vocabulary. Prominent positions were held by leading ministers and, as Leo Pfeffer observes, the body did not hesitate to legislate in matters of religion. Pfeffer's list includes "morality, sin, repentance, humiliation, divine service, fasting, prayer, reformation, mourning, public worship, funerals, chaplains, true religion, and Thanksgiving."

An Episcopal clergyman served as Congressional Chaplain and opened each daily session with prayers. (Unfortunately for the ill-fated Congress, its chaplain was a turncoat who served for two years and then joined the British.) The Congress viewed the churches as prime propaganda mouthpieces and used them as such throughout the revolution. The body even went so far as to set its seal of approval on an American edition of the Bible, and in 1783 proclaimed peace with

England "In the name of the Most Holy and Undivided Trinity."

When attempts to unify the nation proved unsuccessful, the Constitutional Convention met and framed the Constitution as a replacement for the Continental Congress' inadequate Articles of Confederation. The religious atmosphere at the meetings of the Convention was altogether changed from the pious environment that had surrounded the proceedings of the Continental Congress.

None of the fifty-five men who attended were clerics. The name of God was not only omitted as a legislative embellishment—it failed to appear in the Constitution at all. Not even "Nature's God," referred to by Jefferson in the Declaration of Independence, was mentioned. The Convention had no chaplain, and no prayers were said.

At one point, in as eloquent an appeal as he could make, Benjamin Franklin reminded the body that its predecessor assembly had seen fit to pray, and went on to suggest that the Convention should do likewise. Madison quotes him as saying, in part:

> I have lived . . . a long time, and the longer I live, the more convincing proofs I see of this truth—that *God governs in the affairs of men*. And if a sparrow cannot fall to the ground without his notice, is it probable that an empire can rise without his aid? . . . I . . . believe that without his concurring aid we shall succeed in this political building no better than the builders of Babel. We shall be divided by our little partial local interests; our projects will be confounded; and we ourselves shall become a reproach and a by-word down to future ages. And what is worse, mankind may hereafter, from this unfortunate instance, despair of establishing governments by human wisdom, and leave it to chance, war and conquest.
>
> I therefore beg leave to move—that henceforth prayers

imploring the assistance of Heaven, and its blessings on our deliberations, be held in this assembly every morning before we proceed to business, and that one or more of the clergy of this city be requested to officiate in that service.

One would have thought that such an appeal would have moved heaven itself, but it failed to move the Convention. Roger Sherman of Connecticut seconded Franklin's motion. Hamilton, and several others, expressed apprehensions about it. (One remark attributed to Hamilton, but probably apocryphal, has him saying that the Convention needed the intervention of no "foreign power.") A motion was carried that a sermon be preached, at the request of the Convention, on Independence Day, but the final outcome was unfavorable to Franklin's proposal. "After several unsuccessful attempts for silently postponing [the] matter by adjourning," wrote Madison, "the adjournment was at length carried, without any vote on the motion."

It would be interesting to know precisely why the Convention failed to act favorably on Franklin's motion—indeed, why it failed to act at all. Its reaction cannot be explained simply in terms of an absence of funds to employ a chaplain —one reason that was put forward by a delegate—nor can it be accounted for in terms of a difference in religious perspective between Franklin and his peers. They were not that far apart in their views.[4] Prior proposals made by Franklin had been rejected rather consistently by the delegates, who apparently

---

[4] Franklin, as mentioned, was a deist in belief. In 1790, little more than a month before his death, he summarized his beliefs in a letter to Ezra Stiles, President of Yale College, in this fashion: "I believe in one God, Creator of the Universe. That he governs it by his Providence. That he ought to be worshipped. That the most acceptable Service we render to him is doing good to his other Children. That the soul of Man is immortal, and will be treated with Justice in another Life respecting its Conduct in this. . . . As to Jesus of Nazareth, . . . I think the System of Morals and his Religion . . . the best the World ever saw or is likely to see; but I apprehend it has received various corrupting Changes, and I have . . . some doubts as to his Divinity. . . ."

regarded them as passionate but lost causes, somewhat irrelevant to the questions at hand. Such a pattern of rejection would scarcely explain the delegates' negative reaction to the question of prayers, however.

There are, I think, two possible explanations for the Convention's unwillingness to pray. First, the delegates themselves were not the pious sort. The brand of popular piety that may well have appealed to Franklin, despite his deist beliefs, apparently appealed to no more than three or four of the delegates present in Philadelphia.[5] Second, the delegates to the Constitutional Convention—particularly James Madison—had begun to take seriously John Locke's theory of the social contract.

Pfeffer regards the popularization of Locke's Social Contract theory as so much of an accomplished fact as to be "deemed a self-evident truth to the signers of the Declaration of Independence." Its particular application to church and state followed from several arguments.

In *A Letter Concerning Toleration* Locke defines a church as "a voluntary society of men, joining themselves together of their own accord in order to engage in the public worship of God, in such a manner as they judge acceptable to Him, and effectual to the salvation of their souls." "A church," said Locke, "is a free and voluntary society. Nobody is born a member of any church." The state, on the other hand, is "a society of men constituted only for the procuring, preserving and advancing [of] their own civil interests."

It is, observed Locke in 1689, "above all things necessary to distinguish exactly the business of civil government from that of religion and to settle the just bounds that lie between the one and the other." The jurisdiction of the civil magistrate, he said, should extend only to civil matters, and not to the

---

[5] Such is the estimate of support for Franklin's proposal offered by one of his biographers, Bernard Faÿ, in *Franklin* (Boston: Little, Brown, and Co., 1929), p. 505.

salvation of souls. Why? First of all, God has not given any man the authority to compel others to be religious. And second, "the care of souls" should not belong to the magistrates simply because true religion "consists in the inward persuasion of the mind." Coercion by the state can only destroy religion, said Locke, and the Founding Fathers took him seriously.

c) *Disestablishment in Virginia and the Statute for Religious Freedom:* Jefferson was in France in 1786 when the Virginia Legislature passed its famous Statute for Religious Freedom, but his feeling for the importance of the act is attested to by the epitaph he wrote for himself: "Here was buried Thomas Jefferson, author of the Declaration of Independence, of the Statute of Virginia for Religious Freedom, and father of the University of Virginia."

An imposing piece of legislation, the act presumes that the human mind is naturally free, but that by "impious presumption" legislators and rulers have "established and maintained false religions over the greatest part of the world and through all time. . . . To compel a man to furnish contributions of money for the propagation of opinions which he disbelieves," the act states, "is sinful and tyrannical." Truth is sufficient in itself and if left alone will certainly prevail.

The main burden of the legislation was stated as follows:

> *Be it therefore enacted by the General Assembly,* That no man shall be compelled to frequent or support any religious worship, place or ministry whatsoever, nor shall he be enforced, restrained, molested, or burthened in his body or goods, nor shall otherwise suffer on account of his religious opinions or belief; but that all men shall be free to profess, and by argument to maintain, their opinions in matters of religion and that the same shall in no wise diminish, enlarge, or affect their civil capacities.

Jefferson comments in his autobiography that the bill met with opposition, but despite "some mutilations in the preamble," was passed as he wrote it. An amendment proposing a clause which would have referred to "the plan of Jesus Christ, the holy author of our religion" was rejected by a "great majority." The rejection, in Jefferson's view, constituted proof that the assembly wished to protect the religious liberties of "the Jew and the Gentile, the Christian and the Mohometan, the Hindoo, the infidel of every denomination." Freedom of religion, for Jefferson and for Virginia, meant not only the absence of a state church, but liberty for persons of all religious persuasions, Christian or otherwise. As Jefferson himself was to put it years later, "I have considered [religion] as a matter between every man and his maker, in which no other, and far less the public had a right to intermeddle."

d) *Toleration, from Rhode Island to Maryland and Pennsylvania:* "The Baptists," wrote Dean Sperry, "were undoubtedly the most aggressive . . . single religious body in the colonies, so far as the demand for religious liberty was concerned." Certainly few men have argued more eloquently in defense of freedom than the Baptist Roger Williams, as the following quotation testifies:

> And oh! since the commonweal cannot without a spiritual rape force the consciences of all to one worship, oh, that it may never commit that rape in forcing the consciences of all men to one worship which a stronger arm and sword may soon . . . arise to alter.

Spiritual and physical coercion were equally odious in Williams' judgment. A man must be a constant seeker in the realm of the spirit, looking always for the true church which remains elusive and beyond concrete expression. Thus, freedom of religion, for Williams, was not a value to be pursued in itself, but stood as a prerequisite to the search for ultimate religious truth. To deny men freedom of religion meant shackling them to the church of the moment, whatever that happened to be. Compulsion, whether of a spiritual or physical nature, merely served to increase man's sinfulness.

Williams, who had been banished from the Massachusetts Bay Colony by the General Court in October 1639, practiced his heresy in the Rhode Island wilderness. There he proved that his exercise of tolerance could match his theory by extending to the Quakers, whom he disliked, the full measure of religious liberty. The practicability of granting religious freedom was thus proved in America a century and a half before the framing of the Constitution.

Roger Williams was a philosopher and a prophet whose religious beliefs were tested severely. His near-contemporary, George Calvert, Lord Baltimore, was neither philosopher nor prophet, but for purely practical reasons did nearly as much as Williams for the cause of religious liberty. As the church historian William Warren Sweet has put it, Lord Baltimore was "a practical and hardheaded investor in a great land venture, in which his whole fortune was at stake. He founded Maryland upon the principle of religious toleration in spite of his religion rather than because of it."

An important figure in the courts of James I and Charles I, Lord Baltimore unsuccessfully invested £30,000 in an effort to colonize Newfoundland in 1620. Dropping that venture, he attempted to invest in Virginia, but was not permitted to do so. In time, he became the first proprietor of Maryland.

His political career in England cut short by his commitment to Roman Catholicism—he was unable to renounce the authority of the Pope—Lord Baltimore was well aware of the impossibility of making Maryland a Catholic colony. And he was sensitive to the desirability of attracting Protestants to the province. As a consequence, all men of Christian persuasion were granted freedom by the Calverts. (The first Lord Baltimore's son, Cecil Calvert, succeeded him.) Sweet reports that two Jesuits ministered with great success to the early settlers, converting numerous Indians and Protestants to the Catholic faith. They were replaced by secular priests, however, when the news of the conversions reached the English Protestant authorities and they protested.

An Act of Toleration, passed by the Maryland Assembly at the urging of Lord Baltimore in 1649, serves as an example of the tolerance practiced by the province. While providing the death sentence for anyone who denied "the Holy Trinity or the Godhead of any of the Three Persons," the act nevertheless stated that:

> No person or persons whatsoever, within this Province . . . professing to believe in Jesus Christ, shall from henceforth be in any ways troubled, molested, or discountenanced, for in respect of his or her Religion, nor in the free exercise thereof. . . .

In Pennsylvania, William Penn's "Holy Experiment" postdated both Roger Williams and Lord Baltimore. Believing heartily in Jesus' admonition to let the tares and wheat develop together, Penn made freedom of faith and worship an elemental part of the Pennsylvania experiment. His guarantee of tolerance was broader than that offered in Maryland and included all persons who lived "a peaceable and justly" life, and "acknowledged one Almighty and Eternal God to be the Creator, Upholder and Ruler of the world." Thus Jews, Roman Catholics, and Protestants might mingle with the Pennsylvania Quakers without fear of civil restraint.

e) *The European Background:* The dreary chronicle of religious persecutions in Europe is well known. It is enough for now to indicate the depth of conviction among the Founding Fathers by quoting these words of Jefferson:

> Is uniformity attainable? Millions of innocent men, women and children, since the introduction of Christianity have been burnt, tortured, fined, imprisoned; yet we have

not advanced an inch towards uniformity. What has been the effect of coercion? To make half the world fools, and the other half hypocrites. To support roguery and error all over the earth.

With recent tyrannies over freedom of conscience still alive in their memories, it is little wonder that Mr. Jefferson and his colleagues sought to insure a full measure of religious liberty in America.

f) *The First Amendment Is Adopted*: James Madison is rightly regarded as the principal author of the First Amendment. The final wording of the religious clauses of the amendment differed from his first proposal, however, which read as follows:

> The civil rights of none shall be abridged on account of religious belief, nor shall any national religion be established, nor shall the full and equal rights of conscience in any manner or on any pretext be infringed.

A more succinct version was offered by Samuel Livermore of New Hampshire:

> Congress shall make no laws touching religion, or infringing the rights of conscience.

It was Livermore's proposal, writes Canon Stokes, that determined the final form of the wording:[6]

> Congress shall make no law respecting an establishment of religion, or prohibiting the free exercise thereof. . . .

It is clear, then, that Congress sought not only to prohibit the founding of a national church—Christian or otherwise—but also to prohibit any form of aid "respecting" a religion. Church and state were to remain separate and distinct.

[6] See Anson Phelps Stoke's authoritative study *Church and State in the United States* (New York: Harper and Brothers, 1950), Vol. I, p. 317.

THE FOURTEENTH AMENDMENT
AND THE FIRST

What applied to the federal government did not apply to the states. Virginia, as we have seen, had disestablished its church by the time the First Amendment was adopted. Disestablishment in other states came later—1818 in Connecticut, 1819 in New Hampshire, 1833 in Massachusetts. By the time forty years had passed, it was inconceivable that the question of an established church should be reopened in the United States.

The full application of the First Amendment to the various states waited on the passage of the Fourteenth Amendment (1868) and a series of decisions by the Supreme Court. They held that the Fourteenth Amendment, with its provision, "No state shall make or enforce any law which shall abridge the privileges or immunities of citizens of the United States," extended the religious provisions of the First Amendment to the states. In 1923 the Court held that the Fourteenth Amendment provided for the protection of an individual's freedom "to worship God according to the dictates of his own conscience . . . [*Meyer* v. *Nebraska*]." And in 1934 Justice Cardozo wrote (*Hamilton* v. *Regents*):

I assume for present purposes that the religious liberty protected by the First Amendment against invasion by the nation is protected by the Fourteenth Amendment against invasion by the state.

The application of the Fourteenth Amendment was again clarified in 1940 when Justice Roberts declared for a unanimous Court (*Cantwell* v. *Connecticut*):

The fundamental concept of liberty embodied in that Amendment embraces the liberties guaranteed by the First Amendment. The First Amendment declares that Congress shall make no law respecting an establishment of religion or prohibiting the free exercise thereof. The Fourteenth Amendment has rendered the legislatures of the states as incompetent as Congress to enact such laws.

Beginning in 1947, a whole series of opinions made it clear that the Supreme Court took the First Amendment to mean that government—both state and federal—must be strictly neutral in matters of religion, aiding neither this group nor that, and inhibiting none in any way. The only consistent exceptions have involved legal restraints placed on groups or persons who have violated criminal or civil laws, endangered the public health, or the health of minor children in the name of religion. A man would not be permitted, for instance, to play Robin Hood and steal from the rich in order to give to the poor, marry two wives, or refuse to observe reasonable and necessary public health regulations in the name of religion.

How has the Fourteenth Amendment been applied to the First? In 1947 Justice Hugo Black wrote the majority opinion in the *Everson* case, which held that the use of public transportation facilities for church-supported schools was constitutional. His words define the application of the First Amendment in some detail:

The "establishment of religion" clause of the First Amendment means at least this: Neither a state nor the Federal Government can set up a church. Neither can pass laws which aid one religion, aid all religions, or prefer one religion over another. Neither can force nor influence a person to go to or to remain away from church against his will or force him to profess a belief or disbelief in any religion. No person can be punished for entertaining or professing religious beliefs or disbeliefs, for church attendance or nonattendance. No tax in any amount, large or small, can be levied to support any religious activities or institutions whatever they may be called, or whatever form they may adopt to teach or practice religion. Neither a state nor the Federal Government can, openly or secretly, participate in the affairs of any religious organizations or groups and *vice versa.* In the words of Jefferson, the clause against establishment of religion by law was intended to erect "a wall of separation between church and state."

The Court held in the *Everson* case that the state (New Jersey) was not aiding the church. It was simply providing a basic service to the children who were attending parochial schools—much as it provided such basic services as fire and police protection.

Over the next several years the Court decided that releasedtime religious education programs were unconstitutional when held on public-school property (*McCollum* v. *Board of Education*), but that such classes were in keeping with the First Amendment when conducted off the public-school grounds (*Zorach* v. *Clauson*). And it decided that a state might not require an applicant for public office to swear or affirm that he believed in God (*Torcaso* v. *Watkins*).

One would have thought that the American public would have been prepared for the 1962 Supreme Court decision which held that a state-composed prayer recited in New York classrooms was unconstitutional. The public was not. Seldom has there been so violent a reaction to a Supreme Court decision as that which followed the *Engel-Vitale* decision. From the quiet sobriety of a Bishop Pike to the noisy outbursts of a Billy Hargis, dissent to the Court's interpretation of the meaning of separation of church and state was immediate.

THE *ENGEL-VITALE* UPROAR

News of the *Engel-Vitale* decision was first carried by the Associated Press wires at 11:54 A.M. on June 25. The release was terse and to the point. It explained little:

Washington, June 25 (AP)—The Supreme Court ruled today the offering of a 22-word daily prayer in New York State's public schools violates the U. S. Constitution.

The next release, carried by the wire service just eight minutes later, explained that five parents with children in New Hyde Park schools had questioned the constitutionality of the daily recitation of the Regents' Prayer. The prayer was quoted in its entirety:

Almighty God, we acknowledge our dependence upon Thee, and we beg Thy blessings upon us, our parents, our teachers and our country.

One thirty-two-word sentence from Justice Black's majority opinion was quoted, together with the relevant portion of the First Amendment. No fewer than sixty-three words were quoted from two sentences of Justice Stewart's minority opinion. It was noted that Justice Douglas wrote a concurring majority opinion, that Justices White and Frankfurter took no part in the decision, and that the vote was six to one. That was all.

While it could not be said that the wire-service story was slanted, it is worth noting that the story did nothing to illuminate the thinking behind the decision. As Justice Tom C. Clark was to remark later, much of the negative public reaction to the decision was the product of the "haste in which news agencies are forced to cover our [*i.e.*, the Supreme Court's] decisions."

Not touched upon by the first wire-service stories was the fact that Justice Black was extremely careful to indicate that the decision was in no way hostile toward religion. It was based on a considered analysis of the history of freedom of religion in America, on the intent of the Founding Fathers, and on the relationship of the prayer itself to the Establishment Clause.[7] The Court sought to ensure religion an effective place in American life, not to destroy it. It recognized the potentially divisive and destructive effects of governmental intervention in religious matters, and wished to guard against such intervention. As Justice Black wrote in his majority opinion:

> When the power, prestige and financial support of government is placed behind a particular religious belief, the indirect coercive pressure upon religious minorities to conform to the prevailing officially approved religion is plain. But the purposes underlying the Establishment Clause go much further than that. Its first and most immediate purpose rested on the belief that a union of government and religion tends to destroy government and to degrade religion. . . . The Establishment Clause thus stands as an expression of principle on the part of the Founders of our Constitution that religion is too personal, too sacred, too holy, to permit its "unhallowed perversion" by a civil magistrate.

Those who maintained that the Regents' Prayer was, after all, a small, even trivial observance, unrelated to an *establishment* of religion, were reminded that James Madison himself had written:

[7] The provision, "Congress shall make no law respecting an establishment of religion," is commonly known as the Establishment Clause and is distinguished from the equally important Free Exercise Clause: "or prohibiting the free exercise thereof."

[I]t is proper to take alarm at the first experiment on our liberties. . . . Who does not see that the same authority which can establish Christianity, in exclusion of all other Religions, may establish with the same ease any particular sect of Christians, in exclusion of all other Sects? That the same authority which can force a citizen to contribute three pence only of his property for the support of any one establishment, may force him to conform to any other establishment in all cases whatsoever?

In a signed editorial, William Randolph Hearst, Jr., declared that the Hearst papers believed that the Supreme Court had misinterpreted the Constitution and called for an amendment to the First Amendment as the obvious means for righting the wrong done by the Court. The Court, argued Hearst, had used the First Amendment to deprive the people of liberty and to deny the nation's "basic faith in God." Great violence had been done to the intent of the Founding Fathers. The Regents' Prayer, he maintained, "had been carefully worded to avoid offending any minority faith. It was nonsectarian and not mandatory for any child."

The *New York Daily News* editorialized on the decision in its June 29 edition by decrying the "atheistic, agnostic or what-have-you Supreme Court majority." The normally sober *Los Angeles Times* observed that the Court had been "persuaded by a small group of guardhouse sophists to make a burlesque show of the world's first complete declaration of religious toleration." Still another newspaper referred editorially to the "six old goats in long black coats" who were responsible for the majority decision.

A *special* from the Hearst Headline Service indicated that Congress had been shocked, dismayed, angered and embittered by the ruling, and declared that both houses reacted with "swift resentment" by introducing amendments to the First Amendment. "It is anticipated," said the Hearst papers, "that [the amendment] will go through faster than any other amendment ever presented to the nation."

Senate Republican Leader Everett Dirkson did not agree, and was quoted by reporters as remarking, "The proposition of separation of church and state is so ingrained into our people that I doubt that such an amendment would be adopted."

On July 26, Congressional hearings on an amendment to the First Amendment got under way. The testimony heard that day and on August 2 was not as extensive as one might have expected. The exhibits that were printed as a part of the record were voluminous, however. They ranged from a resolution passed by the Annual Assembly of the Disciples of Christ, which approved heartily of the Court's decision, to a statement from the North American and Canadian Diocese of the Russian Orthodox Church, which registered the Synod's "determined support" for the proposed amendment.

By far the most interesting testimony was that offered by Episcopal Bishop James Pike, a lawyer as well as a clergyman. "I believe earnestly that the Supreme Court has distorted the meaning of the First Amendment," said Bishop Pike. "What our Founding Fathers were trying to avoid by the establishment of religion clause was the setting up of a given denomination as the established church of the country." Pike proposed his own wording for a new First Amendment, striking the words "the establishment of religion," and replacing them with "the recognition as an established church of any denomination, sect, or organized religious association."[8] Un-

[8] A motion which proposed a wording similar to Bishop Pike's was defeated—at the time the First Amendment was adopted in its present form—by the first session of the United States Senate in 1791. Like Bishop Pike's proposal, the amendment would have made it clear that Congress was prohibited only from establishing a *particular* denomination or organized religion. It read as follows: "Congress shall make no law establishing any particular denomination or religion in preference to another. . . ." As with Bishop Pike's proposal, the Free Exercise Clause was to follow the "Establishment of denomination or organized religion" clause.

der such a wording, the recitation of the "Hail Mary" or the "Ava Maria" as an official school prayer would constitute "recognition of a given denomination," said the Bishop. And that, he made clear, he opposed. Although Pike willingly acknowledged that a Shintoist or a Buddhist would have found the Regents' Prayer unsatisfactory, he held doggedly to his point of view and declared that local officials should be able to work such things out. (He failed to indicate why school officials could not work out a solution for offended Protestants if the "Hail Mary" were adopted as the official school prayer in a predominantly Roman Catholic community.)

The Bishop also expressed a great concern over what he regarded as a trend toward secularism in the U.S. "Secularism is a religion," he said, ". . . an image of life which includes man and things without God, time and history without eternity, and so forth." He defended the right to be wrong, and the right of an atheist to be an atheist, but argued vigorously for "the American way of life" and our "characteristic institutions," which he described as the "finest flower of the whole Judeo-Christian tradition." He was certain that the Kingdom of God would not rise or fall on the acceptance or rejection of the Regents' Prayer as a part of public-school exercises, but nevertheless felt that the American "middle way" of compromise was imperiled by the Supreme Court decision.

In the days prior to and following Bishop Pike's testimony, no fewer than forty-two proposals for a constitutional amendment were put forward in the House of Representatives alone. They ranged from New York Congressman Frank Becker's proposal, which read, "Prayers may be offered in the course of any program in any public school or other public place in the United States," to Kentucky Congressman Eugene Siler's wording, ". . . this nation devoutly recognizes the authority and law of Jesus Christ, Saviour and Ruler of Nations, through whom are bestowed the blessings of Almighty God."

In a pamphlet entitled "Six Men Against God" Billy James Hargis described the day when the Supreme Court "legislated God out of the public schools" as the "darkest hour" of the nation's history, announced that he was "honestly afraid the consequence of this national sin will be the destruction of the United States and everything we hold dear," and quoted reports claiming that there had been great rejoicing in Moscow over the *Engel-Vitale* decision. Then Hargis turned his anger toward the Justices themselves:

> In the past, I was cautious concerning these projects to impeach Earl Warren. Now it is my earnest conviction that ever[y] member of the United States Supreme Court who either voted to outlaw prayer in the public schools, or was a party to this decision by silence should be impeached. Justice demands it.

He went on to propose that members of the Supreme Court should be elected—either by Congress or the public—to serve limited terms of no more than six years. He did not bother to explain how such a major change of the U. S. Constitution would affect the balance of power in our government.

BIBLE READING AND THE LORD'S PRAYER IN THE CLASSROOM

Less than a year after the *Engel-Vitale* decision, the Supreme Court handed down another controversial ruling on church and state. On June 17, 1963, an eight-to-one majority ruled that no state or locality could constitutionally require the recitation of the Lord's Prayer or the reading of Bible verses in public schools.

The 1963 decision involved two families in two states. In Baltimore, Maryland, the Board of School Commissioners

had required the "reading, without comment, of a chapter of
the Holy Bible and/or the use of the Lord's Prayer." Mrs.
Madalyn Murray and her son, William J. Murray III, both of
them professed atheists, held that the requirement violated
their freedom of religion as guaranteed by the First Amendment.

In Pennsylvania, Mr. and Mrs. Edward Lewis Schempp,
together with two of their three children, brought suit to en-
join enforcement of a statute which required that "at least ten
verses of the Holy Bible shall be read without comment, at
the opening of each school day." Any child might be excused
from the exercises, provided that his or her parent or guardian
furnished the school with a written request.

The Schempps, who were active members of the Unitarian
Church in Germantown, Pennsylvania, found that the practice of reading the Bible, without comment, conveyed religious doctrines which were sometimes contrary to their
religious beliefs.[9] Requesting the school to permit the children to be absent from the exercises was a possible solution,
but it had a twofold negative effect—it subjected the children
to what amounted to a punishment detail by exiling them to
the halls outside their classrooms, and it labeled them as
"oddballs," atheists, or even Communists.

The Murray and Schempp cases came to the Supreme
Court with opposite rulings from the lower courts. In Maryland the majority of a four-judge panel had held that
Baltimore practices were not in violation of the First Amendment. The Pennsylvania trial court found that it was "the

[9] Expert testimony introduced at the first trial corroborated the Schempps'
viewpoint. Dr. Solomon Grayzel noted the absence of the New Testament
from the Jewish scriptures, and pointed out that not only were there parts of
the New Testament which were offensive to the Jewish tradition, but that
the concept of Jesus as the Son of God was "practically blasphemous." Dr.
Luther Weigle, testifying for the defense, made as much of an argument for
the plaintiff by observing that the Bible was "nonsectarian," and then con-
fessing that his understanding of nonsectarian extended only to Christian
faiths.

intention of . . . the Commonwealth . . . to introduce a religious ceremony into the public schools. . . ." And that, of course, was in violation of the First Amendment.

In the majority opinion, Supreme Court Justice Clark, a Presbyterian, wrote:

> The place of religion in our society is an exalted one, achieved through a long tradition of reliance on the home, the church and the inviolable citadel of the individual heart and mind. We have come to recognize through bitter experience that it is not within the power of government to invade that citadel, whether its purpose or effect be to aid or oppose, to advance or retard. In the relationship between man and religion, the State is firmly committed to a position of neutrality.

Justice Brennan, the only Roman Catholic on the Court, observed in a brilliant and scholarly concurring opinion that he could see "no escape from the conclusion that the exercises called in question in [the] two cases violate the constitutional mandate. . . . Nothing in the text of the Establishment Clause," he said, "supports the view that the prevention of the setting up of an official church was meant to be the full extent of the prohibitions against official involvements in religion." He then came to grips with the main problem behind the church-state dispute—the need for peaceful accommodation on the part of the many faiths of a religiously diverse culture. The Founding Fathers, he observed, were aware of the differences among Protestant sects. Today, the even greater religious diversity in America—involving not only Protestants, Roman Catholics and Jews, but "those who worship according to no version of the Bible and those who worship no God at all"—makes offensive many practices which would have distressed no one in the time of Jefferson and Madison. Our interpretation of the First Amendment, said Justice Brennan, "must necessarily be responsive to the much more highly charged nature of religious questions in contemporary society." He observed that the violation of the First Amendment in the Murray and Schempp cases had been more severe than that in the Regents' Prayer case, and declared that the state must remain "steadfastly neutral" in all matters of religion.

To those who would contend that the Supreme Court was banning the name of God from the coinage of the nation, the halls of Congress, courtroom oaths and every other segment of public life, he suggested that the question of religious exercises in public schools presented a unique problem, and argued that the Court must draw a line between the permissible and the impermissible. "The principles which we reaffirm and apply today can hardly be thought novel or radical," he said in conclusion. "They are, in truth, as old as the Republic itself, and have always been as integral a part of the First Amendment as the very words of that charter of religious liberty."

Justice Goldberg, the only Justice of Jewish faith, expressed "no doubt as to the propriety" of the decision. Justice Potter Stewart, an Episcopalian, was not convinced, however, and indicated in his minority opinion that the cases should have been sent back for further hearings. In both cases he saw no more than an attempt, on the part of the states involved, to come to terms with differences of religious belief. There was, he maintained, no clear evidence indicating that governmental authority had been used to coerce belief.

Public reaction to the *Murray-Schempp* decision was less outraged than it had been following the *Engel-Vitale* decision. The Hearst papers once again called for an amendment to the First Amendment. Bishop Pike declared that "secularism by default" was being imposed on the American public-school system, and claimed that the ruling pointed toward the elimination of daily prayers in Congress, at inaugurations, the elimination of the phrase "under God" from the pledge of allegiance, and so on.

Carl McIntire, who otherwise has very little in common with the civil libertarian Bishop, also called for a constitutional amendment and declared, "The establishment of religion, . . . in the context of the Constitution, was simply that we were not to have a State Church. . . . The Court has spoken," he said. "We are to be a godless nation, for anything which partakes of God, appeals to God, is 'religious' and in violation of the First Amendment. It is that plain and simple." He too predicted that the Bible would soon be removed from courtrooms. As a remedy, he suggested the founding of Christian schools where children would "be taught the Word of God." Our coins, he facetiously suggested, might be inscribed with "In pluralism we trust."

Billy James Hargis had calmed down considerably by the time of the *Murray-Schempp* decision, but remarked in his *Christian Crusade* magazine:

> I regard it as shameful that we have permitted these political appointees, most of whom have no past judicial experience and are certainly not qualified to serve on the highest tribunal in our land, to wipe God from the pages of American history with the stroke of a pen [emphasis by Hargis].

Hargis, like McIntire, was concerned about the education of children in schools which he maintained had been "completely stripped of religious elements." The stripping, he said, had not been done by infidels and atheists alone, but by "folk" who acted in the name of religion. An anti-God philosophy, he said, was filtering down to American children and endangering the future of the nation itself.

Curiously, neither Carl McIntire nor Billy James Hargis spent much time drawing analogies between the Court's decision and the atheistic materialism of the international Communist conspiracy. Perhaps they felt that the Kremlin's evil influence was self-evident.

James Francis Cardinal McIntyre, Roman Catholic Archbishop of Los Angeles, was not so circumspect. Speaking in Rome, he declared that the decision "puts us right up against Communism." He went on to say that the ruling "prevents the states from doing anything. It is an attempt to make us an atheist country." The effect of the decision could only mean "that our American heritage . . . [is] being abandoned in imitation of Soviet philosophy, Soviet materialism and Soviet-regimented liberty." The Cardinal's concluding remark was the fervent plea, "May we remain Americans and not become disciples of the Kremlin."

Meanwhile, the National Council of Churches had reminded the public that "teaching for religious commitment is the responsibility of the home and the community of faith . . . rather than the public schools." It warned the churches against the tendency to look to the state as a shortcut means for fulfilling the churches' responsibilities.

Rabbi Joachim Prinz, President of the American Jewish Congress, also found the decision congenial. In his view, it merely underscored the responsibility of the home, the church and the synagogue to take seriously the task of transmitting a spiritual heritage to young people.

Spokesmen for the United Presbyterian Church in the U.S.A. took a similar position. Eugene Carson Blake, stated clerk, and Silas G. Kessler, moderator, released a joint statement in which they said that the decision had "underscored our firm belief that religious instruction is the sacred responsibility of the family and the churches."

The statement was in keeping with a report on "Relations between Church and State" adopted by the General Assembly of the Church a month before. This thirty-eight-page report, which was the work of a three-year study made by a special committee, voiced opposition to devotional acts in public schools, including Bible reading and prayers, but encompassing religious observances and displays as well. The study further expressed the view that "moral convictions peculiar to a religious body ought not be imposed on the general public by law." Dr. Elwin A. Smith, chairman of the special committee, remarked that the Presbyterian church was the first major Protestant body to have "faced up to its responsibilities in a pluralistic society." He was probably correct.

By the time that Alabama Governor George Wallace had publicly stated his intent to defy the Court's ruling, the more bitter opposition had all but died.

THE RIGHT WING AND THE FIRST FREEDOM

What does all this have to do with the Christian ultrarightists? Just about everything, I think. The Christian ultras must be viewed in terms of their response to the unique definitions of religiopolitical responsibility in the United States. Their position, together with their impact on society, must then be evaluated in terms of those definitions.

Let me explain what I mean. There are, I believe, four major Protestant groups which are vitally concerned with the relationship between religion and society, church and state, in present-day America.

First, there are those—represented by men such as Mr. Hearst—who believe in all sincerity that an important facet of the nation's religious heritage has been discarded with each successive Supreme Court decision defining more sharply the line of separation between church and state. The worst that may be said for the members of this group is that they have not troubled themselves particularly about the history of our nation, and that they remain somewhat myopic in their appreciation of the non-Christian religions which assume every day a greater role in the American dialogue of faiths.

The second group, which is perhaps best represented by

Bishop Pike, has read its history and is aware of the religious diversity of our country. But it sees the historical drama as pointing up conclusions which are in sharp contradiction to those held by the Supreme Court. Great tolerance is exercised toward non-Christian faiths, but the group's confidence in the ultimate truth of its own doctrines dissuades it from taking seriously the possibility of even a guarded relativism. It is impossible to say, "My truth is sufficient for me, and I grant to you the possibility that your truth may also be wholly sufficient—perhaps as ultimate as my own." Such an admission would not be denounced as heresy, but it would be classified as grave error. Secularism, for this group, is a kind of sinister antireligion with a negative cathexis all its own, capable of undermining those religious values which are seen as fundamental to cultural cohesion.

Third, there are those groups, who are well represented by Eugene Carson Blake, which fully concur with the lines drawn by the Supreme Court. Their reading of history corresponds with the trend in the Court's decisions. Like William Penn, they are content to have the tares and the wheat grow together until the time of harvest. Their truth is not jeopardized by extending to another group not only tolerance, but the unqualified right to proclaim its truth as ultimate—or as relative, as it sees fit. Secularism is viewed as the mere absence of religion, not as a kind of antireligion.

Fourth, there is the ultra-rightist viewpoint. While separation of church and state is supported in words by this group, it is questioned in fact. Neither the historical basis of church-state separation nor the implications of religious pluralism are accepted. History is rewritten to suit the writers. The many non-Christian faiths of modern America are shunned as unacceptable. Occasionally, they are made the objects of attempts at conversion, but more often they are simply denounced. Non-Christian means un-American. And un-

American means rejected. Completely. Totally. Without possibility of reconsideration.

The Christian ultra-rightists reject the first premise of the American experiment as it applies to religion—the belief that the many *truths* of religion may mingle and contend in a free society, and that a man may believe in one God or in many, or in no God at all. He is free, the premise has it, not because a benevolent state tolerates him, but because freedom is right and sufficient in itself. Our government makes no value judgments in matters of religion—or irreligion. The state will not serve as arbiter in matters of belief or religious practice. On these principles rests the first of the four freedoms.

To the extent that a man's beliefs and convictions are at the very center of what it means for him to be a human being, it is not too much to say that liberty itself is fed by the springs of religious freedom. Reject the notion that the individual is free to believe whatever he chooses—including the most contemptible of heresies—and you have rejected the basis for freedom itself. That, unhappily, is precisely what the Christian ultra-rightists have done.

This is not to suggest that life in a religiously diverse culture is a simple matter. It is not. The best minds search today for sensible solutions to the claims made on society by the individual members of America's family of faiths. To name only the most elemental problem, no one has yet proposed a way in which the transmission of cultural values, together with the particular teachings of this religion or that, may be carried out without our becoming embroiled in endless sectarian battles on the one hand, or an increasingly stereotyped synthesis of democratic values on the other. The direction represented by parochial-school education offers the lure of diversity, but with the certainty of sectarian wrangles. The other direction—that presented by public-school education—suggests eventual cultural sterility brought about by reducing the nation's religious value systems to a common-denominator culture-religion.

We have, to a large extent, given over the inculcation of values to the public schools as the more promising of the two alternatives, but without asking ourselves how we intend to promote the genius of spontaneous self-initiative on which our future as a moral and ethical people depends.

The self-conscious man of this era knows all too well that we are deciding not only who will pass on the democratic inheritance, but just what kind of inheritance will be given over to the next generation.

Our first instinct has been to look to the past. But the past has not been altogether helpful. Symbolic of our dilemma is a moment in the Congressional hearings on the First Amendment.

Senator Hart, who is chairing the committee, remarks with whimsical simplicity, "I wish [the Founding Fathers] were here to visit with us."

Bishop Pike responds: "I do too."

Senator Hart: "I would listen to them . . . more attentively if they brought with them the experience up to the moment of their death, plus the experience of intervening generations, because I think that is the way you have to read the Constitution."

Bishop Pike: "You are quite right, sir, on that."

There is a strange, wistful quality about that exchange—almost as though it were part of a stage play, so close is it to summing up reality, yet treading ever so carefully on the edge of the world of illusion and fantasy.

Sensitive men will feel the need to question history. But they will know that it must be viewed in the perspective of the present. They will realize that America's growing diversity is at once an ennobling fact of our way of life and a frustrating challenge.

The diversification of our religious community means at

least one thing. We are likely to get defensive about what has always meant *religion* to us in the past. Without stopping to think, we may engage in an attempt to bolster up religion from the outside—an attempt that is destined to self-defeat.

Our nation has become not one particle more religious because Congress saw fit to put "under God" in the pledge of allegiance. What is more, the members of Congress, in attempting to play the part of theologians, became mildly ridiculous to anyone who has bothered to think about the matter. They failed to explain why the nation should be *under* God (as in most Roman Catholic and orthodox Protestant Christian theology), rather than *with* God or *in* God (as in the theology of some dissenting Protestant sects and the thinking of many non-Christian religions). And, depending on how one looks at the grammar of the pledge, it is at least possible that our legislators mishandled their modifiers, leaving God, rather than the nation (as intended), indivisible and therefore nontrinitarian (much to the amusement of Unitarians). The question is not a serious one, but it serves to illustrate the wisdom of the Founders in seeing to it that Congress did not, as Jefferson would have put it, intermeddle in matters of religion.

Attempts to make either ourselves or our neighbors more religious by means of Congressional fiat or governmental practice are certain to degrade religion. They can amount to little more than vain efforts to inject into the artifacts of religion the life stuff of a living organism. As such, they must inevitably fail. True religion cannot be coerced into life. Roger Williams knew that lesson. The Founding Fathers had learned it well. Today, we are relearning the elemental concept that democracy in religion means faith in men and in their capacity for finding diverse ways in the realms of the human spirit.

The Christian ultra-rightists would pose no threat to our religious traditions were it not for the fact that these traditions are in flux. Our most thoughtful and responsible thinkers disagree in their conclusions. And into the arena of disagreement step the extremists with their simplistic cant: "This is a Christian nation. It always has been, and we are going to keep it that way."

The extremist harbors a nearly overwhelming eagerness to impose his "truth" on his countrymen—in the form of a Christian Amendment to the Constitution, as an oath of conformity to be taken by all loyal "Christian Americans," as an educational system oriented toward passing on the "true Christian faith." The inevitable outcome is an arrogant attack on those who differ in their beliefs.

The man on the far right has his own definitions of religious freedom. He sees the wall of separation as a sanctified fortress for keeping his private brand of Christianity safe. He uses it to keep out the enemy—*i.e.*, the Roman Catholics, the Buddhists, the liberals, the atheists, the Communists and all the rest. He seeks to limit strictly the public participation of other religious groups, insisting all the while that his religion should be given a favored place. He recognizes that the Constitution permits no religion to attempt to coerce the government, to use the machinery of the state for its own ends. He is quick to cry out when others attempt to do so. He fails utterly, however, to recognize that the same limitations apply to his religion as to others, and he is outraged when the courts tell him that the state may not promote his religious bias.

The right-wing extremist is quick to make political pronouncements in the name of religion whenever they are *his* sort of pronouncements, but attacks unstintingly the man of any other faith who presumes to do the same. He exercises his constitutional right to criticize or persuade his government in terms of his religious values, but denies that right to others.

Were the right-wing extremist talking only to himself there would be little problem. In the absence of any generally accepted image of what our religious freedom means, he is managing to convince others. He has declared so long and so loudly that this is a Christian nation that he is seldom called upon to say what he means. His simple myths are accepted by men who should know better. (I have even had a conservative rabbi tell me that this is a "Christian nation." When challenged, he said he meant small *c*.)

We are in danger of losing our sacred heritage of religious freedom by default—of sacrificing the principles of the Founding Fathers by our ill-informed silences. We cannot afford, I submit, to give the nation's inheritance over to those who have so glibly rewritten its history. Our nation is larger than the strictures of any single faith. The democratic way presumes that truth and justice are the fruits of many points of view contending freely.

One of our deepest responsibilities—perhaps the deepest— is to make the place of the first freedom more secure in America. Only insofar as we exercise our freedom of belief and worship will we develop as a moral people, flexible in the face of changing social conditions, but steadfast in our commitment "to do justly, and to love mercy, and to walk humbly" with our God.

8   Armageddon

PROJECT ALERT WAS one of several "schools" of anti-Communism conducted by right-wing groups in Southern California over the past several years. Held in Los Angeles December 11–15, 1961, the Project was the combined work of the Navy League and the Marine Corps League, and was similar to other schools held from one coast to the other since the radical right launched its first organized activities.

In the course of Project Alert's five-day session, the following bits of knowledge were dispensed to the students: President Kennedy was said to have Communist advisers. ("Red, red-blooded Americans" was the euphemism used.) The "outmoded shackles of democracy" were cited as a hindrance to the military. Anyone opposing war with Russia was called a superpacifist. And it was suggested that the U.S. should invade Cuba, launch a "preventive war" against the U.S.S.R., and hang Earl Warren. The last proposal, and only the last proposal, was withdrawn. The dominant mood of the school was summed up at the closing banquet by a speaker who declared, "Look out Khrushchev! You and your bloody-handed gang and foolish hangers-on are just another tyrant."

Most of Project Alert was far less dramatic, of course. My attendance at several lectures left me with the clear impression that one of the prime requirements for being a good anti-Communist, in the right-wing sense of the word, is an almost limitless capacity for absorbing tedium. I must admit that I was, at times, acutely bored.

Program and speeches aside, however, the reactions of the

Project Alert audience were fascinating. I saw no obvious crackpots in the crowd, no one with bloodshot or catatonic eyes. Everyone looked like a normal, sensible, moderately happy, moderately disgruntled American. What was fascinating about the audience was a quality of another order. It was the group's reaction *as a group* to everything that happened. People had plainly come to applaud, to cheer, to hiss—to react. All speakers were enthusiastically endorsed, regardless of whether or not they had something to say, or how they said it. The audience heard one address after another—many of them highly repetitive—with almost perfect courtesy. It responded to the slogan phrases of the far right with what could only be described as a stimulus-response reaction. All a speaker needed to do was to mention Americanism, free enterprise, atheistic totalitarian Communism, or fuzzy-minded liberalism, and he was applauded soundly. He had merely to chant, "The only *ism* for me is Americanism," and he was answered by clapping, sometimes even cheers. A word would be recited and the audience would respond—almost mechanically, automatically.

This is not to say that a conditioned response is always a bad thing. It is often quite appropriate—at football games, boat races, concerts and the like. But in politics, it may be a most sinister symptom, heralding the end of personal autonomy and preparing the way for the controllers of thought.

But to return to Project Alert. It was a Colonel Mitchell Paige, a retired Marine Corps winner of the Medal of Honor, who declared one morning, "There are those today who would impeach Earl Warren, the Chief Justice of the United States Supreme Court. After having read some sixteen or seventeen of the decisions handed down by this highest court in our land, I was so appalled I felt that impeachment is not the proper penalty, but rather, it appears to me, a more deserving punishment would be hanging." The Colonel's proposal was greeted by applause and approving laughter.

That afternoon, Colonel Paige returned to the stage for a brief appearance. "I want to apologize for stating I would hang Earl Warren," he said. "Really it isn't my feeling he should be hanged."

Again the audience applauded, only this time half of the crowd stood—in honor of Colonel Paige, who had decided that he didn't want to hang the Chief Justice after all.

I find myself wondering what happened to that audience. Is such a response typical of audiences in America today? Do we accept what a speaker tells us and give him our automatic approval, only to increase our approval when he changes his mind a few hours later? I hope not, because if we do our minds are already captive to the man behind the speaker's rostrum, whoever he may happen to be. Speaking for myself, I do not believe that such a reaction is typical of Americans as a whole. Not at all. But it does seem to have a good deal to do with the psychology of extremism.

There were a good many opinions receiving instant approval at Project Alert, and the Colonel's was not the most remarkable. Major General Orvil Anderson received equally generous applause when he proposed that Americans should do away with the "outmoded shackles of democracy" in order to win the cold war. "I believe you must have a commander with authority to order his troops, not committees which waste time," said the General. "These problems depend on professionalism, not public opinion. . . . What a queer strategy our dependence on deterrence which says we'll kill them, too, while we're dying."

General Anderson did not indicate how we could do away with the "shackles of democracy" without doing away with democracy itself. He was unclear as to how military decisions could be turned over to the professionals, without regard for public opinion, without violating Article II, Section 2 of the United States Constitution, which clearly subordinates military authority to civilian. From the General's remarks it was unclear whether he was advocating the circumvention of constitutional principles, their overturning, or something else. He failed to elaborate. But he was applauded handsomely.

José Norman, a plantation owner in Cuba before the coming of Castro, also had military matters on his mind. He proposed a crusade of sorts to the audience by observing that, "If a United States military force of sufficient strength was to invade Cuba in the form of a Crusade, bringing food, medicine, promises of freedom alongside its guns, this could be done with a minimum of bloodshed—if any at all. . . . And if Communist blood is shed, I say it is good riddance of bad rubbish!"

Applause also greeted Los Angeles attorney Loyd Wright when he told the audience that the U.S. government should discard its policy of containing Communism and initiate a "program for victory." At an offstage press conference, Wright elaborated on his views. Our great mistake, he told a reporter for the *Los Angeles Times*, was that we failed to take the initiative and attack Russia in 1946 when we had the atomic bomb and she didn't. Earlier in the same press conference, Wright had outlined his ideas on foreign policy:

> "I would give notice to Russia to get out of the enslaved Baltic nations within a certain time," said the former president of the American Bar Association and one of the founders of the local Project Alert.
>
> "If they didn't get out, I would commence shooting."
>
> Asked whether he proposed Russian cities should be bombed, he said: "We don't have to blow up the whole city of Moscow. But if we do, that's too bad."
>
> He said such an attack should make use of whatever weapons are needed, including nuclear.
>
> Asked if he meant he was firmly committed to the concept of preventive war, he said, "You bet! And I think the American people are in the same frame of mind."

Other Project Alert speakers called for doubling the annual U.S. military budget and for a compulsory Federal plan for the construction of individual fallout shelters. (The characteristic right-wing concern for individual freedom, together with right-wing antipathy toward big government, was suddenly absent.)

Without citing any further examples, it is enough to say that the mood of Project Alert, like that of many similar affairs in other parts of the country, was one of "Let's get on with the war." The majority of persons who attended the school may have thought that thermonuclear war would be horrible, just as all war is horrible. But it represented for them a valid—indeed, for many, necessary—solution to the immediate tensions of the cold war.

A JUST WAR AND THE WORLD OF TODAY

Opinions are divided even on the far right about the desirability of launching a thermonuclear offensive. The John Birch Society, for instance, is committed through its leader to a kind of *de facto* pacifism. Believing as Welch does that pushing the U.S. into making large military expenditures is a part of the Soviet plot to drain our economy, he would have little choice but to watch our military preparedness waste away for lack of funds—were his theories practiced. Welch no doubt is the member of a small, small minority, even among his friends on the far right, when it comes to the armaments question, however.

Most of those on the extreme right have considered carefully the problems posed by Soviet expansionist policies, and the right-wing solution is generally as direct as it is simple. I have heard no summary better phrased than that given by a San Diego, California, radio evangelist in August of 1963.

"World War III is on," he said. "It is on in many fields. . . . Let us hope that the pressures from Christian Americans will continue. . . . Let us be an independent nation and strike against evil where it affects us most."

His conclusion was predictable for a Biblically oriented preacher on the radical right: "The great nations of God's kingdom are at the very door of Armageddon!"

The horror of it is that the preacher may be right. We *are* perilously close to the door of Armageddon, mass annihilation, the wholesale slaughter of entire peoples. Bertrand de Jouvenel has expressed it well: "We are our own Huns." We do our own burning and pillaging. We have perfected the science of reducing whole cities to ashes in an instant, of insuring our military success with such large doses of overkill that we multiply the cipher *death* a hundred times over in order to make certain that the enemy is dead beyond any question.

The year 1945 meant a great many things, but no event was more important than the explosion of the bomb over Hiroshima. It signaled the advent of a new era in human affairs, an era in which policy makers were forced to begin to think of full-scale war as a deterrent only—no longer as an arm of policy.

There are no victors in a thermonuclear holocaust—just the end of civilization as we know it. Thermonuclear weapons are useful only insofar as they deter aggression. Once used, the race for life and freedom is over. It is finished. Civilization might rebuild itself, in time, as the war theorists have proved by their macabre calculations, but the freedom protected by our present state of armed preparedness would not be saved by a war. It would succumb to a fiery death, together with the millions of human beings who would breathe their last breath as the fireball expanded. Modern civilization would yield to primitive anarchy, or to the imposition of rigorous authoritarian controls. There could be no ground of compromise.

All this is generally agreed upon. It is part of the premise on which the U.S. policy of containment is founded. It stands behind the Soviet Union's unwillingness to go beyond brush-fire warfare in its attempts to push its territory outward. The elemental notion that there could be no triumphant nation in a full-scale thermonuclear war is accepted by nearly everyone, it seems, except for those who live in the pre-1945 world of the far right.

The March 1962 issue of the *Bulletin of the Atomic Scientists* hammers home the point with two quotations from a "policy statement" issued by the Air Force Association (a purely nongovernmental association of military men, active and retired, who are interested in the status of U.S. air power):

> Freedom must bury Communism or be buried by Communism. Complete eradication of the Soviet system must be our national goal, our obligation to all free people, our promise of hope to all who are not free.

> We are determined to back our words with action even at the risk of war. We seek not merely to preserve our freedoms but to extend them. . . . Soviet aims are both evil and implacable. The people are willing to work toward, and fight for if necessary, the elimination of Communism from the world scene. Let the issue be joined.

Let the issue be joined, indeed! We might as well write a death warrant for civilization as to conclude the issues of the cold war with the battle cry of the Air Force Association, "The people are willing to work toward, *and fight for if necessary*, the elimination of Communism from the world scene."

The fundamentalist far rightists are generally somewhat more guarded in their declarations of war than are the Air Force Association, Loyd Wright, and their fellow cold warriors. All the same, in terms of their practical consequences, fundamentalist proposals are not markedly different from the more explicit pronouncements on the radical right. Take, for instance, this pronouncement from a tract published by one "Christian":

> Once we face the reality that this is a struggle to the death between the forces of Christianity, and Communism, between Jesus and the devil, between heaven and hell, then we will appreciate our church, our Bible, and our God . . . *as never before* [emphasis in original].

The tract goes on to plead, "May God's Holy Spirit move you to act *now*. It is nearing the midnight hour. The time is five minutes to twelve and the hands of the clock *are moving fast!*"

"Act *now*," says the tract. It does not specify how, but the inference is plain. It is "a struggle to the death." Hence, death for the Communists! Give those bloody merchants of the devil what they deserve. We will be the executioners.

Such a position might once have been tenable for Christians. Jesus spoke of bringing a sword into the world. St. Augustine counseled men to take up arms in a "just war" against evil. (Even so, he called for good will toward an aggressor and did not approve of killing others in order to save one's own life, unless one happened to be a soldier charged with defending the public good.)

Like St. Augustine, Martin Luther regarded war as a sometimes necessary means to peace—a minor misfortune designed to prevent a major one. The sword, Luther believed, could be the civil expression of the wrath of God himself.

Similarly, John Calvin believed that just as the civil magistrate was required to put down rebellion and to suppress crime within his jurisdiction, so also was he required to defend the lives of those committed to his guardianship. The Holy Spirit, in more than one passage of scripture, had declared such behavior to be lawful, said Calvin.

There are other currents in the great river of Christian tradition, of course. The Society of Friends, the Church of the

Brethren, and other groups have radicalized Jesus' beatitude, "Blessed are the peacemakers, for they shall be called sons of God," and have sought to prove the practicability of his injunctions to turn the other cheek and to love one's enemies.

In the main, it is fair to say, however, that just and righteous wars have had a secure place in the thinking of the pivotal figures in the history of Christianity.

The invention of thermonuclear weapons, together with the development of highly sophisticated delivery vehicles, has changed all that. There can be no successful just war when the just turn out to be as dead as the unjust. Or, to put it another way, evil cannot be eradicated when goodness, of necessity, is destroyed along with evil. That is the conclusion of politicians and theologians alike. We must find peaceful solutions to the evils of the modern world. We must learn to contain aggression by means other than war.

The Christian fright peddlers have refused to accept the inevitabilities of the present. They still live in the centuries of the Crusades, believing that social problems may be wiped out with a war. So far as they are concerned, war, in a divided world, is inevitable and they make no apologies for their position. As Carl McIntire put it in a June 1963 letter to his radio audience:

> It is absolutely impossible to have any accommodation with Communism. Moreover, conflict is absolutely inevitable. The two worlds, one of brutality, godlessness, materialism, socialism, *cannot possibly be in peace* with a world of freedom, individualism, where men profess their faith in the living God [emphasis supplied].

Billy James Hargis, as we have seen (Chapter IV), talks about "Christ the Destroyer," reducing the heroic figure of Jesus of Nazareth to one more weapon in the cold-war arsenal of the West. Christ will destroy Communism, believes Dr. Hargis, through the Christian soldiers of America.

Fred Schwarz disclaims any intent to go to war. Cognizant of the destructive potentialities of modern warfare, Schwarz refuses to tell the U. S. State Department what to do in relation to Communism when it comes to the deployment of our nuclear forces. But when he speaks of "The Christian Answer to Communism" he has this to say:

> Christians! to arms. The enemy is at the gate. Buckle on the armour of the Christian and forth to the battle. With education, evangelism, and dedication let us smite the Communist foe and if necessary give our lives in this noble Cause. With courageous yet humble hearts, intelligent yet prayerful minds and dedicated indomitable wills we cry, "We shall not yield! Lift high the bloodstained banner of the Cross and on to Victory."

An elemental Christian injunction has been displaced. Jesus' admonition to "Love your enemies," has been changed to read, "Love your enemies unless they are Communists, and then smite them with all your might." The "bloodstained banner of the Cross" will be lifted high in the name of Christian righteousness, of course, fully symbolic of the ultra-rightists' image of Christian virtue.

POLITICAL NIHILISM AND THE
RIGHT-WING WARRIORS

William S. White is in all likelihood right when, in speaking of the far right in general, he observes, "What is developing here is a political nihilism far more complex and sophisticated than any we have known in my lifetime."

Political nihilism. The words are those of a conservative. They are no part of an idle attack from a disgruntled liberal. Political nihilism *is* the inevitable outcome of the right-wing extremist's position. And the end of nihilism in the second half of the twentieth century is the final nothing made possible by the age of the atom—the destruction of practically everything we hold to be worthful on this planet.

White has also observed that the full anger of the right-wing extremist is seldom directed against race, or religion, or social ills, *as such*, but is hurled against the very world itself.

What do you do with an anger that encompasses the whole world? You propose total destruction. The one "positive" plank in the right-wing platform is the means for destruction. The arms budget should be increased. Our preparedness for war should be stepped up. We should drop our "no win policy" and move on to victory—a victory that would mean death for most of us, including the nihilists themselves. That is the logical outcome of the foreign-policy position taken by the death makers.

What are the immediate implications of such a position? First, there is the matter of our national self-image. Historically, the American people have stood for a policy of self-determination for all nations. National sovereignty, we have maintained, is to be respected even though we may differ radically with the objectives, the philosophy, or the governmental structure of other nations. We have been willing to go to war, but only in the face of clear-cut aggression. As Robert Strausz-Hupe (who is no ranting liberal) put it in A *Forward Strategy For America*, "We reject the strategy of preventive war. The unacceptability of preventive war is one of the axioms on which rests the moral superiority of democratic societies. We reject the assumption that if we do not strike the communists first they will one day destroy us."

That, as I say, is the historic American position. It is also the present policy of our State Department. We may believe that we should counter Soviet propaganda with American information and that we should compete vigorously with the U.S.S.R. (and increasingly with Communist China) in terms of human resources and technology in the have-not nations. But we do not believe in preventive war. Were we to repudiate our ethical heritage in this domain, were we to speak seriously of a war of liberation—of a just or preventive war to save freedom—we would, of necessity, sacrifice the very principles we wish to defend.

The danger is that the fulminations of the new American ultras may be taken seriously, and that in a time of tension— another Cuba, another Berlin crisis—we will consider the possibility of striking first. The possibility is not so remote as it may seem. A change in administration, a reform in the Pentagon, giving the military professionals extraconstitutional authority to act without regard for civilian authority, an unusually aggressive gesture on the part of the Soviets—each could spark the attack that would begin the end.

The moral implications are incalculable. Not only are the principal protagonists involved. The nonnuclear powers would suffer as well. Jainists in Tibet, Indians in Peru, bushmen in Australia would all pay for our folly. The peoples spared the destruction of direct attack would soon suffer the effects of lethal radiation from fallout, the genetic consequences of drifting clouds of radioactive dust.

The wipe-em-out contingent of the far right has little regard, however, for any ethical considerations beyond those involved in the simple preservation of the United States. That their objective is itself unattainable in a thermonuclear war is secondary to the main consideration—the elemental notion that man today is, more than ever, responsible for man. To use our nuclear arms irresponsibly—whether by self-conscious calculation, or as a consequence of fast-paced events—means death.

"The history of man is a graveyard of great cultures that came to catastrophic ends because of their incapacity for planned, rational, voluntary reaction to challenge," says the psychiatrist Erich Fromm.[1] The death makers demonstrate

[1] See Erich Fromm, *May Man Prevail?* (Garden City: Doubleday & Company, Inc., 1961) for a lucid exposition of the psychology of the arms race.

daily their incapacity for dealing with the realities of the nuclear age. Their medieval solutions can only demonstrate the truth of Fromm's observation. History *is* a graveyard of civilizations which were marked for death by their own incapacities for coping with the changing demands of reality. We have only to listen to the advice of the death makers in order to add the American dream to the list of deceased cultures.

THE *DEATH OF EARTH*— ETHICS BEYOND MERE PRUDENCE

The most uncompromising threat from the Christian fright peddlers is the ultimate consequence of their nihilism: the end of civilization as we know it, at best; the death of earth, at worst. (U.S. military strategists summarize the latter possibility with the initials DOE.)

Attacks on civil rights and civil liberties pose radical threats to the way of freedom, but a foreign policy based on the supposition that we must make war on alien cultures can only end in catastrophe. For the first time in history we are forced to take the words of Jesus seriously:

Love your enemies, bless them that curse you, do good to them that hate you, and pray for them which despitefully use you, and persecute you.

Purely prudential ethics can no longer suffice in international relations. We may, at the present moment, be forced to avert aggression with a shield of nuclear power, but we must recognize the fact that that power cannot be used in any "preventive war." While we may not yet be capable of mustering any love for our enemies we must at least learn to live with them.

Before us lie new moral imperatives. War must be replaced as an instrument of international policy by humane approaches. We must learn to innovate, to create, to build new institutions, to construct the machinery for assuring peace among nations.

The western democracies wrestle today with a determined enemy. Let no man mistake the fact. In countering that antagonist we must find ways to speak for freedom and for man. The nations may yet be united. Swords may yet be hammered into plowshares. But it will require unparalleled effort on our part, based on the conviction that the age of warfare is past forever. The ancient phrase, "Love your enemies," comes close to expressing the moral imperative of our era.

9 Sources of the Radical Right

"PATRIOTISM IS THE last refuge of a scoundrel," said England's great Doctor Johnson. It took Ambrose Bierce, an American, to disagree with any telling effect. Patriotism, said Bierce, is not the last resort of the scoundrel. It is the first.

Unfortunately, Bierce was right. Patriotism, like religion and humanitarian idealism, is a ready refuge for hucksters, knaves and professional malcontents. Who would question the motives of a patriot? Who would suggest that his honored place might be sullied by thoughts of personal gain, by a need for power or for glory? The place of the patriot is a post of honor. If he is attacked, so much the worse for the attackers. Have not patriots always suffered for their cause? Have they not always been the object of scorn from the enemies of the state?

The patriot, above all, is a man with a holy cause that invests his life with a meaning, his every action with a purpose. His cause is to him life, energy, wholeness, destiny—a substitute for an affirmative image of himself.

"The less justified a man is in claiming excellence for his own self," says Eric Hoffer, "the more ready is he to claim all excellence for his nation, his religion, his race or his holy cause." Hoffer elaborates on his observation:

> When our individual interests and prospects do not seem worth living for, we are in desperate need of something apart from us to live for. . . . The embracing of a substitute will necessarily be passionate and extreme. We can have qualified confidence in ourselves, but the faith we have

in our nation, religion, race or holy cause, has to be ex-
travagant and uncompromising. A substitute embraced in
moderation cannot supplant and efface the self we want to
forget. We cannot be sure that we have something worth
living for unless we are ready to die for it.[1]

The patriot is always ready to die and, in a thermonuclear
age, to have the rest of us go with him. That is the nature of
his unqualified commitment, which, in theological language,
is pure idolatry—the raising of a worldly cause to the level of
ultimacy.

Perhaps I should say *pseudopatriot*. For the true patriot's
belief is another matter. His is a qualified commitment that
takes into account the finiteness of this world, its institutions
and its movements. His loyalty to his cause is qualified by
his knowledge that there are other causes, some of which may
also be just, and by his appreciation for the fact that the
earth is not the place of absolutes. He is more concerned
with making right the wrongs of his nation than with defending its righteousness. The true patriot sees the promotion of
his cause as clearly secondary to the cultivation of justice,
liberty and the cause of man.

Today's radical rightist is, pre-eminently, a pseudopatriot.
He is the man who is proud to fly the American flag on any
occasion, but quick to attack the civil liberties that that flag
stands for. He is the man in the parade who drives the sharp
foreign car with a placard reading "Buy American," the man
who believes in his country right or wrong, but has no time
for righting its wrongs. His patriotism is his substitute for
thinking about racial injustice in Birmingham; it is his placebo
for easing the pain his conscience might otherwise give him
over the economic exploitation of his neighbor in South America; it is his ready substitute for pondering the antagonisms
of the cold war. He has only to recite, "The only *ism* for me

[1] See Eric Hoffer, *The True Believer* (New York: Mentor Books, 1951)
for a thoughtful analysis of the psychology of the man with a cause and the
movements he may join, or inspire.

is Americanism," in order to feel exonerated from thinking about humanitarianism or altruism.

The first source of the radical right, then, is an escape from selfhood on the part of the individual who engages in a welter of activities in order to conceal from himself the poverty of his personal identity. In that, he is like his extremist counterparts everywhere, regardless of their labels.

The pseudopatriot of today is also a pseudoconservative. The movement to which he belongs is profoundly distrustful of that genuine conservatism which stands for an endorsement of the present order, believes in the viability of American institutions, and yet seeks to bring the harsh injustices of the present order closer to the ideals of the past. As the Columbia University historian Richard Hofstadter put it in a brilliant essay in the anthology *The Radical Right*:

> [The pseudo-conservatives] have little in common with the temperate and compromising spirit of true conservatism in the classical sense of the word. . . . Their political reactions express rather a profound if largely unconscious hatred of our society and its ways—a hatred which one would hesitate to impute to them if one did not have suggestive clinical evidence.[2]

That says something about the identity of the man on the radical right; it also raises the question, *How did he get that way?*

THE SOURCES: SOCIAL AND PSYCHOLOGICAL

The right-wing extremist begins, of course, with his reactions to the world of today. And in that there is a high component of frustration. The man on the far right, like his

[2] Daniel Bell, ed., *The Radical Right* (Garden City: Doubleday & Company, Inc., 1963), p. 64.

contemporaries of more moderate temperament, has seen
Stalinist Russia destroy the exceedingly brief euphoria that
came with peace at the end of World War II. He has heard
his country called "warmongering" and "imperialist" in an
uncompromising barrage of propaganda. He has watched as
one Soviet neighbor after another has turned to Communism
and begun to repeat its slogans. He knows, at least vaguely, of
peasants starved in Russia and in China; he is aware of the
barbed-wire fences that have encircled camps for political
troublemakers in both nations. He remembers that the
U.S.S.R. put the first satellite into orbit and knows of the
accomplishments of Soviet technology. Although he has not
come to terms with the facts of thermonuclear warfare, he
may be at least faintly conscious of the fact that the Soviet
Union could reduce most of the United States, or any other
nation, to rubble in a matter of minutes.

The man on the far right also knows that most of the
people in the world are poverty-stricken. And he is aware that
heretofore primitive nations are moving into the world of commerce, that enslaved peoples are refusing to continue as less
than free.

Add to his disquiet over the world scene concern over the
crises of a Little Rock and a Birmingham, the nagging knowledge that chronic unemployment is not getting any better,
the certainty that a sizable portion of the American population is poorly housed, badly fed and scarcely clothed, and the
fact that the economy is still subject to recessions and probably depressions as well—add all that to the unrest of the
modern American, and he has reason enough to seek a quick
solution to his problems.

The right-wing extremist also has had his unique frustrations not shared by all Americans. He, or his conservative
forebears, were bitterly opposed to the New Deal. Franklin
Delano Roosevelt was viewed as something of a personification
of the excesses of the modern nation state. Any restriction of

individual freedom, any increase of governmental responsibility was looked on as the work of *that man*.

The conservatives held no hope for reform during the Truman administration, but when a Republican was elected many felt that the time to overturn the New Deal had come. The Eisenhower administration accommodated itself to the TVA, REA, Social Security and all the rest, of course, and when it became clear that there was little or no interest in rolling back the New Deal, frustrations mounted. Their hopes trampled on, the unadjusted conservatives turned on the President and his advisers. Calling them *liberals* was not enough. The only word strong enough was *Communists*—or, when niceties were to be observed, *Communist-controlled*. The neighbors, mental-health movements, and the churches were next. The modern world had to go.

The conservative had become the ultraconservative, a displaced person in terms of time, if not geography. He built for himself an image of how things must have been before FDR and stuck to it tenaciously. If only, he told himself, the world of nineteenth-century *laissez-faire* could be restored, stability and individual autonomy would be assured. In time, he began to believe his myth. His frustrations with the world rose in direct proportion to his inability to make it return to his idea of how things once had been.

The man on the radical right has turned out to be something like the businessman who spends a day of intense frustration at the office and comes home to kick the cat. The problems that make the radical rightist anxious cannot be got at—at least not directly—but the neighbors can. Calling neighbors Communists or Comsymps, like kicking the cat, helps to relieve the tension. Blaming international and domestic trouble on the one great evil, *Communism*, converts a diffuse and ill-defined anxiety into a concrete fear.

Anxieties are pernicious and cannot be wrestled with directly. But fears are concrete and invite immediate action, especially if they can be particularized in the person of a friend or neighbor, the man who was elected to Congress last year, or the President in Washington.

That does not say, of course, why one man displaces his anxiety by attacking Communists in every walk of life and another meets his feeling more constructively. What makes the right-wing extremist react as he does? What sort of man is he? What, aside from his extremist stance, sets him apart from his fellows?

Seymour Martin Lipset, Professor of Sociology at the University of California, has some suggestions. He first distinguishes between class politics and status politics. The former develops in times of unemployment or depression, the latter in times of prosperity. Either may be extremist in character.

Those persons most receptive to status-oriented appeals, says Lipset, are of two types: first, there are those who have recently improved their economic position and feel apprehensive about their acceptance by those who already hold status; second, there are those who have long possessed social status, but feel that it is threatened by rapid social change, or by the claims to status made by persons of previously lower status. In other words, those on the way up the status ladder meet those on the way down, or in danger of having to move down. The two groups coalesce and search for scapegoats that can serve as symbols of the status threat they feel.[3]

The pattern, presumably, would hold for the status-anxious from the Know-Nothings through the Ku Klux Klan, and from the followers of McCarthy to the members of the right-wing extremist groups in the post-McCarthy era. In times of prosperity, status frustrations are pooled in an organizational

[3] Lipset's analysis of class politics and status politics as they pertain to the radical right, a term which he invented, incidentally, may be found in the Doubleday anthology cited above, pp. 259 ff.

miasma; the anxieties of its members are then channeled into unqualified hostility toward a common scapegoat.

Richard Hofstadter says much the same thing from the perspective of the historian:

> Paradoxically the intense status concerns of present-day politics are shared by two types of persons who arrive at them, in a sense, from opposite directions. The first are found among some types of old-family, Anglo-Saxon Protestants, and the second are found among many types of immigrant families, most notably among the Germans and Irish, who are very frequently Catholic.
>
> The Anglo-Saxons are most disposed toward pseudo-conservatism when they are losing caste, the immigrants when they are gaining.[4]

The patriotic society serves chiefly as a means for shoring up the pseudoconservative's feelings about his nationality. The first, second, or even third or fourth generation immigrant may still not be fully convinced that he is an American. The "son" or "daughter" of someone who fought in the Revolutionary War may find the family fortune gone, the family name forgotten, personal prestige in doubt. The common meeting ground for the two types of persons may be the local patriotic society.

The problem is uniquely American. It is difficult to imagine an organization to promote Englishism in England, Germanism in Germany, Frenchism in France. The very names stick in the throat. But Americanism? That's different. The creed—and let us acknowledge the fact that it *is* a creed—fulfills a deeply felt need. *Americanism* confirms the ego undermined by doubts about the person's national heritage.

If you doubt this, just question the Americanism of the pseudopatriot. If your questions register, his rising blood pressure will tell you more plainly than his words that his ego is at stake.

[4] *Ibid.*, pp. 71 ff.

There is also a sense in which the superpatriot of the sixties has replaced the hatreds of an earlier era with a more sophisticated stock of antagonisms. It has become disreputable, for the most part, to be anti-Semitic, especially in public. Anti-Catholicism may enliven a conversation, but few regard it as a means for achieving new regard among friends. If one is anti-Negro he must be careful about the company he keeps when expressing his sentiments. Not everyone will understand.

With anti-Communism the situation is otherwise. The ego mileage to be gotten out of anti-Communism is not likely to be impaired by disapproving glances from friends and relatives. The opportunities for self-advertisement are limited only by the number of competing anti-Communists. Moreover, the chance to pin the Communist label on an old-line American—a Harvard graduate, an Eastern Anglo-Saxon member of the Yankee aristocracy—has great potential for ego enhancement. When it comes to feeling superior you can't do much better.

Anti-Communism, which so often turns out to be a substitute label for antiliberalism or anti-intellectualism, has become an acceptable avenue for running down the world. As Hofstadter has observed, Americans are always trying to raise their standard of living; the same effort is now being applied to the standard of hating. The racial arrogance of the Ku Klux Klan has been displaced by the ideological bitterness of the John Birch Society. Hatred for race has been displaced by hatred for ideas. In either case, human beings are the recipients of the hatred. And Negroes, or members of any other minority group, may turn out to be alleged Communists and therefore proper objects for hate.[5]

---

[5] For an example of the racist overtones characteristic of at least some right-wing organizations see the September 1963 issue of the *Bulletin* of the John Birch Society. The entire civil rights movement is reduced to the level of a Communist plot in the following words, ". . . the Communists are running the whole show, for their own purposes, and exactly in accordance with the plans they have laid out, announced, and perfected since this racial agitation in the United States first became a part of Communist strategy."

Since Communists cannot be identified by their physical appearance, it is open season on all those who disagree—Socialists, Democrats and moderate Republicans alike. To hear those on the far right talk, one would think that the worst kind of *Communist* is a moderate Republican. For the members of the John Birch Society, anti-Communism means unrelenting opposition to such notorious "Reds" as Earl Warren and such hateful conspiracies as the United Nations and UNICEF. The typical Bircher would prefer to hand a copy of his anti-U.N. propaganda to a child collecting for UNICEF on Halloween than do something about starving children. There is very little chance for ego enhancement in the latter activity.[6]

Although generalizations about status politics and anxieties over national identity apply broadly to the right wing in general, the John Birch Society represents something of a special case. Its members' politics are identified by Hofstadter simply as "projective politics." Such politics, he observes, involve "the projection of interests and concerns, not only largely private but essentially pathological, into the public scene."

There is much truth in the observation, I believe. Private, personal, individual concerns *may* be projected onto the screen of public affairs. To the extent that the projections represent warped, inadequate, distorted expressions of true selfhood, they will be pathological interpretations of the public life. To Eric Hoffer's observation that the less a man is justified in claiming excellence for himself the more he will claim it for his cause, must be added another: *To the extent that the individual lacks personal integration, the tumult of his inner psychic life will be projected into the public scene.*

---

[6] I have invented no hypothetical incident for the sake of a polemic. The October 1963 issue of the *Bulletin* of the John Birch Society devoted a full paragraph to advising members on how to handle children collecting for UNICEF. In brief, it consisted of telling the Bircher to give the child a piece of candy and an anti-U.N. postcard or a reprint of Representative James Utt's attack on UNESCO and UNICEF.

The nearly universal horror of the mental-health movements (as Communist-dominated) on the part of right-wing extremists is a convincing confirmation of the truth of the generalization.

The social factors—tensions about international and domestic affairs, status anxiety, uncertainty about national identity, and the like—constitute the context from which the individual speaks. His inner psychological conflicts give form to his religiopolitical theories and behavior.

THE FUNDAMENTALIST REVOLT

As Seymour Martin Lipset observes in his book on the social bases of politics, *Political Man*, ". . . extremist religion is a product of the same social forces that sustain authoritarian political attitudes." If political and religious extremism often coexist in the same human being, it is only because the social forces that give rise to the one also produce the other. So too with the psychological aspects of extremism. The man whose religion is primarily a projection of his inner conflicts finds it easy to believe that the White House is occupied by Communists.

The sources of the radical right within American Protestantism are particularly instructive; few movements can tell us more about extremism on the right than what has been called "the fundamentalist revolt against modernity." David Riesman suggests that, in some instances, the fundamentalist revolt may be exceedingly simple. Speaking of the fundamentalist businessman, Riesman observes, "Activist lay leaders in fundamentalist churches sometimes have an opportunity to conduct their church work with a single-minded, businesslike efficiency and pep from which they are restrained in the conduct of business itself. . . ." In the business world there are the labor unions, the intermittent demands and rewards of a free market, government officials to deal with, and so on—all of which play a restraining part in the business life of the activist. Those restraints are removed in his religious and political pursuits. Suddenly, he is free to take part in what Riesman calls the "seemingly dangerous vicissitudes reminiscent on a higher income and educational level of Ku Klux Klan attractions."

To Riesman's insights must, of course, be added the fact that the far right fundamentalist, like his fellow right-wing extremists, resents the drift of world affairs. He too feels a fever-pitch anxiety over successive domestic crises. He shares with his political brothers on the right the creed of Americanism and maintains an unqualified confidence in the gospel of free enterprise. As a crusading member of the Americanist fraternity, the far-right fundamentalist is typically puzzled, if not perplexed, by fellow rightists who turn out to be theologically liberal. He is also astonished, and sometimes incensed, by fundamentalist friends who are neither right wing nor conservative in their political outlook; and he is put off by those who eschew politics altogether, turning to otherworldliness for their salvation.

Right-wing fundamentalism accounts, in large part, for the shaping of "status politics" as outlined by Lipset. In the post World War I era the typical fundamentalist found himself carried along on a temporary economic upsurge, but the depression exiled him from public discussion. In those days it was persons whose commitment was to class politics who were doing the talking. The fundamentalist's notions of frugality and his theories of salvation failed to speak to the man who had not only lost his income and his status, but might conceivably starve before he could discover a way to restore them.

The post World War II era tells a different story. As David Danzig, who has more to say than most men about fundamentalism and the ultra-right, observes, ". . . the truth is that fundamentalism is a growing socioreligious force in [present-day] America."

Writing for the American Jewish Committee journal *Commentary*, Danzig goes on to observe, "With the continuing world crisis, fundamentalism is finding a new political relevance for its doctrines and an arena in which it can exert its growing influence."

Much of the growing fundamentalist strength today follows from increased affluence. Witness Danzig's observation:

> . . . the social base of fundamentalism has shifted markedly, although few political writers have apparently noticed the shift. Its constituency is no longer mainly made up of sharecroppers and poorly educated villagers. Many fundamentalist churches are modern and imposing, financed by wealthy oilmen from Texas and Oklahoma and prosperous farmers in the wheat and corn belts.

In other words, most of the supporters of the fundamentalist right wing are to be found among the newer, but anxious, arrivals on the middle-class scene. Like the European immigrant of a century ago, they have moved up the socioeconomic ladder and brought their religion with them. Their religion is now shaping their social identity. Doctrinal precepts are applied with rigor. The greater the status shift, the deeper the anxiety and the more compelling the application of doctrine.

In application, the fundamentalist world view is not complex. Danzig has summarized it admirably and linked it to its political uses:

> . . . the fundamentalist's apocalyptic conception of the world as strictly divided into the saved and the damned, the forces of good and the forces of evil, has readily lent itself to reactionary political uses. Fundamentalism today supports a superpatriotic Americanism; the conflict with Com-

munism is not one of power blocs, but of faiths, part of the unending struggle between God and the devil. The danger of Communism, therefore, is from within—from the corrosion of faith by insidious doctrines. That is to say, by "collectivism"—the fundamentalist's secular counterpart of atheism.

The root of the appeal, says Danzig, is to be found in "nativist nationalism."

I believe that Danzig's thesis is very nearly correct; I would want only to add that there is more to the appeal than "nativist nationalism." Or, to put it another way, "nativist nationalism" has its own explanation, largely in terms of psychological considerations.

Doctrine, for the fundamentalist, lives a far livelier life than for the more emancipated—or perhaps, moribund—Christian. On an effective application of doctrine depends the whole conceptual framework of the fundamentalist, his ability to interpret reality, his image of himself. Any threat to his world view is therefore regarded as demonic—the work of the devil, calculated to overthrow his understanding of himself.

He is right about that, of course, and we should not be surprised when he marshals his psychic energies against an invader. He would have to revise his entire way of thinking about the world in order to avoid responding to the demands of reality with an attack. Such an option is not ordinarily available to the anxious man.

The fundamentalist's nationalism, though rooted in American soil, is close to being a self-image projected onto a screen of diffused time. I say "diffused" because the fundamentalist view of history demands little rigor in definition. Little heed is paid to historical sequence or fact. The Founding Fathers all become Bible-believing Christians and Alger Hiss becomes the framer of the United Nations Charter.

Given this qualification, in terms of the roots of "nativist nationalism," I think that Danzig is talking sense. He runs into major difficulty when he begins applying his theory to cases, however. He errs by identifying Welch with the fundamentalist tradition and calls the Rev. James Fifield of Los Angeles both a fundamentalist and a leader in the nativist movement. Fifield *may* be a leader, but he is most certainly not a fundamentalist.

Danzig mentions Schwarz and Hargis in the same breath, as though they both stood for Christian fundamentalism as he defines it, when, in fact, Schwarz has taken no position on one of the essentials of fundamentalist belief as listed by Danzig—the premillennial return of Christ. More important still, Schwarz's fundamentalism is an altogether covert affair, always in second place to the anti-Communist cause. Hargis' fundamentalism is overt and militant. Schwarz's nationalism is scarcely nativist, even though his hearers' response probably is. There is no question about the nativist character of Hargis' Christ-centered Americanism. And so on.

The point I want to make is not that Danzig's thesis is mistaken because it breaks down when he attempts to apply it to particulars, but rather that it needs refinement. It applies, with qualifications, to the Schwarz-Hargis-McIntire syndrome.

Elsewhere, Danzig makes another point, and it is worth our consideration. We are mistaken, he says, if we think that the fundamentalist minority has developed anti-Communism in order to win religious popularity contests. Anti-Communism, he observes, has always been a part of the fundamentalist mentality. It happens that the viewpoint was largely irrelevant until the present juncture in world affairs; suddenly, the perspective is relevant, and although it may represent a false alternative in our search for an answer to the challenge of Communism, it is still an alternative. We cannot dismiss it with a facile claim that it represents a public-relations ploy. It is more than that.

It would be interesting to examine the career of Billy Hargis to see if he were preaching anti-Communism in the early 1940s. Schwarz's dedication to anti-Communism seems to be a matter of record, of course, and Carl McIntire has merely changed the priority of threats. Communism has not always been at the head of the list for him, but it has been on the list.

The same might be said for any number of fundamentalists on the far right. The emergence of the fundamentalist minority is no capricious phenomenon, fated to wither with the next drift in international affairs. It is an integral part of our culture, and we shall have to learn to live with it.

The great pity is that the emergence of any minority, fundamentalist or otherwise, is generally accompanied by a good deal of defensive maneuvering on the part of the group concerned. With fundamentalism, the result has been the proclamation of its private virtues in stark opposition to other, usually dominant, cultural values. The assertion of values has been absolute. So also has been the nonfundamentalist's denial of those values. We have thus lost the opportunity to share in whatever insights the fundamentalist minority might develop, were it permitted to get off the defensive. By treating the group as one more among the "undesirables" we have abandoned whatever latent capacity for creative genius it may have.

THE CONVENTIONAL CHRISTIAN ULTRAS

Data on the radical rightists within the mainstream of Christian orthodoxy is harder to come by. Generalizations are more difficult to make. But, in terms of what must be primarily impressionistic judgments, the right-wing Episcopalian, Presbyterian, Lutheran, or Methodist is likely to be: 1) a person with at least a high-school and probably some college education, 2) an individual whose exposure to the traditions and doctrines of his church has been brief or nonexistent, 3) a person with more than a normal quotient of hostility toward those who seek to transform the world through social reforms, and 4) an individual with a strong need for some source of authority apart from himself.

In addition, the radical rightist who sits in the pews of the conventional Protestant church is at least as likely as his fundamentalist friends to feel gravely anxious over international and domestic affairs. He too may suffer from status anxiety and may attempt to achieve some sense of self-naturalization by proclaiming his Americanism.

What sets him apart from the Biblical fundamentalist? His education, for the most part. He has learned too much to scoff at the theory of evolution; he cherishes no stereotype of the Communist college professor. He may believe in free enterprise, but he does not make a creed of it or attempt to baptize it with verses from the holy scriptures.

For all that, this Christian on the far right is often wholly ignorant of the history of his own church. (The fact does not stop him from arguing vigorously for his favorite innovation and claiming history as his defender, however.)

Judging by reports from denominational officials, this breed of far-right Christian may be one of the first examples of a type we have been predicting would show up for some time now. For as long as most of us can remember, educators have been telling us that our increasingly segmented education would someday produce partial individuals—engineers who would know no history, chemists who would know no political science, historians who would know nothing of physics, linguists who would be ignorant of technology. Today, we are surprised when chemical engineers speak *ex cathedra* on political questions with all the wisdom of first-day kindergarten students. We are shocked when men with college educations in mathematics fabricate simplistic historical myths.

We should not, I submit, continue to be surprised. The ignorance that makes it possible to believe that the United Nations is a subtle device for imposing a Soviet-controlled police force on the American people, or that John Foster Dulles was a Communist, is no less ignorance because the believer of the myth happens to hold a B.S. in engineering. He is a victim of the arrested development built into our educational system. We have provided for political and religious illiterates, who are otherwise well-educated—at least within the limits of their specialization.

Anxiety over this knowledge gap comes close to being a defining characteristic of the radical right. It is difficult to summarize its significance, but one leader on the far right, speaking to a select audience made up of those most dedicated to the cause, once stated it as well as anyone: "We believe in plain freedom of enterprise, simple truths we can understand. We believe in God and we say so. But no—*they* don't. And something is wrong with us. We don't sit around and apologize because we aren't intellectually superior to them." He then went on to attack what he called "latent socialists."

THE SECURITY-CONSCIOUS

One final item must be added to our review of the sources of the radical right—the effect on the American public of security measures taken by nearly all levels of government, government agencies, and those industries which work under government contracts. Several million Americans are affected, directly or indirectly, by the loyalty programs instituted since the beginning of the cold war. The schoolteacher, the government worker, the engineer who works for a defense industry—all are scrutinized in terms of their loyalty. No fewer than six million persons are involved in the federal loyalty program alone.[7]

It would be surprising if it were otherwise. Soviet armaments had to be taken seriously from the beginning of the cold war. Sabotage, espionage and the pirating of military secrets have been valid concerns. Our industrial security program was the direct outcome of the arms race.

Whether security precautions taken in the nondefense sectors of government, or loyalty programs instituted in public-school and higher education may be similarly justified is another question. In any case, the security program was a defensive reaction toward what we saw plainly as potential aggression.

From the beginning, abuses of the loyalty program were given great publicity. Senator McCarthy's name was soon known to every American. Instances of employee dismissals over security questions, from Oppenheimer to local engineering draftsmen, generally made headlines. Their vindication, if it was secured—and it sometimes was, years later—was secreted away in the back pages.

Moreover, it soon became evident that there was more to the loyalty program than the maintenance of national security. Political motivation entered in. The investigative powers of Congress were used to harry dissenters from within the administration itself to heretical college professors at Swashbuckle U. Inquisitorial methods were used by Senate and House committees alike. Legitimate investigative powers were then cited as the rationalization for the public exposure of political adversaries.

[7] The figure is that cited by Gerard Piel, publisher of *Scientific American*. For a thoughtful appraisal of our security system and its impact on our national well-being see Gerard Piel, *Science in the Cause of Man* (New York: Alfred A. Knopf, 1961), pp. 113–133.

What has been the over-all effect of our loyalty program? Herbert Hyman, Professor of Sociology at Columbia, has put it well:

When millions of individuals, located everywhere, are brought under official scrutiny as possible security risks, it validates the belief that everyone ought to be regarded with suspicion, and it legitimates the idea of investigation itself, whether performed by professional officials or by amateurs.[8]

Although the loyalty program of the sixties is happily no longer the program of the fifties, some of the abuses persist. The public remains apprehensive, particularly in the field of industrial security, despite the fact that executive orders and Supreme Court decisions have clarified the rights of employees. The evidence suggests that the security program functions reasonably well in the defense industries today; there is little basis, in terms of the facts, for the typical employee to fear a witch-hunt. All the same, he is cautious. The past, he knows, is never wholly past. It is better, he maintains, to err on the side of timidity than of boldness. One never knows when the spirit of McCarthy may be exhumed.

Into this arena of trepidation steps the right-wing radical. His strength is built on the fears of the security-conscious, who silently give him a right denied to him by the Constitution—to play the inquisitor. He subjects the religion and the politics of his fellow citizens to relentless scrutiny. Everything must fit into his twofold scheme of the universe. A man, a viewpoint, or an activity is either good or it is evil. Your religion and politics—and mine—are neatly classified. If you disagree with him you are clearly on the side of Satan.

[8] The quotation is from Professor Hyman's contribution to *The Radical Right*, entitled "England and America: Climates of Tolerance and Intolerance," p. 246.

THE FEELINGS OF AN EXTREMIST

How does it feel to be a member of the radical right? It is difficult to say from the vantage point of one outside of the movement. But I am certain that I will never forget the feeling communicated to me in a conversation I once had with an employee of a Southern California business which was then engaged in a full-scale anti-Communist campaign. Many of the company's employees spent numerous hours traveling the Southern California freeways to show films, give lectures and distribute literature to a great variety of community organizations.

I met this particular employee one evening after a showing of the film "Operation Abolition." We talked for some time, and in the course of our conversation he told me something about himself—far more, I suspect, than he intended to convey. What he said moved me deeply, so deeply, in fact, that I wrote it down. Speaking of Communism in the United States, he said, "The American public is so uninformed. If you know anything at all, you feel like a wizard. It's a tremendous ego builder."

That confession, if it may be called a confession, is a rather touching thing, isn't it? A human personality wanting to be someone, something—anyone, anything at all. But to be real, to have an ego, a sense of purpose.

Think of how it must feel to believe, as this young man did, that the civilization we live in will shortly be taken over by the aggressive armies of a ruthless, inhuman state—to believe that all of us, every last one of us, will become subject slaves alike. Think of how it must feel deep inside to believe that a Communist master plan of conspiracy is even now being executed and that the western nations are being taken over, willingly relinquishing their freedoms, simply because they are blind to what is happening.

The fear that follows from such beliefs must be altogether compelling. At least I am inclined to think of it that way.

The moment one identifies with anxieties of such magnitude it is no longer difficult to imagine why the extremist strikes out at reality as he does. He must, you see. He has been hurt by the world—badly hurt. And he is striking back. A perfectly understandable thing. He wants to repudiate the more sinister aspects of his image of reality. In this there is an overwhelming urgency.

Anti-Communism may serve as the expression of the extremist's sense of urgency, but it is not the urgency. Let us be clear about that. Extremist attacks stem not from the compelling fact of anti-Communism. No *anti*, taken by itself, can shake a person to the depths of his being. The overwhelming urgency felt by the extremist is at once the product of the social forces that shaped him, and the fruit of the psychological patterns that make him vulnerable to images of impending disaster. The overwhelming threat may be to his image of himself as a human being, but it is never seen as such. If it were, he would cease to project his anxieties onto the world and come to terms with himself.

10   The Inquisitor Is Answered

On October 23, 1963, three officers of the John Birch Society appeared before Municipal Judge William B. Keene in Torrance, California. They were charged with disturbing the peace. Their plea was "guilty."

On November 7, 1963, the three defendants were fined $225 each and sentenced to ten days in jail. Judge Keene, who labeled the behavior of the defendants as "adult delinquency," suspended the jail sentences, but nevertheless placed all three on probation for two years. He was quoted as telling the men that their behavior "violate[d] every basic precept of freedom of speech."

The court case had grown out of a meeting held in Torrance by a local human relations committee in an effort to provide residents with factual information on problems in integration. Disbanded when hecklers made it impossible to continue, the meeting was later reconvened at the request of a large segment of the audience. Not all of the scheduled speakers appeared after the meeting reconvened, but the audience did hear an impromptu speech by a Birch Society officer who responded to the chairman's appeal to the hecklers to provide a spokesman for their position.

Part of the disturbance was later described by Carl Pearlston, Jr., General Chairman of the event, in the following terms: "A woman dressed in red, white and blue walked up and down the rows slamming seats up and down. They've also developed a neat trick of everybody coughing." Others present reported that booing and heckling of a more conventional sort had helped to break up the meeting. Unfortunately for the hecklers, the moderator of the discussion was Charles F. Catterlin, Torrance city prosecutor. It was Catterlin who brought the case before Judge Keene.

The incident is instructive. When individuals or groups willfully attempt to thwart the bases of our democratic society—such as freedom of speech and freedom of assembly— we must be willing to challenge their attempt, and if necessary, to seek legal remedies. That, after all, is what the laws are for. To fail to challenge fable peddled as fact, to avoid coming to terms with tactics of harassment and disturbance is to fail to give democracy its due. It is to grant to those who oppose the way of freedom the right to destroy whatever aspects of freedom happen to displease them at the moment.

Legal remedies are, of course, something of a last resort. It is generally possible to come to terms with an adversary before it becomes necessary to meet him in court. And the place to begin, in my judgment, is with public opinion.

DALLAS AND THE CONSCIENCE OF THE NATION

"What is uniquely disturbing about the emergence of the radical right in the 1960s," says Daniel Bell in *The Radical Right*, "is the support it has been able to find among traditional community leaders who have themselves become conditioned, through an indiscriminate anti-Communism, . . . to judge as respectable a movement which, if successful, can only end the liberties they profess to cherish."

Sadly, Daniel Bell is right. I have had community leaders tell me that they supported a project for human rights or civil liberties without qualification, only to request a moment later that I keep their support confidential. Friends might be distressed; campaign funds might be cut off; a church board might protest. I have known of nationally prominent figures who, privately and confidentially, offered their full support to protodemocratic endeavors only to request that their names not be used because, according to their own accounts, they never publicly support anything more controversial than a fund for crippled children. Most distressing of all, I have seen public figures give apparently unqualified backing to projects for social justice, only to work quietly behind the scenes in an effort to keep things in hand, or to cancel plans altogether.

Why? Daniel Bell has given us the answer. The radical right has been accorded—by some public figures, at least—a stature that it does not deserve. Bishops, state legislators and city councilmen alike, while not assenting to the antidemocratic bias of the right-wing extremists, have nevertheless thought it better to maintain a sanctified silence than meet head on a flurry of criticism, or a minor opposition campaign.

Such generalizations demand qualification, of course. What may be true in Los Angeles is not necessarily true in San Francisco. What may be true in Chicago may not be at all true in New York City. And, one must note, even the most extremist-ridden of cities may occasionally find the courage to repudiate the excesses of some of its citizens. When a woman lambasted Adlai Stevenson with an anti-U.N. sign and a man spat on the Ambassador, following his October 1963 appearance in Dallas, civic leaders sent Stevenson a telegram saying that they were "outraged and abjectly ashamed of the disgraceful discourtesies you suffered at the hands of a small group of extremists."

The "small group," according to a UPI dispatch, had numbered about seventy persons. Earlier, Mr. Stevenson's United Nations Day address had been repeatedly interrupted by hecklers.

Not only were the city fathers of Dallas willing to speak up in the face of such behavior, the Dallas *Times Herald* published a front-page editorial declaring, "Dallas has been disgraced. There is no other way to view the storm-trooper actions of last night's frightening attack on Adlai Stevenson. The jeering, bullying mob was not attacking the United Nations. It was battling the right of you and me to hold our separate beliefs." The paper went on to say that such a "misconstrued, misguided brand of patriotism is dragging the name of Dallas through the slime of national dishonor."

The prompt and decisive action taken by Dallas leaders no doubt went a great distance toward discrediting and curbing the extremist element in that city. When President Kennedy arrived in Dallas less than a month later his welcome could not have been more cordial. Gone were the signs of extremist hatred, the placards of radical dissent. No mass demonstrations foretold the tragedy that was soon to befall the President, his family and the nation.

At 11:50 A.M., central standard time, on November 22, the President, together with Mrs. Kennedy and Texas Governor and Mrs. Connally, left the crowd at Dallas Airport and began the drive into Dallas in the presidential limousine. The crowds were enthusiastic. The chief executive and his party were impressed by the warmth of their welcome.

At 12:30 P.M. an assassin's bullet hit the President. Another hit the Governor. Then a third shot—the President had been hit again. He was pronounced dead by physicians at Parkland Memorial Hospital at 1:00 P.M.

At 1:35 P.M., following the murder of Dallas policeman J. D. Tippit, Lee Harvey Oswald was arrested by Dallas police. He was soon to be charged with the murder of the President of the United States as well.

As Oswald's background became known, a grief-stricken and outraged public learned that extremism could speak without warning, public notice or fanfare.

When it was learned that the accused murderer of the President was a self-proclaimed Marxist with a history of pro-Communist and pro-Castro activities, the left wing was quick to disassociate itself from him. Lee Harvey Oswald, said spokesmen for the Fair Play for Cuba Committee, of which Oswald was said to be the local chairman, is unknown to us. We have never heard of him.

Perhaps they never had. But the Communist Party headquarters in New York City had, if an account in the November 27 edition of the *New York Times* was to be believed. According to an assistant district attorney in Dallas, Oswald's papers included letters from the New York office of the Communist Party of America. Written on official letterheads, they showed a "working friendly relationship" between Oswald and the party. One letter advised him on how to set up a chapter of the Fair Play for Cuba Committee and went on to say how to avoid "nosy neighbors."

There was nothing to indicate that the Communist Party was involved in an assassination plot. But it seemed certain that an emotionally unbalanced young man, who had found the teachings of Marx and Engels congenial, had attempted to become a Soviet citizen, and had been an admirer of the Cuban regime of Fidel Castro, was the assassin of John F. Kennedy.

The world was never to discover guilt, innocence, or motivation from the lips of Lee Oswald. They were closed by a bullet fired at point-blank range. Before the funeral of the President was over, the world press wondered aloud about the stability of the United States and speculated on the possible motivation for the second assassination.

Dallas residents began a painful reassessment. The day that the President was murdered the December issue of *Redbook* magazine had reached many of its readers. It contained an article entitled "What Are Americans Like?"—a report on the attitudes toward Americans held by European school children. It began with these words by way of summary:

The average American is, of course, a Texan. He eats lots of breakfast and gets fat so he has to go on a diet because he likes to look skinny. He calls everyone "sweetheart" and is bad to colored people. If he doesn't like who is President, he usually shoots him. . . .

Astute observers were all too aware that such an image represented more than simply the viewpoint of European school children, revealing a truth about the European image of the American way, Texan or otherwise.

In Dallas, Mayor Earle Cabell voiced the sentiments of many residents when he spoke of the deep shock which the city had felt following the assassination. The act, he said, was that of one man, in no way representative of the way the citizens of Dallas felt about their President. But the murder *had* happened in Dallas, and the city soon began what was to become an agonizing reappraisal of its political crosscurrents. Ironically, the assassination of a President, apparently by a left-wing extremist, was the occasion for deep thought about the extremism on the right which had been polluting the local waters of democratic discussion.

On November 26, Mayor Cabell called on Dallas citizens to "exemplify the fundamental principles of the nation which we love," and asked the churches and synagogues of the city, in particular, to speak "with utmost candor both of the ideals of truth and of the shortcomings of our community so that we may be guided into the paths of right." There was much for the clergy of Dallas to consider. On hearing the news of the assassination of Lee Oswald, a crowd assembled across from the city hall had cheered. Numerous man-on-the-street radio and television interviews had indicated that a great many Dallas residents approved of Jack Ruby's action. "Give us an eye for an eye and a tooth for a tooth, and never mind about the cumbersome machinery of justice," seemed to have been the prevailing sentiment. Said one woman, "It's a good old western custom to take the law in your own hands."

One Dallas minister, a Baptist, recalled the cheering crowd across from city hall and declared that such a repudiation of the American system of justice was the "most chilling sound of those dreadful four days."

A Methodist minister, the Rev. William H. Dickinson Jr., spoke of a "nice, respectable dinner party" held two days before the murder of the President, where a "bright young couple" told their friends that they "hated the President of the United States—and that they would not care one bit if somebody did take a shot at him."

Episcopal Bishop C. Avery Mason declared that America had been placed under the judgment of God and pointed to the assassination as "but the evidence of an evil among us which is too lightly regarded, and too frequently ignored."

Probably the most searching words spoken by any minister in Dallas that week were those of the Rev. William A. Holmes. In a sermon delivered on Sunday, November 24, at the Northaven Methodist Church, Mr. Holmes observed that the phrase "We take no responsibility for the death of this man" was fast becoming a slogan for Dallas. It was not enough, said Mr. Holmes, to dismiss the assassination as the work of "one madman and extremist."

"I am well aware," he continued, ". . . that the man charged with the assassination of our President has admitted to being a Marxist and left-wing extremist. But, my friends, whether extremism wears the hat of left wing or right wing, its by-products are the same. It announces death and condemnation to all who hold a different point of view. . . . There is no city in the United States which . . . has been more acquiescent toward its extremists than Dallas, Texas. We, the majority of citizens, have gone quietly about our work and leisure, forfeiting the city's image to the hatemon-

gers . . . in our midst. The spirit of assassination has been
with us for some time. . . ."

Mr. Holmes then reviewed what was comparatively recent
Dallas history: an incident three years earlier in which the
then Vice-President and Mrs. Johnson were spat upon and
cursed in the lobby of a Dallas hotel; the Stevenson incident
less than a month before. It was in Dallas, said Holmes, that
"fourth-grade children in a . . . public school clapped and
cheered when their teacher told them of the assassination of
the President. . . .

"In the name of God," asked the minister, "what kind of
city have we become?"

Mr. Holmes acknowledged that he loved Dallas and held
it in high regard, but declared that the "vocal, organized and
unorganized extremists" had taken over the city. "By our
timidity, we have encouraged the aggressor," he said. "By our
paralysis we have given safe-conduct to reactionaries; . . . by
our small prejudices and little hates we have prepared the way
for monstrous and demonic acts. . . ."

Holmes called on his parishioners and on the city to continue to debate the issues, but in the spirit of "mutual for-
bearance and good will." The place to begin to change the
temper of Dallas, he said, was with the children of the city.
They were not born "hating the President of the United
States." Next, there was the neighborhood extremist to consider. "When the extremist across the street or down the block
starts spewing his epithets and hate," said Holmes, "he must
soon discover he has a contest on his hands, as we confront
him with sanity and love."

On November 26, a CBS television news program carried
portions of Holmes' sermon. The following day the Associated
Press reported that Dallas police had placed the minister and
his family under guard. Apparently, his remarks had not been
taken lightly by those who still had violence on their minds.

A controversy developed over the accuracy of Holmes' allegation that school children had cheered the news of the death of the President. The Dallas school system issued an official denial, but the *Dallas Morning News* reported that a teacher in a local junior high school had confirmed the minister's statement. She acknowledged, however, that the majority of students had "felt a sincere grief and showed remorse." Fellow teachers in other schools, she said, had reported similar incidents. Eleven local Methodist ministers issued a statement endorsing Holmes' sermon and stating that they could "document times over the exclamations of approval by school children at the death of President Kennedy."

As Dallas residents argued over the behavior of their children, others wondered that the main points of Holmes' sermon could have been so easily missed—that hatred and violence are the by-products of extremism, and that sanity and love were needed in Dallas if the city were to come to terms with its conscience.

Recovering from nearly fatal wounds at Parkland Hospital, Governor John Connally reflected on the tragedy and voiced what was probably the view of the majority of Texans. It was possible, he said, that the death of the President might so shock and stun the people of the nation and the world that they would recognize "the cancerous growth that's being permitted to expand and enlarge itself upon the community and the society in which we live. . . ." The assassination, he continued, "could have occurred in any other city in America. It is nothing more than a manifestation of an extremism on both sides— . . . the genesis of our self-destruction, if we're ever going to be destroyed." He then called for a realization of the simple virtues of reason, tolerance and knowledge in place of the hate, the passion, and the prejudice that had come to the fore in Texas and in the nation.

On the same day that Governor Connally made his observations, the western edition of the *New York Times* carried an Associated Press dispatch which reported that in

Tacoma, Washington, "a leader of the ultraconservative Citizens Council . . . resigned because of President Kennedy's assassination. . . ." In a letter to the head of the state organization, J. (Bud) Nelson had observed, "Though it was a left-wing Communist who wantonly assassinated our President, I feel that every radical, left and right, had his hand on the rifle butt and finger on that trigger. We are all guilty (morally) of fomenting hatred of one sort or another. . . ."

Nelson's words anticipated, in a sense, those of President Johnson, who declared in his first speech to Congress, "The time has come for Americans of all races and creeds and political beliefs to understand and respect one another." The President then offered a deeply felt plea: "Let us put an end to the teaching and preaching of hate and evil and violence. Let us turn away from the fanatics of the far left and the far right, from the apostles of bitterness and bigotry, from those defiant of law, and those who pour venom into our nation's bloodstream."

For a few days it seemed as though President Johnson's words would be heeded. But before the shock over the tragic events had faded, the purveyors of fear and hatred were back at work. One spokesman for the Communist Party had no more than expressed her grief over the death of the late President than she launched into an attack on American "fascists" and the far right wing, claiming that despite Mr. Kennedy's virtues he had sometimes been the captive of right-wing propaganda. While she praised the late President as an effective proponent of world peace and civil rights, she claimed that he was, nevertheless, still a representative of the capitalist class.

Communists, she said, had never advocated individual violence. Lee Oswald was only one highly disturbed individual, in no way representative of Communist philosophy or methods. She observed that the far right had already begun to attack systematically the Communist Party as though it were directly responsible for the assassination. The attacks, she implied, were the product of a carefully coordinated effort to further smear the name of the party. She then turned to a systematic attack of her own on the far right, speaking as though she fancied that it held a monopoly on hatred and so was responsible for most, if not all, evil on the American scene.

Some of the attacks on the far right were more direct, if less sweeping, and extended even to the most respectable of conservatives. In an exclusive report from the *Chicago Tribune*, Senator Barry Goldwater was described as "stunned and shocked by receipt of a number of abusive telegrams and letters, some containing threats of a violent nature." Senator John Tower of Texas had also received threatening letters and wires, and had moved his family from his Washington home for several days because of what he regarded as the potential for violence. No one was arguing that *this* hate was being peddled by right-wing extremists.

Meanwhile, Carl McIntire declared in a letter to his radio listeners, dated the day of the President's funeral, "It is late but not too late for us to awake and fight for our freedom. The death of the President came in the providence of God." But, said McIntire, God would "overrule" the assassination, "if we will stand for righteousness and truth." He renewed his attack on Communism and offered listeners a packet of materials entitled "A Communist Kills Our President and the Right Wing Is Blamed."

The John Birch Society ran full-page advertisements in newspapers from one coast to the other. "The President of the United States has been murdered by a Marxist-Communist within the United States," the ads began. Lee Harvey Oswald was a Communist, the Society declared, and "when a Communist commits murder he is acting under orders."

So also with Billy James Hargis, who told the readers of *Christian Crusade* that "*Mr. Kennedy was assassinated by a*

*communist, whom I feel time will reveal was a man con-
nected with the communist conspiracy, and was acting under
orders . . .* [emphasis by Hargis]" Hargis further observed
that, to his way of thinking, the assassination was calculated
*"not only to destroy the President of the United States, but to
create panic within the country and to create distrust and
suspicion of the anti-communist forces of the country* [em-
phasis by Hargis]."

Neither the Birch Society nor Hargis mentioned the fact
that press accounts had reported that the F.B.I. file, which
had already been turned over to the Warren Commission,
indicated that Oswald had acted alone.

SHAPING OPINION

Despite the continuing war of charge and countercharge
between the left wing and the right wing, there was reason to
think that the American public, as a whole, had been moved
by the tragedy to reassess the place of extremist claims and
campaigns, to look more carefully at the programs offered by
professional dissidents whether old or new to the scene.

Unfortunately, the systematic hate campaigns, the propaganda of vilification that preceded the Stevenson incident in
Dallas, and forced something of a national reassessment
following the assassination, had gone on in the past, ignored,
winked at, even endorsed by public officials in many an
American community.

If it is true, as Emerson suggests in one of his essays, that
". . . the ancestor of every action is a thought," the time to
deal with extremist behavior—left or right—is when it emerges
as extremist thought.

I am not suggesting repression. The grossly mistaken must
be assured of their freedom of opinion, for theirs is the free-

dom to be wrong. I am suggesting that errant nonsense must be refuted as such. We must be willing to enter into open encounters with falsity whenever it is proclaimed as truth, giving it the lie before it can begin to eat at the vitals of the free society.

Civic leaders have, at the very least, a clear-cut responsibility to refuse to lend their names to those groups and their affiliates which have established records of manufacturing unsupported and unsupportable allegations. So long as an extremist group is small and relatively unknown, silence may be the best policy, but once its existence and its charges are a matter of public knowledge, it behooves those in positions of public responsibility to make themselves heard. Charges should not be left hanging in the air, resembling so many vultures.

As an official of the National Council of Churches once put it, "We try patiently and perseveringly to answer all charges, no matter how irresponsible, mischievous and cockeyed they may be. . . . We ignore none of it, but, in a process akin to building a house of truth brick by brick, do our best to set the record straight with all who seek to know."

In the same spirit, the International Convention of Christian Churches (Disciples of Christ) has put together a set of guidelines for the information of its two million members who may meet with extremist religiopolitical activities from time to time. According to an account in the October 14, 1963, edition of the *New York Times*, the denominational body pointed out that "in recent years certain organizations have made a practice of labeling individuals as subversives, dupes of some foreign power or un-American."

The *Times* quoted the statement itself as observing, "Christians are cautioned against lending support to such groups. Although frequently having the name 'Christian' in their titles, such organizations use a number of un-Christian methods and state positions which are antithetical to the Christian faith."

Sometimes charges made on a local level need more direct refutation. There was a time in Los Angeles when it was almost doubtful whether the word *democracy* could be said out loud at a public meeting without inviting a chorus of protest. A number of pseudopatriotic carnivals had been held in the area. The Supreme Court had been attacked, the United Nations declared a seat of treason, the administration in Washington named as part of the over-all conspiracy to make America Communist. Mental-health associations, PTAs and church councils had been denounced as Communist or pro-Communist.

The refutations had been few, so a group of civic leaders developed plans for still another rally in the rally-ridden city, this one to stand *for* the traditional American form of government and American institutions. Harold Fey, editor of the *Christian Century*, happened to be in town during one of the steering committee meetings and contributed the opening phrase to an affirmation that began, "In these troubled times, we desire to speak a resounding word of faith in the democratic process."

The affirmation went on to speak of "apostles of discord" who "use innuendo against churchmen, educators and leaders in government to serve their own political ends." It declared, "We do not want totalitarian extremism in any form, be it Communism or the authoritarianism on the right," and concluded with a concise summary of American ideals and a call to a Town Meeting for Democracy.

The Rev. John Burt, an Episcopal clergyman and President of the Southern California Council of Churches, presided at the Meeting, which brought over five thousand persons to Los Angeles' Shrine Auditorium to hear Clifford Case, Republican Senator from New Jersey, and Eugene McCarthy, Democratic Senator from Minnesota, speak eloquently of the democratic process.

What did the Meeting accomplish? Haskell Lazere, secretary of the steering committee and director of the western region of the American Jewish Congress, later summed it up by saying, "The Meeting was a mass response to the radical right to demonstrate that the sane moderates were a representative majority . . . not to be stampeded by the Birchers, the witch-hunters and the book burners." The Town Meeting also served a less public function, Lazere observed, by letting individual moderates know that they were not alone in their feelings of apprehension about the extreme right, and what was more important, in their confidence in the democratic process.

FROM VIOLENCE TO COMMITMENT

Mass meetings may sometimes be of little help to local organizations that have been hard hit by extremist or extremist-inspired attacks—particularly when those attacks include physical violence.

I shall never forget the evening of March 31, 1963. I had no more than been installed as the incoming president of the San Fernando Valley chapter of the American Association for the United Nations, at a dinner meeting in a Sherman Oaks country club, than word came that our office in nearby Encino had been bombed.

The damage was fairly extensive. The carpet was ruined, windows shattered, a number of gifts in the gift shop damaged, curtains and literature burned, and many of the records destroyed. Whoever had planted the bomb, which we were later to learn was a crude, lead-pipe affair capped at both ends, was deadly serious in his apparent intent—to do as much damage as possible to the office without killing anyone or blowing up the whole building.

We had no more idea who had exploded the bomb than we had had the year before when bombs were exploded at my home and at John Simmons'. It seemed clear, however, that whoever exploded the bomb had no special affection for the United Nations and what the organization stands for. California Governor Pat Brown probably summed up the feelings of most Californians when he wrote me:

"This was a disgraceful, un-American act, and I want you to know that I am deeply concerned about it and other incidents like it.

"Your association is doing significant work in helping carry the message of a peaceful solution to world problems through the United Nations. I feel sure that the people responsible for bombing your office, and other acts against your organization and the United Nations itself, are not familiar with your objectives and those of the U.N.

"This latest incident indicates we need a vigorous information program about the United Nations. . . ."

What happened during the next several weeks might well serve as a model for other organizations besieged by extremist attacks. The membership, quite without any pep talks or grand gestures, went to work on the basic jobs of the organization with renewed enthusiasm. The bombing was seldom mentioned. Extremist attacks, in the form of letters and telephone calls, were answered as they were received, but they took no inordinate amount of time. Damage to the building was repaired and the gift shop was restocked. Plans went ahead for a community conference on the United Nations at San Fernando Valley State College. More literature was distributed to those who requested it. Additional speaking engagements were booked. New members were signed up. In short, the organization turned its full attention to its purposes for being.

Similarly, both those organizations which face harassment from disruptive paper "members," and those whose meetings are plagued by unfriendly visitors have found that their best defense has been to keep their attention focused on their reasons for existence. Just as organizations that were harried by left-wing extremists a decade or more ago found that the most effective countermeasures consisted of doing the job already agreed upon and sticking closely to democratic procedures, so also the disruptive tactics of right-wing extremists must fail in the face of a continuing concentration on the tasks at hand.

Patterns of responsible behavior have a way of working themselves into the structure of an organization. It is the voluntary association that is loosely defined and poorly oriented toward its primary purposes which finds itself in trouble when the opposition moves in.

It is also the minister who never thinks of discussing questions of social justice until those questions are of critical importance who finds himself under attack when he finally speaks up. The minister who consistently concerns himself with social issues may be criticized by those outside his community of faith, but he will, in all likelihood, enjoy the support of those within it.

There is a deeper reason for his concern, of course, and it has to do with the roots of his faith. As James Luther Adams of the Harvard Divinity School once put it, "Christianity is no longer an optional luxury for me. Salvation does not come through worship and prayer alone, nor through private virtues which camouflage public indolence. Time and history are fraught with judgment and fulfillment."

The judgment and fulfillment of time, Professor Adams made clear, are to be found only by the man who is willing to take time seriously—that is, "to act as a Christian and as a citizen through socially effective institutions." The church itself, he said, must "decide unequivocally whether it means business, whether it will play a constructive role in the dynamic process that makes history meaningful."

If the church cannot, or will not endeavor to "make history meaningful" through its efforts to come to terms with the arms race, economic exploitation, or racial prejudice, then it is not truly a church. It is one more society for brotherly irrelevance, a club for the comfortable and the pious. It may speak to aches and pains in the private lives of men and women, but it cannot speak of life and meaning. The man of religion—whether clergyman or layman—who finds himself constrained from speaking of justice, equality or mercy by censorious looks on Sunday morning had better ask himself whether he is in a church, or in the mere semblance of one.

The Rt. Rev. Arthur Lichtenberger, Presiding Bishop of the Protestant Episcopal Church, has put it well:

> The Church is to be concerned with all that affects man's life in this world, with economics and politics and public morality. Those individuals and groups in our country today, who in the name of the gospel and patriotism tell us that the Church must not speak out on such public issues, do not, I submit, understand the gospel or know the meaning of true patriotism. The Church cannot be a refuge from the disturbing and threatening events of our time. . . .

A history of involvement with the problems of social justice is a good indication that a church or a minister is less likely to be vulnerable to extremist attacks, but the reason for involvement is far less prudential. It involves the very *raison d'être* of religion: *the quest for meaning and its realization in the lives of men.* The prophet Amos perhaps said it better than any man when he expressed God's disinterest in feasts and solemn assemblies, declaring on behalf of the Lord, "But let justice roll down like waters, and righteousness like an ever-flowing stream."

THE TONE OF PUBLIC LIFE

Much of our capacity to deal realistically with extremism, right or left, comes from the tone of our public life—an intangible and difficult thing to describe, much less to change or reform.

A psychology of fear has never been an effective means for dealing with social problems of any sort; yet that is often the first resort of those who would cure us of our ills. The House Committee on Un-American Activities sends up distress cries over internal Communist activities and urges legislation on Congress which, once passed, soon drives the party underground. "Ironically," the Committee then declares, with official after-the-fact wisdom, "the latest Party moves to bury its apparatus deeper underground have been in response to legislation which Congress enacted in an effort to bring Communist activity into the open."

We must not repeat the mistakes which Congress has made in relation to Communism when dealing with extremism on the right. Neither in terms of legislation, nor in our public life, can the psychology of fear solve our dilemma. Extremist groups, of whatever caste, are not likely to yield to repressive measures. Repression, moreover, carries within it the seeds of the destruction of the very liberty we seek to preserve.

To date, neither Congress nor the administration has seen any reason to attempt to deal with the radical right by means other than debate and discussion of the issues. The emphasis has been on a constructive appraisal of the dangers inherent in extremism, on an appeal to the good sense of the average American, and on informing the public of the facts. In November of 1961, President Kennedy described what was to be his administration's position by observing that "there have always been those on the fringes of our society who have sought to escape their own responsibility by finding a simple solution, an appealing slogan or a convenient scapegoat." He urged Americans not to heed the "counsels of fear and suspicion," but to "prove we think our country great by striving to make it greater." The direction of history, he said, "is on the side of liberty—and so, for all time to come, are we."

In refusing to prefer charges against Dallas extremists some two years later, Ambassador Stevenson similarly offered a temperate solution to extremism. "I didn't want them to go to jail," he said. "I thought it would be better if they went to school."

When neither institutional freedom nor a man's reputation is at stake—and when physical violence, endangering life and property, is not a question—an educational remedy is to be preferred over a legal one. It is doubtful whether the right-wing extremist would listen long to Mr. Stevenson, or seek anything resembling honest information. All the same, some-one may get through to him, and a vigorous public-information program can do much to improve the tenor of our national life.

Beyond that, we who have inherited the way of freedom have a responsibility to defend our heritage. The channels of communication must be kept open. Those who would bra-zenly set fire to the houses where freedom of inquiry dwells must be repudiated for what they are—the enemies of freedom and of the democratic heritage.

As the inheritors of freedom, we have a trust of incalcula-ble value committed to us. In the name of that trust, we must refuse to let those persons whose narrow strictures make them fit candidates for any totalitarian state, ancient or mod-ern, have the final say as to what the Constitution means —whether in terms of extralegal interpretations, or in terms of gross revisions of our legal process. We must stand with Jefferson and his party of small *d* democrats by saying ever-lastingly *nay* to all those who would establish their latter-day aristocracies. We must have the courage to choose for free-dom, and when action is called for, we must act. Above all, we must defend and practice the most precious elements in our democratic heritage—the right to assemble freely and to speak without restriction.

Our democratic way has a life and a vitality greater than most of us know, and any antidemocratic movement must reckon with its strength. To cite but one example, despite

Mr. Welch's unequivocal repudiation of democracy, local chapter leaders in more than one part of the country speak openly of the Birch Society as a "democratic organization." Democracy will not be put down easily, for the democratic sentiment lives in the thought patterns, the feelings, the convictions of every American.

What is true of one extremist group is true of another. Our history as a democratic people is on our side, and our national temperament will continue to reflect that history so long as conscientious men care to maintain their liberty.

THE FINAL ANSWER

The greatest threat from right-wing extremism makes itself known on a personal, rather than on a public level, however. It is simply that we who oppose extremism may become like it. Not in terms of ideas. I am not afraid of that. But in terms of our attitudes and modes of dealing with persons. It was Adolph Hitler, as I remember, who remarked that the great strength of the totalitarian state is that it forces all those who fear it to become like it. Like all totalitarians, Hitler had great insight into the defensive workings of the human personality. The great danger from authoritarianism *is* that those who oppose it will take the authoritarian stance. In attempting to counter the arbitrary and the coercive, we ourselves may easily become arbitrary and coercive.

The psychiatrist Viktor Frankl, in recounting his experiences in a Nazi death camp, tells how some of the prisoners behaved after they were released. Freedom was too much for them. Having been faced with unrelenting tyranny, they themselves became tyrants, minor versions of those who had enslaved them. Unable to live with their newfound freedom, they relinquished it for the anonymity of the faceless tyrant.

Having been the oppressed, they sought to become the oppressors.

The psychology of the experience which Frankl describes is not limited to the extremes of an Auschwitz. Or, perhaps, the truth is simply that the potential for an Auschwitz is always present in human affairs. In any case, my point is this: authoritarianism begets authoritarianism. The first answer to fulminations is likely to be counterfulminations. The first reaction to violence is likely to be violence. The first response to an attempt at dehumanization is to play the part—that is, to *become* dehumanized and to insist that one's adversary is a block of wood, a social dinosaur, an insolent crackpot.

The great danger from the radical right is that the man who is attacked will let his attackers rule him by shouting authoritarian answers into the wind in a vain attempt to return the sentiments of his attackers.

The true answer to the radical right—or to any other form of authoritarianism—is the nonauthoritarian answer implied by the phrase "the democratic method in human relationships" and made real in every encounter that is truly humanistic.

Do you recall the Grand Inquisitor scene in Dostoyevsky's novel *The Brothers Karamazov?* Jesus appears in this poetic fantasy, you may remember, for a brief moment in sixteenth-century Seville. He returns to earth for a few hours. And there he faces the Grand Inquisitor himself.

Locked in a cell in the palace of the Holy Inquisition, Jesus is interrogated by the old man, a mere caricature of a human being, a living lie to everything that he stands for outwardly. He is the essence of arbitrary, coercive authority, the spirit behind a hundred thousand burnings, for it is he who has taken the terrible burden of human freedom upon himself in order to spare mankind. It is he who, in his benevolent wisdom, has relieved a feeble, faltering, impotent mankind of its responsibility to be human.

There is no place for a Jesus in the theology of the Grand Inquisitor. The seal of finality has been placed upon the work of the Rabbi from Nazareth. His work of old has been corrected by the church, and it is necessary that he be dealt with speedily.

"Tomorrow Thou shalt see [the] obedient flock . . . hasten to heap up the hot cinders about the pile on which I shall burn Thee for coming to hinder us," the Inquisitor tells Jesus. "For if any one has ever deserved our fires, it is Thou. Tomorrow I shall burn Thee. . . ."

Without saying a word, Jesus brings the Grand Inquisitor to admit to himself, perhaps for the first time, that he is not what he stands for in the view of the world—that he is, in fact, in league with Satan. Or, as we would put it in today's idiom, that his public image is a façade for his private life, which has little to commend it, everything to condemn it.

The only answer given by Jesus is silence. . . . Silence . . . . And a kiss, before he steps out into the night of Seville.

Now I am not suggesting that we should all become like Jesus, not even like Dostoyevsky's image of Jesus. Not at all! Sainthood is reserved for those on whom the mantle rests lightly. For the rest of us, it constitutes an aping of goodness and, as such, is necessarily hollow.

What I am suggesting is that the figure of Jesus here represents the humanistic answer to authoritarianism—an answer that does not have to include so much as one word, but is an answer all the same. It is an answer without compromise, yet one that permits the full acceptance of the personhood of another. It is the ability to say No to fear-driven ideas, to warped systems of thought, to the demonic in human affairs —to say No to arbitrary authority while saying Yes to the person held captive by his fears.

Most of us will probably never have to face an Inquisitor with the power to attempt to bend our thoughts to fit his own. And then again we may. It makes little difference. Our answer should be the same, an answer born of the democratic spirit.

The most decisive encounters with the radical right may never occur on the lecture platform, in the newspaper, or in the conference room. More likely, they will happen when neighbor meets neighbor, when friend encounters friend. What does one say to right-wing extremism when it exists in the person of a friend or neighbor, in the person of a parishioner, or a colleague? How then does one speak to it?

One begins, I believe, with the democratic spirit in human relationships. And by that I mean nothing more complicated than simply listening, at first. I suggest that when we meet another person who has something to tell us about the things that concern him deeply we might begin by listening and entering into a kind of unspoken contract—a contract that says, "I will listen as carefully as I can to what you have to say, remaining attentive to you as a human being as I listen. Perhaps then we can converse."

No word need pass between us proclaiming the fact, but it may be that if we listen honestly, with an unaffected effort to understand, we will discover that the other person has also entered into our unspoken contract. We may find that mysteriously, without any fanfare or trumpets, a conversation has begun between us.

There is risk in this, to be sure. One must always risk something of himself whenever he dares to seek authenticity in human relationships. The risk is multiplied when ideas, convictions, sentiments, separate us from another person. There is then the danger—perhaps the certainty—of rejection. We must find it in ourselves to take that risk, knowing that our encounter may come to nothing, but that it has the potential for fulfillment.

It may happen, of course, that we will find ourselves modifying our own convictions as we listen, that we will discover that part of what the other person has to say speaks to us of truth.

We may have to relinquish some of our most treasured notions about how things are in this world of ours. But what of it if our commitment is to reason and to a full relationship with the world? It may just be that the person with whom we talk knows something we need to learn.

There is no need to capitulate to the fears and anxieties that torment our adversary. To do so would be to renounce our own selfhood. What is important is that we maintain our integrity as persons, while initiating a conversation in values which has the potential for penetrating the skull of at least one of the participants.

Now it may seem as though I am talking in contradictions —first an emphasis on the importance of countering the radical right in its attempt to usurp constitutional principles; then a suggestion that we should listen sincerely to the proponents of extremism. First, an uncompromising defense of the freedoms of speech and assembly; then, a willingness to consider seriously the contentions of those on the far right.

The contradiction is one of appearance only. It conceals a polarity that is basic to our world, the polarity between our common life and the world of inner experience. Both the social dimensions and the interpersonal aspects of extremism must be considered. To neglect one is to be satisfied with a fractured, half-acknowledged reality.

Man must live in social relationships, with the institutional components of the human community. They constitute the prerequisites for human relatedness. Insofar as social institutions are just and equitable, insofar as they are *for* man, fashioned to his needs and to his meanings, we may hope for significance in our encounters. Whenever our social arrangements are false or unjust, we may expect the meeting of persons to be fragmentary and broken, triumphing over the lifeless machinery of institutions and conventions only with great effort.

"I never met a man I didn't like," said Will Rogers, creating an aphorism that has built itself into the texture of American life. With all respect for the great humorist, I would prefer to be able to say that I have never met a person I couldn't relate to. It's the relationship that is all-important, you see—even if it must be one of hostility and negation, for in that there is still the quality of humanity.

Authentic relationships cannot be contrived, invented or manufactured. They happen by the grace of a world of complexities far too fragile and too numerous to be set down. They follow from an openness of being. As Martin Buber has expressed it, "Only he who himself turns to the other human being and opens himself to him receives the world in him."

I am, of course, discussing more than an answer to extremism. I am talking about what is at the heart of the universe, of life, of sense and nonsense, of longing and frustration, joy and grief. I speak of the elemental ground of being in which man lives and loves and dies.

The behavior of the extremist is the wounded reaction of one who is estranged from his being—no more estranged, perhaps, than some whose cries are stifled, or resolved in the commerce of human affairs, but still estranged. He is unable to converse meaningfully with his fellows and so must resort to an incestuous substitute for relationship by turning to a world of bromides, stereotypes and clichés. He repeats the formulas of conspiracy that unite him with those who share his alienation. The camaraderie he feels is a substitute for an overcoming of his estrangement, a collective substitute for being.

And so we must speak to him not as an extremist, but as a person, a human being whose first need, in common with the rest of us, is to relate. "The fundamental fact of human existence is man with man," says Buber. The first fact of human life is not the aggregate—the social institutions, the conventions of men. Nor is it the individual, isolated and alone with himself. It is "man with man," or more exactly, what happens between man and man. In this is the cosmos struggling for expression, the universe asking to be known, the face of God there for those who have eyes to see.

The world is never neutral. It is a place of elemental separation and pain, a place of restlessness and ruin, a place where evil walks in daylight as well as darkness because men are estranged from their primal being. The world plays host to revelries and joys, to high moments of exaltation. But when the everlasting ego caves in on itself and a man can at last see clearly, he may discover that his being is one with all being.

For the present we must content ourselves with fragments of meaning, with momentary intimations of a reconciliation. If we move with the certain knowledge that all men were created from the same clay, seeking to remedy injustice and to open ourselves to the being of others, we have done what we can.

The final answer to the radical right must follow, I believe, from a coherent view of reality. If your view is not my view, so be it. The important thing is that we discover in our views of life, whatever they may be, a capacity for structuring human relationships, for speaking truthfully to men. My own conviction is this: The answer to right-wing extremism is an answer with the strength of humanity on its side. It is all that follows from the elemental word *democracy*.

Index